SOCCER IN MIND

CRITICAL ISSUES IN SPORT AND SOCIETY

Michael A. Messner, Douglas Hartmann, and
Jeffrey Montez de Oca, Series Editors

Critical Issues in Sport and Society features scholarly books that help expand our understanding of the new and myriad ways in which sport is intertwined with social life in the contemporary world. Using the tools of various scholarly disciplines, including sociology, anthropology, history, media studies and others, books in this series investigate the growing impact of sport and sports-related activities on various aspects of social life as well as key developments and changes in the sporting world and emerging sporting practices. Series authors produce groundbreaking research that brings empirical and applied work together with cultural critique and historical perspectives written in an engaging, accessible format.

Rachel Allison, *Kicking Center: Gender and the Selling of Women's Professional Soccer*

Jules Boykoff, *Activism and the Olympics: Dissent at the Games in Vancouver and London*

Diana Tracy Cohen, *Iron Dads: Managing Family, Work, and Endurance Sport Identities*

Cheryl Cooky and Michael A. Messner, *No Slam Dunk: Gender, Sport, and the Unevenness of Social Change*

Andrew M. Guest, *Soccer in Mind: A Thinking Fan's Guide to the Global Game*

Jennifer Guiliano, *Indian Spectacle: College Mascots and the Anxiety of Modern America*

Kathryn E. Henne, *Testing for Athlete Citizenship: Regulating Doping and Sex in Sport*

Jeffrey L. Kidder, *Parkour and the City: Risk, Masculinity, and Meaning in a Postmodern Sport*

Alan Klein, *Lakota Hoops: Life and Basketball on Pine Ridge Indian Reservation*

Michael A. Messner and Michela Musto, eds., *Child's Play: Sport in Kids' Worlds*

Jeffrey Montez de Oca, *Discipline and Indulgence: College Football, Media, and the American Way of Life during the Cold War*

Joshua I. Newman, Holly Thorpe, and David L. Andrews, eds., *Sport, Physical Culture, and the Moving Body: Materialisms, Technologies, Ecologies*

Stephen C. Poulson, *Why Would Anyone Do That?: Lifestyle Sport in the Twenty-First Century*

Courtney Szto, *Changing on the Fly: Hockey through the Voices of South Asian Canadians*

Nicole Willms, *When Women Rule the Court: Gender, Race, and Japanese American Basketball*

SOCCER IN MIND

A THINKING FAN'S GUIDE
TO THE GLOBAL GAME

ANDREW M. GUEST

RUTGERS UNIVERSITY PRESS

New Brunswick, Camden, and Newark, New Jersey, and London

Library of Congress Cataloging-in-Publication Data

Names: Guest, Andrew M., author.
Title: Soccer in mind : a thinking fan's guide to the global game / Andrew M. Guest.
Description: New Brunswick : Rutgers University Press, [2022] |
    Series: Critical issues in sport and society | Includes bibliographical references and index.
Identifiers: LCCN 2021015412 | ISBN 9781978817319 (paperback) |
    ISBN 9781978817326 (hardback) | ISBN 9781978817333 (epub) |
    ISBN 9781978817340 (mobi) | ISBN 9781978817357 (pdf)
Subjects: LCSH: Soccer—Social aspects. | Soccer fans—Social aspects. |
    Soccer—Psychological aspects. | Sports and globalization. | World Cup (Soccer)
Classification: LCC GV943.9.S64 G847 2022 | DDC 796.334—dc23
LC record available at https://lccn.loc.gov/2021015412

A British Cataloging-in-Publication record for this book is
available from the British Library.

♾ The paper used in this publication meets the requirements of the
American National Standard for Information Sciences—Permanence
of Paper for Printed Library Materials, ANSI Z39.48-1992.

www.rutgersuniversitypress.org

Manufactured in the United States of America

For
Kris and Pete,
always there with love and support

CONTENTS

PREFACE AND ACKNOWLEDGMENTS

> Football always seems the most important of the least important things.
> —Jürgen Klopp, manager of Liverpool FC

This is a book about mixing global soccer with social science to explore ways to enrich experiences of the sport, while also learning some psychology, sociology, and related academic perspectives along the way. Much of the book was written during 2019 and 2020, just before the COVID-19 pandemic interrupted soccer around the world and before racial justice movements in the United States challenged conventional ways of thinking about sport and society. In some ways, the timing was inauspicious for the project; the dramas of 2020 disrupted the deeply embedded patterns and meanings in soccer analyzed throughout what follows. In more ways, however, that disruption vividly exposed the general need to think about soccer differently.

At the start of the pandemic, it was shocking to know that Gianni Infantino, the head of FIFA, saw the same need for change, articulating an impetus for new perspectives in global soccer after the game was forced to temporarily shut down: "Football will come back, and when it does we'll celebrate coming out of a nightmare together. There is one lesson, however, that both you and me must have understood: the football that will come after the virus will be totally different . . . [more] inclusive, more social and more supportive, connected to the individual countries and at the same time more global, less arrogant and more welcoming. We will be better, more human and more attentive to true values."

The idea of making the game "more human" is essential to this book, and to the very social science of soccer. I doubt Infantino, as president of international soccer's governing body, meant the exact same thing I mean, but the social science perspectives used in the chapters that follow depend upon a centering of human experience. Global soccer is many things. It is recreation, business, spectacle, pastime, tool, institution, outlet, and more. But each of those depends upon people making the game part of their lives and communities. The goal of using psychology, sociology, and social science to explore and explain soccer is to learn how the game intersects with those lives and communities.

The early returns from the restart of elite global soccer during the COVID-19 pandemic were mostly discouraging. The professional men's game came back first with "ghost games"—soccer without fans organized primarily to fulfill television contracts and provide a commercial spectacle. Youth soccer, grassroots soccer, women's soccer, school soccer, and most other forms of the game were pushed aside and largely disregarded. Player health and safety was only considered insofar as it made the televised spectacle possible. National teams and most other authentic representations of community were marginalized in favor of contractual obligations to professional clubs.

In other ways, however, the events of early 2020 put the human essence of soccer on vivid display. Initial efforts to televise the men's Bundesliga (the first league to return) were nearly unwatchable due to a total absence of atmosphere. Broadcasters had to provide fake fan noise in order to make the games seem real. People around the world found creative ways to connect and play, using new technologies to train, learn new skills, and remind themselves that soccer only really requires a very old technology: the ball. Social movements commandeered the televised spectacle, forcing broadcasters to acknowledge that Black Lives Matter and compelling the powers that be to recognize sport as a social, cultural, and political space.

The evolution of soccer as a social phenomenon and as a human experience, in other words, is ongoing. This book offers ways of thinking about soccer without going much deeper into the specifics of the impact of COVID-19 and racial justice movements on soccer (in part because their impact can only be fairly evaluated over time). The book does, however, strive to offer ways of thinking that allow anyone interested in soccer to better understand relationships between the global game, the social world, and individual lives in the past, present, and future. The hope is that this type of thinking can be a fun way to deepen engagements with the game, to learn some social science, and to help make soccer's evolution "more human."

My own experience of writing this book was significantly enriched by some humans that matter to me. I'd particularly like to thank Sara Guest for being the best reader I know, always ready with opinions and giving of time, and Zane Guest for bringing enthusiasm to his dad's project and bringing a sense of purpose to his dad. I'm also grateful to have great readers among my circle of friends; Mike Kaufman and Adam Davis don't like soccer as much as I do, but they like good writing and pushed me thoughtfully to make mine better. Professional colleagues and soccer scholars including Rachel Allison, Jules Boykoff, and John Turnbull offered incisive readings and constructive feedback at critical points for the book's drafting, generously sharing an impressive mix of academic wisdom and thinking fandom. I also feel lucky to have been part of the Football Scholars Forum for almost ten years of "intellectual peladas" about soccer books, with Peter Alegi and Alex Galarza serving as magnanimous team captains.

The writing of this book also benefited from prior efforts to write about soccer as a thinking fan. Spending almost a year between 2009 and 2010 writing brief weekly essays for the now defunct Pitch Invasion blog sparked some of the ideas included in what follows, as did periodic efforts to write outside conventional academic outlets for blogs such as the All-rounder and Engaging Sports. I've also drawn here on some of my more conventional academic writing; chapter 2 borrows, by permission of Taylor & Francis, from Andrew M. Guest and Anne Luijten, "Fan Culture and Motivation in the Context of Successful Women's Professional Team Sports: A Mixed-Methods Case Study of Portland Thorns Fandom," *Sport in Society* 21, no. 7 (2018): 1013–1030; chapter 7 is a slightly updated version of Andrew M. Guest, "Soccer Saves the World?" in *Playing on an Uneven Field: Essays on Exclusion and Inclusion in Sports*, ed. Yuya Kiuchi, reprinted by permission of McFarland & Company, Inc., Box 611, Jefferson NC 28640.

Though the rest of this book draws more on this type of scholarly work than on soccer coaches, the quote at the opening of this preface from Liverpool's Jürgen Klopp seems a helpful way to start thinking about a very social science of soccer. In the macro context of a global pandemic, an overdue reckoning around racial justice, and whatever of society's challenges come next, soccer is indeed among the "least important things." But in the micro context of people's daily lives soccer can be among the "most important" ways to be in that society—offering physical, interpersonal, communal, and intellectual engagements that shape many days and, however subtly, many lives. Soccer is important, in other words, primarily when it becomes what this book strives to understand: a more human game.

SOCCER IN MIND

Croatian national team player Josip Šimunić, caught up in the emotion of qualifying for the 2014 FIFA World Cup finals, led the crowd in a "For the homeland!" chant associated with the fascist *Ustaše* movement. He was suspended by FIFA for ten games, and missed the World Cup. Marko Lukunic/ Pixsell Images.

CHAPTER 1

Lenses

Psychology, Sociology, and the Ways Soccer Explains Us

IN NOVEMBER 2013, a capacity crowd of nearly forty thousand fans at Maksimir Stadium in Zagreb, Croatia, celebrated one of the great moments for any team competing in international soccer: by defeating Iceland 2–0, the Croatian national team had qualified for the 2014 World Cup in Brazil. Amid the ecstasy, someone made the fateful mistake of handing a microphone to Josip Šimunić.

Šimunić was a hard-tackling defender for the team, and at the age of thirty-five this was almost certainly his last chance to play in a World Cup. Alone on the field but for a cameraman tracking his every move, Šimunić moved with a manic and youthful energy that belied his gangly six-foot, five-inch frame, his receding hairline, and his perpetual five-o'clock shadow. Having participated in the international soccer tradition of trading jerseys with one's opponent, he was wearing only a white long-sleeved undershirt, shorn of any team logos, and in his hands he waved a blue Iceland jersey like a magician's scarf. As he dramatically gesticulated with the jersey and microphone, he screamed to the crowd, repeating *"Za dom spremni"*—"For the homeland!" In perfect and immediate synchrony, a large portion of the crowd responded "ready!"[1]

The stadium was pulsating with raw emotion and symbolism—demonstrating the rare capacity of soccer, as the most global game, to host dramatic stories about people and places. Unfortunately, the story that day had no happy ending. Šimunić's chant, it became clear, was a reference to a hateful nationalist cry used by the fascist *Ustase* pro-Nazi regime that ruled Croatia during World War II. Šimunić, despite protesting innocence ("some people have to learn some history"[2]), was suspended through the World Cup and never again played for the Croatian national team.

To make Šimunić's story even more symbolic, it turned out that his dangerous moment of nationalist frenzy followed a lifetime spent mostly nowhere near "the homeland." Though Šimunić's parents were Croatian, he was born and raised in Canberra, Australia, and he developed into a world-class soccer player at the Australian Institute for Sport—a famous talent factory for Australian Olympians.[3] Prior to his World Cup suspension, Šimunić was best known for earning three yellow cards in a 2006 World Cup match between Croatia and Australia. Though two yellow cards usually results in a red card ejection, the English referee in the game had erroneously attributed one of Šimunić's early yellow cards to an Australian player because he was confused by Šimunić's Australian accent.[4] Professionally, Šimunić spent the majority of his career playing in Germany with teams in Hamburg, Berlin, and Hoffenheim, and his wife was a Canadian Croat. Though he ended his career with Dinamo Zagreb and served for several years postretirement as an assistant coach for the Croatian national team, it seems plausible to suggest that Šimunić's emotional nationalism was less a product of his actual home as it was his way of making sense of the type of splintered and imagined identity that so powerfully shapes our twenty-first-century lives. As a general rule, our brains like to use shortcuts and imagine that people are intrinsically something: Croatian or Australian; fascist or patriotic; heroic or depraved. But people don't actually work that way. Neither does soccer.

Šimunić's story is less a morality tale and more a prompt for questions of the type that will organize this book. What is it about soccer that inspires raw emotional fervor that is rarely so vividly on public display? How is it that a game can so powerfully shape identities and enmities? What do players themselves reflect about the places they represent, and what does it take to become great? What are the constructive and destructive ways people can learn to deal with the emotions of the game? How do we make sense of a story such as Šimunić's when soccer is so often portrayed as a unifying force? Can soccer, as a globally shared cultural form, actually do good in the world?

These types of questions are premised on the idea that soccer offers distinct opportunities for understanding societies and selves. Stories like those of Josip Šimunić create opportunities to learn about culture, immigration, and tribalism in contemporary global society, while also offering chances to reflect on how human performance, socialization experiences, and psychology mix into the things we do on the field and in our daily lives. This is not, of course, why most people watch, play, and love soccer—mostly we enjoy the game because it is fun. I get that. But for many of us who enjoy soccer, complementing the fun of soccer with what I call "thinking fandom" offers opportunities for a richer and more meaningful experience with the game.

Thinking fandom here means approaching soccer with a broad intellectual curiosity and an engaged critical consciousness, going beyond winning and losing to think about the meanings of the game. The type of thinking fandom offered in this book employs lenses from social science, most often drawing on concepts, research, and theories from psychology and sociology. The beauty of social science lies in its ability to apply useful tools and methods from science to the incredibly complex social realities of human experience. Soccer, like much of the rest of our lives, is infused with patterns that become evident through systematic investigation. It also takes place in a messy social world that bears little resemblance to a tightly controlled laboratory. Soccer's global appeal depends on its humanity, and a science of soccer—particularly one focused on human experience—depends on understanding its very social nature. By the end of this book, I will also argue that a social science version of thinking fandom might just help make soccer itself better.

To further explain the social science lenses applied in these pages, this chapter begins with three examples of how soccer explains us, using psychology, sociology, and a bit of autobiography to introduce the perspectives that frame the chapters that follow. The three examples, which are also underlying themes for later chapters, include the ways in which soccer shapes our identities, illuminates cultural pluralism, and interweaves our emotional and rational selves. This chapter then shifts to considering specifics of how psychological and sociological perspectives can help us better understand soccer, society, and ourselves. The chapter uses examples from the men's and women's World Cups, along with examples from famous players, to take advantage of the familiarity of high-profile elite soccer to most fans. But the ways of thinking about soccer introduced here should apply beyond the elite level for anyone who enjoys watching, playing, coaching, or just being around the game in all its many guises.

Finally, the end of this introduction explains and defends what may have already triggered some sensitive fans of the game: my preference for the word "soccer" over the word "football." There are few better ways to make

English-speaking fans cranky than this particular semantic debate. But the debate itself embodies some of the personal, psychological, and sociological complexities that make the game emotionally resonant, narratively compelling, and a vital space for social science. While some of the appeal of soccer is its seeming simplicity—ultimately the game is twenty-two players trying to get the ball across a line—much about soccer is more complicated, and more interesting, than it first appears.

How Soccer Explains Us (and Me)

In 2004 the American journalist Franklin Foer published a popular book on soccer and global affairs titled *How Soccer Explains the World*, offering a theory of globalization based on case studies ranging from the Celtic-Rangers rivalry in Scotland to Pelé and corruption in Brazil to suburban soccer families and culture wars in the United States.[5] While the book's theory of globalization received mixed reviews, its ambitious title reflected a growing awareness among academics and serious journalists that soccer was more than just a mass distraction. The opportunities global soccer provides for thoughtful (and fun) analysis have since spawned enlightening historical work, exemplified by David Goldblatt's magisterial *The Ball is Round*, and eclectic economic thinking, such as that in *Soccernomics* by Simon Kuper and Stefan Szymanski.[6] It has also supported entire academic journals (*Soccer & Society* published its first issue in 2000) and a growing community of scholars who draw on a variety of academic disciplines to analyze the game, such as the U.S.-based Football Scholars Forum and the UK-based Football Collective.[7] The goal of this book is to build on that burgeoning body of work with something in between humanistic histories and econometric analytics—and to borrow some inspiration from Foer's title by focusing on how soccer explains us.

I've become interested in the ways soccer explains us partially because the game is a significant part of how I explain myself—and that, in turn, helps frame the perspectives throughout this book. I like to think I've lived through just the right times to be an American, and a social scientist, who loves the game. In the year I was born, 1972, the National Federation of State High School Associations estimates there were 78,510 boys playing high school soccer in the United States and 700 girls. Forty-seven years later, in the most recent data available from the 2018–2019 school year, the total had increased more than tenfold, comprising 459,077 boys and 394,105 girls.[8] This doesn't include the estimated three million boys and girls registered as youth soccer players with clubs outside of schools, but it does give a sense that the last four decades have coincided with an astonishing growth of soccer in the United States. I don't exactly know why my parents put a soccer ball in my crib; neither of them had ever played the game (though, like many American men of his generation, my dad picked up the game recreationally in middle age). But I do know that it became a central part of my identity through a lifetime of playing, coaching, watching, and studying the game in locales ranging from Michigan to Malawi and North Portland to Northern Ireland.

Soccer also exposed me to the intriguing intersections between sports, lives, and communities, leading me to look for ways to understand the broader meanings in the game. Playing college soccer in the middle of Ohio with a collection of teammates and coaches from around the world led me to study in Ireland and serve in the Peace Corps in Malawi. Both experiences were grounded in my joining competitive soccer teams while abroad that offered insight into diverse cultural contexts. A brief stint as the captain of the minor league professional (and short-lived!) Cincinnati Cheetahs led me to question the assumption that professional sports is a necessarily healthy goal for a young player or for community investment. Coaching future national team players with the Illinois Olympic Development Program led me to recognize the unpredictable mix of ability, dedication, access, training, opportunity, and luck that leads to elite talent development. Working with inner-city soccer programs in Detroit and Chicago public housing communities led me to develop an enduring curiosity about how soccer might do some social good. Along the way I also found an outlet for my intellectual curiosities about soccer, and sports more broadly, through more academic study, earning a master's degree in sports studies at Miami University and then a PhD in human development at the University of Chicago. Though my dissertation work was a broader investigation of psychological adaptation for children in Chicago public housing communities and Angolan refugee camps, soccer was my entry point into each community.

In recent years, after my days of playing and coaching transitioned to a more academic life as a professor of psychology and sociology at the University of Portland in Oregon, I've taught a variety of social science courses (from lifespan development to a quadrennial offering on the World Cup) that have furthered my appreciation for just how easily a game can intersect with a life. In his classic formulation of development through the lifespan, Erik Erikson situated ego identity as our central developmental task.[9] Starting with the emergence of a self-concept in early childhood, through the active identity exploration of adolescence and emerging adulthood, to the shifting and deepening of life commitments during middle and later life, the human mind is primed to affiliate and differentiate in ways that craft a distinct sense of self. Although that process, which some psychologists call "identity work," is shaped by a wide range of forces, from families to schools to communities, for many people like me sports provide an emotionally engaging opportunity to explore and connect.

The way soccer lends itself to identity work offers a first example of how the game can help explain us. For many, soccer starts interacting with our identity as we play the game at a young age. For many kids, being a soccer player means connecting to physical activity and being part of a team. I first fell in love with the game because a soccer field was a place I could have fun, feel competent, and engage with my friends around a shared challenge. Elite players now often have to fully commit their identities to soccer at very young ages, in ways that risk what Eriksonian psychologists might call "identity foreclosure"—identity commitments that lack the type of healthy exploration important to longer-term well-being (a topic discussed more in chapter 5 on performance psychology). But most of us diversify our identities through relationships, careers, politics, religion, interests, and other social commitments that compose a reasonably stable self-concept, with soccer and sports as just one particularly fun anchor point.

In crafting our self-concepts, soccer also provides points of communal identification and social comparison—particularly in the capacity of teams to represent cities, nations, or ideologies. This is part of how Josip Šimunić came to identify with Croatia through soccer, and to encourage Croatians to identify themselves with their team. It is also why every World Cup I briefly identify more as an American than I do in non–World Cup years. And it is the source of an ongoing identity crisis around the fact that I grew up in Seattle as a fan of the old North American Soccer League (NASL) Sounders but am now a card-carrying citizen of the People's Republic of Portland—spending much of my year following Seattle's archrivals, the Portland Timbers and Thorns. In most practical ways Seattle and Portland are not that different as cities, but soccer makes local fans feel psychologically compelled to layer identity differences onto the obvious similarities.

Soccer fandom more generally is another prompt for identity work, facilitating our natural tendency to affiliate with groups that have clear identity markers (such as colors, jerseys, and scarves), along with opportunities for group distinctions through competition. While fandom will be discussed more extensively in chapter 2, the point here is that soccer fields provide a rare space where communities put themselves on display—so much so that in his oft-cited discussion of nationalism the social historian Eric Hobsbawm argues that "the imagined community of millions seems more real as a team of eleven named people."[10] An "imagined community," according to social theorist Benedict Anderson, is a way of creating a sense of nation or community, despite few visible boundaries and diverse populations, through the simple fact that people perceive themselves to be part of that nation.[11] The eleven named people on a World Cup soccer team, and soccer team identification more broadly, have become significant mediators of those perceptions and, in turn, of our communal identity work.

The universal tendency for us to identify and affiliate does not, however, suggest that fandom means the same thing all over the world. As anyone who has watched games in different parts of the world knows, culture matters. I think, for example, of the contrast between my experience watching a top-division game in Iceland—where the main obstacle to getting into the stadium was all the bicycles kids had strewn haphazardly (and unlocked) around the entrance gate—and watching a top division game in Scotland, where a child (and his father) had to be extracted from the stands with armored police protection for impulsively cheering when the away team's English striker scored a cracker of a goal. Fan cultures vary dramatically, playing styles vary some, and the game itself offers a fertile empty field to be filled with meanings by the social contexts in which it takes place.

This tendency toward cultural pluralism is a second theme that becomes clear when watching soccer through social science lenses. While some like to think of soccer as good or bad, fun or boring, simple or complicated, here we will take soccer itself to be something like what some academics call an empty or floating signifier: "a symbol or concept loose enough to mean many things to many people, yet specific enough to galvanize action in a particular direction."[12] Soccer, from this perspective, is mostly an empty—or at the very least neutral—space that gets filled in with meanings by the people and places that play, watch, and ascribe significance to the game. Analyzing how this works will be key to chapter 3, which contrasts different cultures of the game. But the cultural pluralism of soccer also explains something about how people think, feel, and behave—with a foundation of underlying universal human tendencies, and then many socialized differences in how those tendencies manifest. Culture and socialization experiences are not all-powerful: soccer in Brazil isn't totally distinct from soccer in England. But culture also isn't trivial. There are real differences between what the game means in Mexico and what it means in the United States, and real reasons why U.S. soccer has had a hard time capitalizing on the rich diversity that should be a strength for our national teams.

Answering the question of how the United States might best take advantage of its cultural diversity to fuel soccer success also depends on a third example and theme for the very social science of soccer: that the game necessarily interweaves our emotional and rational selves. There is a purely aesthetic appeal to athletic artistry. Think here of Messi gliding past defenders with the ethereal balance and touch of a dancer, or Marta spinning and juking like a white-water current. There is also a raw emotional joy to getting wrapped up in an intense competition—the ecstatic release of goal in extra time after a tactical master class, or the cathartic schadenfreude of seeing a conniving opponent sent off for the denial of a goal-scoring opportunity. But those base aesthetic and emotional experiences are counterbalanced by our more reasoned understandings. If we didn't grow up in Argentina or Spain, we gather information and make intentional decisions about whether we consider ourselves fans of Messi and Barcelona. We read about Marta's background to learn whether her bravura is more influenced by the romanticized Brazilian samba style or by her fighting against the patriarchal history of Brazilian soccer. We study tactics to learn about breaking down a high-block defense with vertical passing, and we interpret rules to make judgment calls about who constitutes the last defender. And American soccer fans alternate screaming chants of "U-S-A" and singing "I believe that we will win" with copious time debating whether there will ever truly be an American soccer style or an American soccer superstar.

We can do any of these as distinct acts—enjoy the aesthetics, immerse ourselves in the emotions, engage the reasons and the rationale—but a core premise of this book is that they are better together. This is also a premise of human psychology. As psychologists from classical Freudians to contemporary neuroscientists have recognized, our minds are divided. We constantly navigate between our basic instincts, call them the id or the limbic system, and our higher-order reasoning, whether the superego or neocortex. And the human experience is about finding ways for it all to work together—to interweave our emotions and our rationality in a way exemplified by soccer as one of the most globally shared human interests. It then follows that the more we understand the game, the better the game gets.

My own relationship with soccer has evolved over the years, just as the game itself has evolved in the United States and globally. And while soccer is no longer as much of an anchor to my identity, the opportunities I've had to learn about the game through travels, research, teaching, playing, and ongoing fandom in locales ranging from Mexico to Tanzania, from South Africa to England, have indeed made the game better to me. I've continued to play in men's league and pickup games as my aging body allows—the game is still a hub for my social life, as it is for so many around the world. And I've also continued to coach when the opportunity arises, but mostly at the grassroots level with teams such as the middle school group down the street where immigrant boys from Haiti, Mexico, Nigeria, and elsewhere found their way to recreational soccer for its remarkable ability to simultaneously connect them to their international roots and their new American community.

I also have to admit that I've tried to quit the game a few times. As my body ages, I've wondered if it was really worth the frustration of playing with only memories of peak performance. As I settled into my academic career as a social scientist, I've wondered if I shouldn't pay more attention to topics other than sports and games. But the more I've thought about it, the more I've realized that the game is an invaluable way to engage with a pluralistic world. It has also proven to be a fun and enriching space to employ the social science lenses I've honed, like soccer skills, through many years of practice. So, what specifically do those lenses look like?

Social Science Lenses: Psychology, Sociology, and Soccer

A defining characteristic of most social science is its centering of human experience and human society. Social science starts with the scientific method—asking questions based on existing knowledge and theory, exploring those questions systematically using empirical research, and drawing conclusions based on identifying meaningful patterns. But social science, in contrast to the natural sciences, is also heavily leavened by the complexity of people and the messiness of human societies. There are few definitive laws for the social world, but there are meaningful patterns that become evident through systematic observation and through comparing ideas, theories, and experiences. Those meaningful patterns are there in soccer culture just as they are in every other social landscape.

For an example, let's return to a recent World Cup—but this time on the women's side. The 2015 Women's World Cup in Canada was the seventh iteration of the tournament, and the largest yet with twenty-four teams qualifying for the finals. While the tournament itself was a rollicking affair highlighted by spirited newcomers such as Cameroon and Costa Rica and championship rivalries such the United States versus Japan, the social organization of the tournament was defined in part by soccer's sexist history. FIFA has been sponsoring a men's World Cup since 1930, including thirty-two teams in the final since 1998, and had hesitated to even share the World Cup name with women at their first sanctioned championship in 1991 (calling the tournament the "First FIFA World Championship for Women's Football for the M&M's Cup").[13] FIFA didn't want to associate its "World Cup" brand with the women's game (though apparently it was less worried about marketing candy). Even the 2015 version in Canada, a country that has historically been more supportive of women's sports than most in the world, was notorious for having the tournament games played on artificial turf fields—a surface that is expressly prohibited for the men's tournament because it's not considered top standard. It is not hard here to see a meaningful pattern.

During that 2015 tournament I had the treat of making a trip up the West Coast to Vancouver, British Columbia, to watch several games at BC Place stadium on the central island of one of the world's most beautiful cities. The stadium is mostly a soulless concrete dome, and FIFA and its corporate sponsors did all they could to paper the facility with bland sloganeering such as "she believes" and "to a greater goal." But the games themselves were often magnificent; the aesthetics and emotions of athletes in their prime playing for their country rarely disappoints. And the American television audience clearly agreed. The U.S. games in the 2015 Women's World Cup garnered the largest television audiences of any soccer games, male or female, ever televised in the United States. These ratings were not quite Super Bowl level, but they were significantly higher than the average ratings for the NBA and NHL championship finals.

What explains the mass appeal of the U.S. women's team despite FIFA's efforts to marginalize the women's game? I think it has as much to do with psychological and sociological phenomena as it has to do with soccer phenomena. The women do indeed play great soccer. But as some dismissive commentators point out, elite women's teams also have average differences in strength and speed that make head-to-head competition with elite men's teams challenging. There are practical reasons that sports of all sorts are divided by gender (though those reasons, and even gender itself, are also more complicated than they seem). So we can't love women's soccer only for the absolute level of the competition.

Instead, taking a psychological perspective, it becomes clear that our motivations for watching sports of all types are rarely just about the absolute competitiveness of a team. If so, only the world champions would ever have an audience (and no one would ever watch the American men's national team!). If so, Americans would never fill one-hundred-thousand-seat stadiums for college football and Texas would never have high school football stadiums that seat nearly twenty thousand fans. If so, we'd only ever watch heavyweight boxers and completely ignore the little guys like Manny Pacquiao and Floyd Mayweather. Psychologically there are at least two important things going on here. One is related to what psychologists call "social identity theory," which is the idea that our behavior and attitudes are often guided by powerful needs to affiliate with groups.[14] One reason we like to watch teams that we perceive to represent us in some way is because fandom helps us with our identity work. We watch the Women's World Cup because it makes us feel part of something beyond our selves. A second reason is related to "hedonic adaptation" and the remarkable ability of the human psyche to adapt. On average, people with a reasonable amount of money are just as happy as the wealthy because the more we have, the more we adjust our expectations. We can enjoy soccer of all types, beyond a minimum decent standard, as long as we appreciate what we are looking for. We watch the Women's World Cup not only because the athletes are bigger, faster, and stronger, but also because it is fun to watch players who are savvy, skillful, athletically gifted, and represent us in all our human complexity.

These quick takes are the result of applying a psychological lens to soccer, even if they don't even scratch the surface of all the psychology involved in playing and coaching the game. A psychological lens draws our attention to human experiences by clarifying the patterns of thoughts, behaviors, and emotions that make something like soccer so fun, challenging, and engaging. Psychology helps us understand fandom, performance under pressure, participation motivation, and all the various ways the human mind shapes our experience of the game.

We'll also need more sociological perspectives to widen our attention and understand the broader social forces shaping soccer. One other reason the U.S. Women's National Team (USWNT) is so popular in the United States, for example, is because they win. A lot. The USWNT has won four of eight Women's World Cup titles and four of six Olympic gold medals prior to 2021, and the U.S. television audience likes to support winners. But why? Why do U.S. fans get so invested in patriotic display, and why is the United States so good at women's soccer? Here we need to understand something about culture and social structures, both key components of a sociological lens.

From a sociological perspective, it is clear that a wide variety of nations and societies use sports of all types to promote patriotism and unity. A national sports team of any sort offers a powerful visual representation of country as people that is rare elsewhere in global affairs—patriotic photos of a United Nations delegation just don't have the same punch. The United States has been particularly eager to leverage the emotional appeal of sports, with social historians such as Mark Dyreson arguing that "more than any other nation, the United States has politicized its Olympic participation."[15] Americans put a high cultural value on patriotism, at least in part because American culture has a relatively short and dynamic history compared to many other parts of the world. We like to see nationhood as a competition, and sports are perfect for that vision.

American culture also heavily promotes "American exceptionalism"—the doctrine that there is something unique and special about the American system. Scholars such as Andrei Markovits have argued that sports as a whole represent a form of American exceptionalism in that we've mostly preferred our own historically odd games (baseball, anyone?).[16] And the relatively shallow roots of soccer in the United States have allowed for women's soccer to become another exceptionalism—a space where the United States is distinct in promoting almost as many participation opportunities for women as for men.[17]

But U.S. success in women's soccer is not just about cultural values. The opportunities for girls and women to play in the United States were mandated through the application of Title IX, legislating equal opportunities in educational settings, to sports in a way that created a huge talent pool. Certainly part of the reason the U.S. women are so good and so popular is because at a micro level they play with great attitude and effort. And that is the dominant discourse around their success. But from a sociological perspective we also have to recognize the macro level: according to FIFA statistics, well over half of the women's soccer players in the world live in the United States and Canada (despite those countries only accounting for about one-twentieth of the world's population).[18] Though it sounds tautological, the United States is so good at women's soccer at least in part because we have (a lot of) women playing soccer.

These ideas help to introduce how we might apply sociological lenses, or what is often called "the sociological imagination," to soccer. The sociological imagination, which C. Wright Mills famously described as an awareness of how our personal experiences relate to wider society, helps us see the ways social forces shape how soccer is played and, more importantly, the significance the game takes in people's lives and communities.[19] A sociological lens helps us understand the social and cultural meanings in the game, emphasizing the ways in which individual experiences of soccer intersect with wider social forces.

In this book sociological interpretations will primarily work in tandem with psychological perspectives, though sometimes the material will also call on cultural anthropology, economics, political science, and any discipline that offers useful insights toward a very social science of soccer. Those lenses and insights are used in the chapters that follow to analyze and interpret a selection of key topics representing three broad areas: the macro level of soccer as a global phenomenon (including chapter 2 on fandom and chapter 3 on global soccer cultures), the micro level of soccer players and performances (including chapter 4 on talent development and chapter 5 on soccer psychology), and the ways soccer itself can be fashioned as a social good (including chapter 6 on the social impact of star players and mega events and chapter 7 on soccer for development initiatives). The selection of topics is not exhaustive. Instead, each chapter is an exercise in crafting a very social science of soccer that can be readily applied to other aspects of the game. Building through the chapters is a vision of thinking fandom, and a way of thinking about soccer as a social phenomenon, that will come to fruition in the final chapter. In that chapter I more directly unpack what it means to be a thinking fan and suggest examples of what thinking fandom might look like in practice. The intention throughout is to show how a very social science of soccer can offer a more enjoyable, enriching, and effectual experience of the game.

The hope of the book is that a better future for soccer can come to fruition through a more thoughtful engagement with the meanings of the game. A very social science of soccer approaches the game in a way that prioritizes people and places over profit and performance. This may seem naïve in an era when the global game has become big business, and when many fans just want their teams to win regardless of the costs. But the argument here is that the social essence of soccer is exactly what has made it so popular. It would, in other words, be equally naïve to assume that cold business analytics can tell us more about the game than considerations of human experiences and interpretations of social forces. There are patterns to the social world around soccer, along with patterns in the game itself, that can be illuminated by systematic research and reasoned theory, but those patterns are embedded less in natural laws and more in the messiness of being human and the quirks of a game that humans love.

Why Soccer (Rather than "Football")

One of the most peculiar quirks of soccer is its name. Anyone who has discussed or written about the game with a mixed audience knows my preference for the word "soccer" is not a choice to be taken lightly: the "it's football, not soccer" Internet meme is a creative semantic battleground that often makes explicit the emotional fervor with which fans of the game take sides. People with too much time on their hands have created images of characters ranging from Morpheus in *The Matrix* to SpongeBob SquarePants to Gene Wilder as Willy Wonka screaming (in bold font and all-caps) that the game is called "football." Some have added snarky illustrations annotating the "foot" and the "ball" in pictures of Manchester United players in action next to the "hand" and the "egg" in pictures of the Dallas Cowboys playing America's game. Academics have taken note: the economist Stefan Szymanski and language scholar Silke-Maria Weineck wrote an entire book in 2018 "on the history, emotion, and ideology behind one of the Internet's most ferocious debates."[20] The name of the game itself, in other words, can offer one last introductory example of watching soccer through social science lenses.

It is true that logically the game should be called football; it is, after all, primarily (though we must admit not exclusively) about using one's feet to kick a ball. But one of the points of bringing social science into the discussion is that pure logic cannot explain much about soccer. It is not logical to spend so much of our time watching grown men and women kick a ball; it is not logical to invest our identity in the happenstance of a ball crossing a line; and it is not logical to invest hopes for large-scale social change in a game. To understand these things, we have to understand the context.

The context is that "football" is such a good and simple name that lots of different varieties have staked a claim. Most of the bitterness is about American gridiron football usurping the term, but some other popular global varieties include Gaelic football, Australian rules football, and the one that probably started all the trouble in the first place: rugby football. The historical record, as smartly strung together by American writer Steve Hendricks in a 2015 letter to the rest of the world and published by *Sporting Intelligence*, suggests that the origins of "soccer" lay in efforts in the mid to late 1800s by English prep schools to distinguish between "Association football" and "Rugby football."[21] The word "rugby" had an easy enough ring to it but calling a game "association" didn't roll off the tongue. So, following English prep school traditions of abbreviating words and adding an *-er* suffix to make them sound convivial (coffee or tea with your brekker?), "soc" was pulled out of "association" and given the *-er* ending. The word "soccer" basically— and ironically, given contemporary assumptions that "soccer" is just an Americanism—seems to come from aristocratic British schoolboys trying to sound casually cool.

Through parts of the twentieth century the terms "soccer" and "football" were used in largely interchangeable ways in both British and American media. The economist (and coauthor of both *Soccernomics* and *It's Football, Not Soccer*) Stefan Szymanski has analyzed the popularity of each term in newspaper reports and book titles since 1900, finding that the word "soccer" only declined in popularity in England once it started to become popular in the United States. No less an English soccer icon than Sir Matt Busby, manager of Manchester United in the 1950s and 1960s, used the term in the title of his autobiography, *Soccer at the Top*. By the time soccer started gaining traction in the United States, American football was too well established to avoid confusion on this side of the pond—so the word "soccer" took hold.[22]

Szymanski speculates that "the penetration of the game into American culture, measured by the use of the name 'soccer,' has led to backlash against the use of the word in Britain, where it was once considered an innocuous alternative to the word 'football.'"[23] Taking this diplomatic argument a bit further, the name of the game itself has become another of the irrational but deeply meaningful points of rivalry and tribalism provoked by kicking a ball.

Steve Hendricks in his "Letter from America" also points out that it is not just Americans who call the game "soccer":

> Canada, South Africa, Australia, New Zealand, and a goodly share of Ireland do. In South Africa, even the Afrikaners call it *sokker*, and in Canada, the Québécois, who loathe every other English word, use soccer unmodified by so much as a circumflex. Britain is alone among the world's major English-speaking countries in banishing the term. In fact, wipe us 320 million Americans off the map (a tempting thought, I know), and the world would still have more than 100 million soccer-inclined speakers in the above five countries. Rather puts your 64 million football-inclined speakers in perspective, what? Toss the United States back in, add countries where English isn't spoken but where soccer reigns supreme (as in Japan, which uses *sakkaa*) or where soccer has parity with football (as in the Philippines, where it's *saker*), and the world's soccer speakers number more than half a billion. Truly the sun never sets on the British linguistic empire.[24]

Ultimately, like so much about the game, the great football-versus-soccer debate stirs up a rich brew of emotions, allegiances, and meanings. That, to me, is what makes it all so fascinating. I'm glad Brits and Anglophiles prefer the term "football." It makes it more fun for Americans to prefer the term "soccer" (to say nothing of Italians calling it *calcio*), and it provides convenient reinforcement for the example themes introduced earlier in this chapter. First, the name of the game itself involves identity claims, situating us linguistically, culturally, and interpersonally. Second, recognizing the multiple names of the games requires acknowledging the game's cultural pluralism. While the fundamental rules are the same everywhere, the meanings depend heavily on social, cultural, and psychological context. And third, the names we choose jumble our emotional and rational selves in ways that make it all the more entertaining. I happen to think the name "soccer" is more rational than the name "football," given all the many football codes around the world. But I'll admit to my own psychological bias: there is a pique of pride and playfulness involved in poking the "it's football, not soccer" crowd.

The ways in which anger wells up in many anglophiles when Americans talk "soccer," along with the resentment that burns in many American soccer fans when our own teams opt to define themselves as United FC (Football Club), emerge from the same brain network that made Josip Šimunić think it was a good idea to celebrate Croatia's World Cup qualification with a neofascist chant. Soccer just has a way of engaging all the different dimensions of the human experience. As such, it is worth noting that while Šimunić never again played for the Croatian national team, he did go on to help produce a documentary film in an attempt to clear his name.[25] Šimunić, in other words, got caught up in the irrational complexity of the game and decided that he needed to explain. He wants the world to know that his moment of nationalist frenzy was not as simple as it appeared. And while I have no interest in defending Šimunić, I have nothing but sympathy (along with the remainder of this book) for the idea that soccer is much more than it first appears.

Under a massive American flag unfurled over the crowd at the 2010 FIFA World Cup game between the United States and Algeria, played in Pretoria, South Africa. Author photo.

CHAPTER 2

Fans

Losing Your Mind and Finding Your Place

F OR U.S. FANS THE 2010 WORLD CUP IN SOUTH AFRICA offered an emotional jumble of the type that makes enjoying soccer an enduring paradox: it simultaneously torments and compels. The U.S. team's first two games in the group stage included a surprising draw with England (thanks to a comical goalkeeping mistake) and an enervating draw with Slovenia (thanks in part to controversial refereeing decisions), setting up an anxious final group stage game with Algeria for the potential joy of advancing to the second round. I had gone to great expense and put in extensive effort to be there for all three games, and part of my reward was to be wracked with the conflicts of fandom: an intense mix of anxiety and excitement that seemed all the more strange for being about a game in which I had no real stake. In retrospect I can't help thinking about it like a social scientist: why, anyway, does soccer mean so much to fans, and is fandom really worth investing so much of one's self?[1] As the kickoff of the U.S.–Algeria game approached, however, I was deeply in the moment.

The game was scheduled for Loftus Versfeld Stadium in an upmarket section of Pretoria, with pregame festivities on the surrounding streets including an iconic World Cup mix of singing, chanting, face painting, and drinking (mostly by the Americans). There was also much flag waving on both sides and just a hint of tension. When, on my way to the game, I passed a particularly large group of Algerian fans stationed in front of an outdoor restaurant banging drums and determinedly waving large Algerian flags, I felt the uncomfortable urge to give wide berth. I knew rationally there was no real threat but my autonomic nervous system accelerated anyway: shorter breaths, a faster heartbeat, small prickles of sweat. Emotions, those capricious drives motivating a significant part of soccer fandom, were starting to take over.

My own usual approach to fandom, befitting my academic interest in soccer, tends to be stoic and cerebral. This very book is largely an argument for thinking fandom—for recognizing the virtues of applying an intellectual curiosity to the game that makes observing, interpreting, and learning as rewarding as emoting. Even sitting in attendance at the World Cup, I usually only get back up on my feet when the rows in front require it because of their own enthusiasms, like standing for a corner kick or to cheer a goal. During the U.S.–Algeria game, however, the game built such tension through ninety minutes of scoreless back-and-forth that by the end the whole stadium was on its feet and ready to burst. As if to accommodate, several minutes into injury time the U.S. team executed one graceful move from the U.S. goalkeeper's hands to a midfielder's run to a striker's cross to a defender's miscue to a slotted finish by U.S. star Landon Donovan. The tension broke. The U.S. fans erupted with ecstasy. And I was right in the middle of it.

Unthinkingly and uncouthly, I leapt from my seat and started screaming in a high-pitched staccato that hadn't passed my lips since boyhood. I unabashedly began hugging and slapping hands with strangers, friends, and compatriots. Seemingly out of nowhere, a massive American flag unfurled like a wave climbing my section of seats; I frantically grabbed the fabric to do my part and make sure it kept moving overhead. I completely lost myself in a florid moment of patriotic fervor, with light shimmering through my red, white, and blue ceiling amid huddled masses of people with whom I most shared in common ninety minutes of soccer. Simply put, and in the tradition of soccer fans all over the world, I lost my mind.

This capacity of soccer to cause otherwise rational people to lose their minds is just one of many curious dimensions of fandom we can start to understand through social science. The jumbling of our emotional and rational selves triggered by soccer is an underlying theme of this book and a very human tendency. And fandom is, by definition, a very social experience. To be a fan means to appreciate something beyond our selves, and a significant part of enacting fandom is joining a community—real or imagined, local or global. We are compelled not just because of emotional connections, but also because of social connections that situate us in our communities and society. This chapter will draw on several specific social experiences of fandom to unpack the meaning of those connections, including examples from my own research on fans of the Portland Thorns (the top-drawing women's professional team in the world) and from rivalries such as those between Portland and Seattle and between the United States and Mexico.

This chapter will also explore the paradoxes of fandom by starting with a small dose of classic social theory and a selective overview of contemporary research. The idea is not to offer a comprehensive review of how to understand fandom; that is a task that would require a book of its own (and there are already several).[2] Instead, the intention here is to use theory, research, and relevant examples to suggest that fan experiences are indeed worthwhile because they can be among the most deeply human parts of the game. People are conflicted. Feeling both tormented and compelled by soccer, whether from the stands, from the field, from the sideline, or from the couch, involves the human mind in all its complexity. The question thus becomes not just why soccer means so much to fans, nor only why soccer sometimes makes us lose our minds, but what about the human mind makes people so compelled by a game?

Fandom as Human Nature

In hindsight, long after the fervor of my 2010 U.S. goal celebration passed, I think of that moment as my most powerful experience of what eminent sociologist Emile Durkheim described as "collective effervescence." Durkheim discussed the phenomenon in his 1915 book *The Elementary Forms of Religious Life*, offering a deeply sociological account of group religious rituals as moments when society is made manifest and internalized.[3] These moments often feel meaningful because of the intense emotional and physical elevation in group actions—dancing, yelling, singing, fighting, and so forth. The result is a buzzing feeling of leaving one's self and being immersed in the energy of a group. Most soccer fans know the feeling; it is a reason we still go to games in person despite our high-definition TVs at home, and part of why we get an eerie sense of dissatisfaction from the fan-less "ghost games" common during the COVID-19 pandemic. The power and universality of that feeling is also a reason to consider deeper elements of human nature embedded in soccer fandom.

Durkheim's concept of collective effervescence emerged from a context far removed from contemporary global soccer: a study of Australian Aboriginal communities and their religious rituals around the start of the twentieth century. Reading that study, it is not hard to imagine him talking about my experience at the 2010 World Cup, or the experience of many fans when deeply immersed in moments of soccer drama. Durkheim writes:

> When arrived at this state of exaltation, a man does not recognize himself any longer. Feeling himself dominated and carried away by some sort of an external power which makes him think and act differently than in normal times, he naturally has the impression of being himself no longer. It seems to him that he has become a new being: the decorations he puts on and the masks that cover his face figure materially in this interior transformation, and to a still greater extent, they aid in determining its nature. And as at the same time all his companions feel themselves transformed in the same way and express this sentiment by their cries, their gestures and their general attitude, everything is just as though he really were transported into a special world, entirely different from the one where he ordinarily lives, and into an environment filled with exceptionally intense forces that take hold of him and metamorphose him.[4]

The "decorations" here are not incidental. Moments of collective effervescence are inextricably linked with totems, symbols which themselves become sacred and remind members of a society of their collective values. For Durkheim writing about Australian Aboriginal communities around the start of the twentieth century these might be sacred animals or a figure crafted in the shape of a sacred plant. For the U.S. soccer fans that day in Pretoria, and for soccer fans all over the world, the totems are the jerseys, scarves, and flags that we use to signify our fandom and our social identities.

The social identities embedded in collective soccer experiences at a World Cup, despite ancient roots, are often intertwined with modern nationalism. The blunt chants of "U-S-A" at global sporting events such as the World Cup are not just mind-numbing in their repetition—they are identity claims and assertions of patriotism. The distinctive prompts for those claims at an international soccer match, as described by sociologist Sven Ismer, start with collective rituals: singing the national anthem, or chanting words and rhythms that have shared meanings for a national group (think of the U.S. fans with their "I believe that we will win" chant, or Icelandic fans with their "Viking thunderclap").[5] The identity prompts continue with the emotional charge of goal celebrations or other competitive moments, along with the physical sequelae of hand slapping, hugs, and bodily communion. The prompts are further accentuated by the media's tendency to promote patriotism as a way of creating sentimental connections for viewers and advertisers. The whole mix becomes a potent brew of emotional nationalism. I personally get emotional watching a Banco de Chile commercial from the 2014 World Cup featuring an appeal by the crew of Chilean miners who were dramatically rescued after sixty-nine days trapped underground.[6] When the miners plead for the national team to remember that *"para un Chileno nada es imposible!"* my arms erupt in goosebumps. And I've never even been to Chile.

This type of emotional nationalism is another example of how fandom can cause us to lose our rational minds, though it is also easy to spot its downsides of jingoism, xenophobia, and hostility. While emotional nationalism may sometimes seem mindless, it fits with classic understandings of how the human mind activates through socially meaningful rituals. The psychological foil to Durkheim's sociological account of religious experience, for example, was William James's 1902 book, *The Varieties of Religious Experience.*[7] James focused on the individual within religious rituals, and argued that religious experiences are most distinct in their feelings of transcendence, with the universality of that feeling revealing something about human nature and neural capacity. Though James did not have the tools of neuroscience in 1902, his account was a forebearer of more contemporary research exploring how neurotransmitters, hormones, and brain activity associate with intense emotional experiences of all types—including sports fandom.

For one example from the soccer world, consider the research on the testosterone of fans watching the 1994 World Cup final between Brazil and Italy. As described by Eric Simons in his book *The Secret Lives of Sports Fans: The Science of Sports Obsession*, psychologist Paul Bernhardt used the opportunity of the game to gather saliva samples from fans at a Brazilian watch party and an Italian pizzeria in Atlanta.[8] When the game ended dramatically in penalty kicks with the Italian Roberto Baggio sending his spot kick well clear of the crossbar, Bernhardt lost most of his sample of Italian fans—they were too depressed to participate. But the ones that had enough left to provide spit samples supported the hypothesis: testosterone shot up for the Brazilian fans, and dropped for the Italian fans.[9] As Simons describes it, "These groups, sitting in sports bars more than two thousand miles from site of the game, watching twenty-two soccer players that none of them knew personally, were so invested in the outcome that they had essentially the same testosterone response that the players themselves did. Whether the competition was direct or vicarious didn't appear to matter."[10]

Our fandom, as with all human experiences, is deep in both our brain and our body. My loss of control that day in South Africa in 2010 was as physiological and neurological as it was sociological. But my physiology, and my brain, is not just something that independently creates soccer fandom—my physiology and my brain are simultaneously cause and effect. Simons explains: "The hormonal response is not just unadulterated reflex. What we humans do is adulterate our reflexes. Whether you have an outcome-related testosterone increase depends entirely, researchers say, on that individual psychology. It depends on how you think, how you care about the team, how your personality responds to life."[11]

Sports take on meaning, in other words, because they channel a recursive loop between physiology, identity, and society. In the years since 2010 I have periodically returned to that U.S. goal versus Algeria through a YouTube montage interspersing the emotional reactions of U.S. fans around the world, from a basement in Arkansas to a bar in Berlin (the video is accessible via an online search for "Landon Donovan Algeria goal celebrations"). The four-minute video never fails to make me emotional; the joy and relief of diverse groups of fans responding to an unexpected goal again triggers my autonomic nervous system with a baby version of my response that day in the stadium. And that emotional response, in turn, is shaped by the years I've spent playing and watching soccer that have made the game itself part of my identity. That identity, also shaped by years of elementary school pledges of allegiance to the flag, is immersed in my social milieu: coming of age in a particular time and place where soccer was a safe space for an urban, coastal, middle-class American male to engage a global curiosity (and perhaps just a bit of global competitiveness).

This recursive loop ultimately provides a universal template for fandom and reinforces that the underlying physiology of fandom is based on shared neural hardware. But it also results in diverse manifestations. Algerian fans that day at the World Cup also combined physiological reactions, communal identity, and social meanings—but the result and the mix made for a very different set of experiences. And for every American fan who feels the effervescence of belonging through soccer, there are many who may also feel the ire of exclusion due to the complicated natures of both American identity and American soccer culture. Following William James and leveraging the global appeal of soccer, we can learn as much from considering the *varieties* of fan experiences as from identifying a universal template. The varieties, in fact, help us to understand both the similarities and the differences of fandom. What, then, might more contemporary research and theory on fandom look like in a distinctively modern soccer space?

Fandom as Values

The Portland Thorns franchise, part of the National Women's Soccer League (NWSL), has played only since 2013, but in the initial years of its existence it quickly became, by the metric of regular average attendance, the most popular women's professional sports team in the world. From a social science perspective, this raises a rich opportunity to think about fandom and how the game matters. What kindles contemporary fandom? Why do large groups of people attach themselves to a new team in a new league to enjoy a version of the game that has been historically marginalized and still has trouble garnering popular attention? Why, when the average team in the women's Bundesliga draws only one thousand fans per game, when most NWSL teams draw between two thousand and four thousand fans per game, when the WNBA averages around seventy-five hundred fans per game, and when more than half the men's teams in Major League Soccer average less than twenty thousand fans per game, do the Portland Thorns average nearly twenty thousand fans per game (even when an uncooperative schedule takes away many of the star players for large chunks of the season)?[12] Answering these questions motivated me to spend a good part of the 2016 Thorns season observing, interviewing, and surveying fans, and offers insight into both conventional and alternative ways of thinking about the social science of fandom.[13]

What constitutes a conventional view of fandom in the contemporary scholarly literature? Most existing research on sport fan motivation comes from a sports business perspective and attends to the sports that usually draw the largest mass audiences: American college and professional football, basketball, and baseball, along with European soccer. This research tends to categorize fan motivations into a variety of interacting types that might be easy to guess without intensive empirical work. Common examples include having opportunities to escape life's problems, being able to bet on outcomes, enjoying the simple entertainment value of sports spectacle, experiencing emotional stimulation, and benefiting from the self-esteem boost we get when our team wins.

That last motivation is oft-cited by sport psychologists, who use the acronym BIRGing (Basking In Reflected Glory) to describe the motivating satisfaction of having a team one cares about do well.[14] Even though I rationally know that whether the Thorns win or lose has nothing to do with me as a person, I feel a nice boost when they win and a significant deflation when they lose. And some years they have lost a lot. Fortunately, any highly identified fan has a whole host of psychological coping strategies to manage such disappointment. As laid out by prolific sports fandom researcher Daniel Wann and colleagues, every moment of BIRGing can by counterbalanced by times of CORFing (Cutting Off Reflected Failure).[15] Fans use a wide range of psychological strategies that include "outgroup derogation" (Seattle is a bunch of sellouts anyway); "biased attributions" (how can a league call itself professional with that type of refereeing?); "magical thinking" (we've been cursed ever since that one championship season); and "downward social comparison" (at least we're better than . . .). The classic study of BIRGing even found that fans were more likely to describe a victory with the pronoun "we" (*we* played an amazing game) as compared to descriptions of losses (*the team* just didn't seem to try)—automatically disidentifying as a way of maintaining public and self-image.[16] The human mind is remarkably adept at deploying these types of coping mechanisms. They serve as a sort of psychological immune system that simultaneously allows us to maintain our self-concept and ensures the English national teams maintain their fans despite decades of close-but-not-quite World Cup performances.

Beyond psychological coping mechanisms, fans of losing teams have an additional reason to stay invested: each other. Another influential psychological theory of fandom proffered by Daniel Wann and colleagues is the "Team Identification-Social Psychological Health Model" of fandom, where sports matter in providing a sense of community and social bonds.[17] As the famous Liverpool song assures: with deep fandom "you'll never walk alone." And as Wann's research shows, sports fans get psychological health benefits from the real and symbolic social support that comes with shared identification and investment. Sometimes the social bonds of team identification are brief (as with the anonymous Americans I found myself hugging in South Africa). But sometimes they are deeper; sometimes our teams become places of personal belonging and meaningful relationship.

These types of social bonds mattered to many of the Thorns fans we surveyed in 2016.[18] In responding to open-ended questions about motivations for their fandom, nearly a third of Thorns fans brought up the particular enjoyment of the sense of community and comradery around Thorns fandom.

One fan described the experience through a particularly psychological lens: "The Thorns organization has changed my life. I used to suffer from depression, and it could get especially bad during the summer. The Thorns gave me a home, and a type of genuine joy I've never experienced before. The players and the coaches are all incredible people and I'm incredibly excited for every single game or experience with the organization I get. I've also made some of my closest friends through the Thorns."

This feeling of social connection is not distinct to soccer fandom. Religious groups or even book clubs might provide something similar. But when soccer fans feel part of a supporters' culture it often accentuates such feelings; in the surveys of Thorns fans, "supporters' culture and atmosphere" was the single most popular category of response to a question of what they enjoy and appreciate about the Thorns. A close second was the quality of the soccer, the players, and the team, while the third most frequent type of response involved appreciating the opportunity to explicitly support women. In other words, while fans do want to be impressed by the physical performance they are paying to watch, they are equally interested in being emotionally engaged and feeling like they are part of a social experience and a value equation that seems right.

As another Thorns fan explained during my research: "I call Thorns games Yelling Church. I get to be loud and move around and send out positive affirmations of skilled, fit women for two hours. Being a Thorns supporter is for me also a political/economic statement of gender equality. . . . By supporting the NWSL (and the Thorns in particular since our association with Timbers fan culture, Providence Park's audiovisual production values for broadcasting games, and the high-profile players on the team all make us a great exemplar of what could be happening all over the place) I am creating economic demand for pro women's sports."

This type of values-based fandom seemed especially prominent among Thorns fans, but different versions are wrapped up with much global soccer fandom. Soccer clubs talk intentionally about having an identity (or, in more business-focused contexts, about building a brand) because they are trying to define the values and meanings associated with their team and community. These vary from place to place, from team to team, and from supporters' group to supporters' group, but the appeal of defining club identities lies in the ways it can create symbolic connections with existing and prospective fans.

Another social scientific explanation for fandom from another part of the world—this time based on a study of Israeli soccer fans—emphasizes "the symbolic experience" of fan identity as one of three key dimensions of fandom, alongside more "affective-emotional experiences" and more "cognitive experiences."[19] The affective-emotional experience in this scheme is based both on the excitement of the game and the emotional satisfaction of being part of a collective, while the cognitive experience is based on a more rational cost-benefit analysis of how much to invest in fandom.

The symbolic experience is where our soccer fandom becomes a part of our social identity. This is where being a fan of Celtic in Glasgow takes on meaning because of the club's history as a Catholic icon in a religiously and politically divided society. It is where being a fan of Barcelona signifies Catalanism for those concerned with regional autonomy in Spain. And it is where being a Portland Thorns fan means identifying with a particular blend of American progressivism that emphasizes inclusion and empowerment—at least for groups such as women and LGBTQ+ communities. As one Thorns fan explained in a survey response: "I love the [Thorns] fan culture, the opportunity to see world class soccer for $13, the inclusive and welcoming atmosphere in the north end. Even at Timbers games my boyfriend and I hear homophobic remarks, get called fags, etc. NOT at Thorns games."

The idea that part of the attraction of the Thorns is that fans themselves have created an "inclusive and welcoming atmosphere" suggests a bottom-up process of defining the symbolic experience of Thorns fandom. The fans themselves have created their own value equation. With the Thorns this bottom-up process is complemented by top-down support from the team's business operators—who deserve credit for creating a high-quality professional environment, where women's soccer is taken seriously and elite athlete can put their skills on display. But that professional environment also exists in places that have been significantly less successful in drawing fans to women's league games (including England's Women's Premier League and Germany's *Frauen-Bundesliga*). The difference for the Thorns is the grassroots supporters' culture.

The particular culture of Thorns fandom may not work everywhere and may not be appealing to all fans; many fans enjoy sports precisely because they can offer the illusion of an escape from the culture wars. Many go to Thorns games because it seems like a reasonably priced family outing that promotes good role models for kids. Or because they think the uniforms look cool. Or because following the team makes them feel cool themselves. In one influential sociological taxonomy, Richard Giulianotti suggests a range of four fan types including supporters, followers, fans, and flâneurs—with flâneurs most attracted to the marketing and brand image of a team, and supporters most invested in a team's culture and identity.[20] Most major soccer teams have fans of all types. Ironically, however, it is Giulianotti's "supporters" type who creates the authentic symbolic experience of a team culture that then gets monetized through an appeal to the "flâneurs" type.

The dependence of the top-down business of soccer on the bottom-up culture created by fans is particularly evident for the Portland Thorns. But, it also represents a broader tension between business and culture in many parts of the soccer landscape. Soccer teams in most parts of the world originated as social clubs rather than as business franchises, but most fans recognize that the game is now big business. Fans seem to respond best, however, when that business leaves significant space for bottom-up fan cultures that satisfy more social needs. In this regard the success of the Thorns is similar to the success of professional men's teams such as Liverpool, Celtic, or Barcelona that have existed for more than a century; they are defined largely by cultures that reinforce their values and their social identities. Thorns fandom, in this example, integrates a history of appreciating good soccer, an embrace of women's sports as a site for empowerment, and a progressive emphasis on inclusion that fits the broader social ethos of Portland as a city. Thorns fandom, in other words, is like most versions of soccer fandom around the globe in allowing people to express their values and identify with a socially constructed group.

Fandom as Social Identity

One of the seminal, and perhaps oddest, analyses attempting to apply a social scientific lens to the culture of soccer was Desmond Morris's 1981 book *The Soccer Tribe* (revised and republished in 2016).[21] Morris, a well-known English zoologist, explained his process of applying a scientific lens to the game: "It soon became clear that each centre of soccer activity—each soccer club—was organized like a small tribe, complete with a tribal territory, tribal elders, witch doctors, heroes, camp followers, and other assorted tribesmen. Entering their domain I felt like an early explorer penetrating for the first time some remote native culture."[22] Though Morris's analysis of the game veers too far into a deterministic type of sociobiology for my tastes, his meta-phor of a soccer tribe resonates with a large body of social psychology research on group identity. Despite mass commercialization and the best efforts of modern sports marketers to commodify soccer, soccer fandom endures as a way to fulfill one of our most elemental psychological needs: to belong.

People have evolved as eminently social creatures—as the psychologist Roy Baumeister phrases it, we are the "cultural animal."[23] The diversity of human societies is largely explained by our human capacity to learn, adapt, and negotiate social relationships. The fact that humans are the only animal with complex language, complex social rules, and complex self-awareness means that we are distinct in our ability to create and re-create cultural mean-ing systems. But these complex abilities also interact with more basic instincts. We are, after all, still animals, and our minds as much as our bodies are adapted to survive and reproduce. One such adaptation, according to both evolu-tionary and social psychologists, is our compulsion to identify with groups of the type that soccer has a particular capacity to produce.

Often discussed under the modern rubric of social identity theory, the compulsion to identify with groups has ancient roots.[24] Through our evolu-tionary history it was helpful for both survival and reproduction to know who was with us and who was against us. The mind evolved to categorize people into two basic groups: us and them. "Us" we are more likely to help and trust. "Them" we are more likely to deprecate and fear. "Us" is Portland and "them" is Seattle. "Us" is the U.S. Men's National Team and "them" is Mexico's El Tri. "Us" is Liverpool and "them" is Manchester United. Or vice versa.

Perhaps the most amazing thing about this basic us-versus-them instinct is how quickly and easily it can be activated when the conditions are right. The seminal research on the topic in psychology was Muzafer Sherif's 1954 "Robbers Cave Experiment."[25] Sherif was a social psychologist at the Uni-versity of Oklahoma interested in group behavior, which prompted him to devise a classic experiment that was elegant in its simplicity. He took a group of boys, intentionally selected for their homogeneity and unfamiliarity with each other, to summer camp at Robbers Cave State Park. The trick was that the boys were randomly assigned to two separate groups and isolated from each other for the start of the camp—adopting group names "the Rattlers" and "the Eagles" (coincidentally but meaningfully for American soccer fans, one of the first influential supporters' groups in Major League Soccer was DC United's "Screaming Eagles").

After an initial period of bonding, the boys learned of the other group, and the researchers began arranging competitions on a ball field. There was almost immediate animosity: name-calling, efforts to self-segregate, raids of group camps, and, in fine supporters' group tradition, the exchange of derogatory songs. The researchers added a final phase where they created situations in which the groups had to work together, and suddenly everyone started to get along again. It was a simple study making a profound point: there was no difference between the two groups of boys until they became comparable groups.[26] Any of the "Rattlers" could just as easily have been "Eagles" in exactly the same way as, I suspect, many Manchester United fans could just as easily have been for Liverpool with a few small twists of fate.

Another powerful example that psychologists find illustrative comes from several decades ago, when an Iowa schoolteacher named Jane Elliot brilliantly demonstrated the power of us-versus-them as a way to address racism with her elementary school students in the wake of Martin Luther King Jr.'s assassination in 1968.[27] One morning, she told her class of third-graders that they were going to do an activity in which they would be divided for a few days by the color of their eyes. The kids initially thought it sounded like fun. First, the blue-eyed kids received the privileges, while the brown-eyed kids put on colored scarves marking their out-group status; the next day the statuses were reversed. By recess time that first morning, the kids were brawling on the playground because *us* started mocking *them* for having brown eyes. In Jane Elliot's words: "I watched what had been marvelous, cooperative, wonderful, thoughtful children turn into nasty, vicious, discriminating, little third-graders in a space of fifteen minutes." Substitute "soccer fans" for "children," along with "ninety minutes" for "fifteen," and the quote still works quite well. To say nothing of the scarves.

Soccer and supporters' groups are an excellent laboratory for stimulating hostile versions of us-versus-them instincts. In my own corner of the United States, I've long been struck by how the Portland Timbers versus Seattle Sounders MLS rivalry creates artificial distinctions and significant enmity. Having spent the first eighteen years of my life in Seattle, and the most recent seventeen in Portland, I can say with confidence that the cities and the people share exponentially more similarities than differences. Yet, as one Seattle fan "two-stick" crowd sign proclaimed in faux-biblical verse style during a Sounders versus Timbers game, "Thou art our neighbor, but we f***ing HATE you. ECS 12:1" (with "ECS" standing for Emerald City Supporters).

The power of fan groups to inspire groundless hate was particularly stark for me at a U.S. Open Cup match in Portland several years back when a Timbers two-stick making its way around the sold-out crowd had a stark black-and-white illustration of a large rifle captioned with "KELLER—DO THE COBAIN." The message here was directed toward Sounders goalkeeper Kasey Keller and was a clear allusion to the suicide of Seattle grunge music icon Kurt Cobain. But the inappropriateness of the message went beyond its cruel trivialization of suicide.

At that point in his career Kasey Keller had played only twelve games for the Sounders, returning to his hometown after an itinerant sixteen-year career in Europe. He had, in contrast, played more than one hundred games for the U.S. Men's National Team—the nation to which, despite occasional efforts to declare its own people's republic, Portland still belongs. What's more, Keller had more connections to the city of Portland than any single player on the field for the Timbers that day. Keller had been an all-American at the University of Portland and was widely credited as a key player that allowed legendary coach Clive Charles to make UP a national soccer power (Charles now is one of only five members of the Timbers' Ring of Honor). Keller even played ten games for a previous minor league incarnation of the Timbers in 1989. In contrast, the Timbers' starting eleven that day had exactly zero players with any childhood or college roots in Portland—and at least one player on the roster who told me during an interview that he'd not even heard of Portland, Oregon, until he stepped off the plane his agent had booked for him (the only "Portland" he knew was in Maine, so he was confused about why his flight from the East Coast had stopped for a layover in Denver!). Yet, for the simple fact of putting on a Sounders uniform to play for *them* in a game against the Portland Timbers as *us*, in the minds of some fans Keller should die.

Of course, even these fans would not expect their admonition to be literal. Another occasional appeal of sports fandom is that it creates a liminal space where we can say and do things that we don't expect to be taken seriously. But the fact that we let our rational minds be distorted by the emotional, often deeply irrational, instincts of our fandom in soccer spaces is a serious example of the conditions that intensively enhance group social identities to feel primal.

The developmental psychologist Judith Harris crafted an entire "group socialization theory" synthesizing research on the importance of our social groups to human development—and it is remarkable how well the key ingredients for making group membership psychologically significant mesh with soccer fandom.[28] Integrating research on social identity theory, in her popular work Harris suggests these ingredients include competition and an emphasis on points of contrast (inherent in any game that involves keeping score), proximity (evidenced around the world in the phenomenon of the local derby), explicit markers of group membership (as per the aforementioned team scarves and replica jerseys), and socially defined membership criteria that often associate with implicit norms and expectations (including the types of political commitments that make some fan groups famous as either "left-wing," such as Saint Pauli FC in Germany or the Thorns and Timbers in Portland, or "right-wing," such as SS Lazio ultras in Italy or Battalion 49 with New York City FC).[29]

These last examples of how soccer affiliations can bleed into political affiliations also highlight the limits and complexities of group social identities. Not all Thorns or Timbers fans are leftists, and very few NYCFC fans have sympathies with right-wing extremists. Every individual fan navigates a distinct place within the social worlds of soccer, and fans make conscious decisions about how far to take their fandom. Even the primal instincts so powerfully triggered by soccer fandom are tempered by the rational parts of our mind. Our fandom drives us to be part of meaningful groups, but also requires us to make intentional choices about what groups will be most meaningful.

Fandom as Identity Work

The fact that the social identities of fandom are often triggered by rivalry reminds us that fandom involves choosing sides. These choices are not entirely conscious or intentional. My emotional connection to the U.S. national team is based almost entirely on the fact that I was born and raised in the United States. In every World Cup I've watched, the United States has been my team. Many other fans likewise identify with their teams because of their community, their family, or other deep personal connections. But at some point, most fans start to think about their affiliations and make conscious decisions about what they mean. Even with my U.S. fandom, at various points I've made decisions about whether I'm going to literally and figuratively drape myself in the American flag during U.S. games. Those decisions are shaped more by my rational mind than by my early socialization experiences.

My fandom helps to shape my way of being American, just as my being American shapes my fandom. The international dimension of soccer, and particularly international rivalries, offers a rich example of how fandom can be important as identity work.

International rivalries stoke both fandom and identity work in part because they often involve ethnic and geopolitical considerations. Take, as just one of many possible examples, the United States versus Mexico. The social and psychological aspects of this rivalry have so many dimensions that it has merited its own academic book: *Perspectives on the U.S.–Mexico Soccer Rivalry: Passion and Politics in Red, White, Blue, and Green*.[30] In the foreword, journalist and professor Andrés Martinez, who grew up in Chihuahua, Mexico, with an American mom and a Mexican dad, explains the significance of the rivalry:

> Sports have traditionally been the one form of global pop culture not dominated by the United States. Like our aversion to the metric system, Americans' aversion to the world's most popular sport in favor of our own games (whose insularity we mask with fictions like "the World Series" and calling the Super Bowl winners "World Champs") was long a staple of American exceptionalism. When I was a kid, the United States posed no threat to Mexico at soccer. And that was an important salve for Mexicans' identity. The gringos had grabbed nearly half of Mexico's territory in the nineteenth Century and become the world's dominant power in the twentieth—and dominant in so many aspects of life—that it seemed only right for Mexicans to be able to *golear* the Americans every so often on the soccer pitch.[31]

In recent decades the U.S. Men's National Team (USMNT) has become an occasional threat to Mexico's regional soccer dominance, including a dramatic knockout-stage win in the 2002 World Cup that led to the American's best-ever showing in a men's world championship. And, as Martinez points out, other tensions between the two countries have amplified as debates about immigration dominate political discourse on both sides of the border.

These undercurrents magnify elements of each fan culture that exist even aside from the rivalry. The U.S. fan tendency to put hypernationalism on display around USMNT games, through endless chants of "U-S-A," limitless iterations of American flag wear, and ceaseless assumptions of national superiority, regularly dip into the kind of mindless patriotism that has earned U.S. citizens abroad the moniker of "ugly American." At the 2010 World Cup, after the collective effervescence of the Algeria win, Dave Zirin, writing for the liberal-progressive magazine *The Nation*, questioned whether fans' reactions to Team USA amounted to "joy or jingoism."[32] Zirin noted how, in the wake of the victory, American sports radio emphasized dismissive stereotypes of Algerians (quoting one host as proclaiming "When I think of Algeria, all I think about are terrorists and Abbott and Costello movies") and implicitly framed the World Cup as a civilization contest. Zirin asked: "Why can't we just recognize that Algeria played gallantly against a better U.S. team, which won by the skin of its teeth? Why must an insanely miraculous athletic victory also be a reinforcer of cultural supremacy?"

Though Zirin's piece was mostly a set of balanced thoughts evaluating his own reaction and that of sports radio programs in his hometown of Washington, DC, he was immediately pilloried by some fans. "You must be either a biased foreigner or a self-loathing American," read a typical online comment. "If you don't take simple joy from American victory," commentators seemed to be saying, "then you can't be one of us; you must be one of them."

The jingoism embedded in national team fandom sometimes goes further into racist stereotypes. Researchers writing about the U.S.–Mexico rivalry found that at U.S.–Mexico games it is not uncommon to hear American fans shout (often at a safe passing distance) phrases from loaded American political discourse such as "go back to Mexico" or "f**cking wetbacks."[33]

On the other side of the equation, a subset of Mexican fans has made it a "tradition" to chant a homophobic slur at every opposing goalkeeper upon the occasion of every goal kick. Though there has been some spirited debate about whether the term *"puto"* (sometimes translated as either "faggot" or "male prostitute") is *really* homophobic, the consensus in the global soccer community is that it is indeed designed to deprecate a class or people and is inherently discriminatory.[34] But that same global soccer community can't quite manage to stop it.

After some denial and obfuscating, FIFA and Mexican soccer officials have tried in recent years to end the chant through a combination of cajoling (including public relations campaigns where Mexican soccer icons try to tell fans that the chant isn't welcome at their games), fines (according to *The Guardian*, there were fifty-one fines for homophobia during the 2018 World Cup, with the eleven fines to the Mexican federation being the most for any single group), and threats (including the possibility of abandoning games or playing home games without fans allowed to attend), with only limited success.[35] At this point the simple act of doing the chant has become a perverse point of pride for some fans of the Mexican team—an effort to maintain a distinct fan culture that doesn't respond to top-down dictates. In a way the Mexican fans who won't give up their *puto* chant are asserting a type of fandom that is agentic and self-expressive, bearing a resemblance to other active fan cultures that advocate for causes authorities may not always appreciate. In such cases, fandom can become more important than game outcomes themselves.

Fortunately, there are other, more robust and inclusive versions of Mexican fandom—particularly evident in the way fandom can create space for Mexican Americans to craft bicultural identities. One set of particularly rich chapters in the academic book on the U.S.–Mexico soccer rivalry delves into the rituals and experiences of fans from Mexican immigrant families who both implicitly and explicitly see soccer as a chance to navigate biculturalism. For example, in the chapter "Food-Ball: Tailgates that Enculturate Before US-Mexico Fútbol Matches," Roxane Coche and Oscar Guerra argue that while tailgating parties in stadium parking lots were historically linked with "American" sports such as gridiron football, Mexican American fans "have gone further than just adopting tailgating before *fútbol* games, they have also adapted it: a new type of tailgating revolving around high-quality food and family, instead of junk food, friends, and drinking games, has emerged."[36]

As one female Mexican American fan, a member of the Pancho Villa's Army supporters' group that is specifically for Mexico fans in the United States, explained to Coche and Guerra:

> You know when it comes to being Mexican, we have to have that empowerment around us all the time. So, a tailgate event for [the] army is all when we are doing better. So when we empower each other, in a positive, loving community family-oriented way, everybody is more happier. Because you want your kids around, you want to pass that tradition on. I've been watching soccer since I was three years old with my dad. So, the fact that I can bring my grandma to a tailgating event, and she can have a nice time, alone is enough for me to want to be a part of this, about us coming together as a whole and cheering on Mexico. So we are empowered, when Mexico wins, we win. We feel like the country is doing better.[37]

In a separate analysis of how Mexican American fans use soccer to help navigate their biculturalism, Coche, Meân, and Guerra argue soccer provides a space to work through potential stressors for individuals who sometimes feel betwixt and between.[38] They note in particular the tendency of Mexican American fans to support the Mexican national team, leading to occasional accusations of a lack of appreciation for their lives in the United States. But for many fans it is not an either/or proposition. As one Mexican American explained to Coche, Meân, and Guerra:

> I'm always with Mexican people so I don't have to explain myself. If you're in Arizona you know I'm wearing shorts and I have a big Cardinal tattooed on my leg so they know that if it's tattooed on my body, you know the cardinal the NFL symbol, they know it's American. I mean my mom and dad are Mexicans, I'm Mexican-American so the fruit doesn't fall far from the tree you know what I'm saying? I mean it is just the way it is. People have to accept it, so do I root for Mexico during the baseball classic? No, of course not, because that's different. There're certain sports that are specific genre. When you come to football soccer, I root for Mexico, but when it comes to baseball, I'm American all the way.[39]

This ability to switch allegiances may, Coche, Meân, and Guerra argue, relate to the relative quality of the teams and the BIRGing phenomenon in fandom generally. They find, for example, that for women's national teams Mexican American girls and women tend to find the USWNT easier to support than the Mexican women's national team, in part because the U.S. team is more established as a world power.

The main point, however, is that soccer fandom creates spaces for people to engage in a dynamic range of human needs, including the complicated identity work required by globalized geographical flows. For Mexican American fans this space is often healthy and constructive, allowing them to navigate the challenges of biculturalism. U.S. citizens and Mexican Americans who also happen to be El Tri fans are staking pluralistic identity claims through rituals including food, family, music, language, and community, all of which are wrapped up in soccer. But soccer fandom can also create hostile spaces—opportunities to derogate immigrants or reinforce homophobia. National rivalries thus reflect both the best and the worst of fans, reminding us that the intense jumble of emotions and reason provoked by fandom makes for a paradoxical, and deeply human, mix.

Fandom as Human Experience

After my own intense identity experience as a fan of the U.S. team in its game against Algeria at the World Cup in 2010, I found myself lingering in the Pretoria stadium feeling simultaneously exhausted and exhilarated. Along with most of the U.S. fans there that day, I had stayed in the stands long after the final whistle, basking in the glory of the game and knowing that once we left the vividness of the shared emotions, our collective effervescence, would quickly dissipate. We were physically drained, even those of us nowhere near the field, but psychologically animated—testosterone (and maybe just a bit of alcohol) was pumping through our brains and bodies. No one wanted it to end. I still treasure that moment, and I loved the entire experience of being a fan at that World Cup. But, as a social scientist, I remain conflicted about what "losing my mind" over a soccer game, a game that mattered to me largely due to an imagined sense of community, says about me.

There is a way in which fandom brings out the worst of us. It can sometimes cause us to rabidly endorse unthinking commitments, engage in jingoistic taunting, and accept insular social identities. This chapter has largely elided soccer hooliganism because it is a fringe part of soccer fandom, but it is easy to recognize hooliganism as an extreme version of much that is described above. Fandom can also lead us to engage in only superficial forms of community, devoting ourselves to rituals, values, and motivations that go little beyond brand allegiance and consumer entertainment. Fandom can sometimes even take us away from things that matter more—our families, our friends, our work, and time we might spend on healthier recreations (such as playing, rather than watching, the game). Being a fan, when the fates conspire, can be a pain.

But, of course, fandom can also bring out the best of us. In the right context it can be immensely gratifying to sometimes lose our minds. My moment of screaming abandon in that South African stadium was an all-too-rare ecstatic experience. My transitory sense of community, my brief moment of pride in being American, was a rare moment of patriotism. The way global soccer can allow fans to express values and help us find our place in the world can be a worthy way to engage the identity work that is essential to our development. Being a fan, on the right day, is a joy.

The complicated feelings I have about my own soccer fandom, in other words, may just make that fandom an embodiment of the conflicted nature of human experience. Fandom has roots in primal neurobiology—the neuronal and hormonal rush triggered by soccer—but that rush is calibrated by the values and identities we invest in our teams. Fandom activates a primitive sort of group identity, but that identity can be used constructively by reflective fans to situate and cultivate their sense of self. Fandom reflects much about our individual psychology, but it also helps us find our place in the social world. Soccer fandom both torments and compels us, in other words, because it activates the human mind with all its conflicting emotions and complicated reasons. At its worst and at its best, caring about soccer makes us feel human.

Brazilian national team players appeal for help for the chronically under-supported women's program after a loss in the 2007 Women's World Cup final. National cultures of soccer often embed implicit and explicit bias, including as related to gendered support by federations. Jonathan Larsen/Diadem Images/ Alamy Stock Photo.

CHAPTER 3

Cultures

Soccer Is Familiar, Soccer Is Strange

S EVERAL DECADES AGO, while serving as a Peace Corps volunteer in the Republic of Malawi, I spent a season playing and coaching as the only non-African in the Malawian Super League—the most powerful cross-cultural experience of my soccer life.[1] It was a disorienting year. In terms of soccer ability I would have been about an average player in the league, but the exoticism of my presence—the tall, slow, floppy-haired White guy—made for strange expectations. And in my own mind I employed a more extreme version of soccer exoticism, an affliction that builds on the human tendency to attend excessively to differences and make soccer into a space for othering. That season, combined with deliberately acquired social science lenses, challenged me to think hard about the meaning of culture, the power of culture, and the way culture does (and does not) express itself in soccer. It also challenged me to realize that the diversity of a global game virtually begs a thinking fan to engage with deep cultural questions. If we want to really understand the game we have to explore what cultural comparisons can teach us about soccer, and what soccer might teach us about culture.

During my season in Malawi I thought I saw an exoticized version of culture everywhere. I found local playing styles so heavily reliant on exuberant and expressive ball skills that I couldn't recognize much tactical awareness. The chronological age of players proved shockingly fluid, with my teammates and opponents adjusting how old they claimed to be according to situations and whether it was better to seem older (when experience was required) or younger (when scouts might be looking for potential to grow). Regular references to *juju* or black magic as a major determinant of game outcomes struck me as both farcical and fascinating. Even the meaningless jargon used to exclaim a moment of skill or excitement, like the *waka waka* phrase later made famous by Shakira at the 2010 World Cup, felt fabulously exotic.

These feelings of cultural difference were particularly evident around the biggest game of the year for my team, against league leaders Bata Bullets. At the time Bullets were one of the two most popular teams in Malawi, and my team was near the bottom of the table. Though we usually drew mediocre crowds, any game against Bullets was a major attraction—and the day of the game my team was buzzing with excitement for a full stadium and a big stage. I was both impressed with my teammates' confidence and worried we were in for a thrashing. My confusion was magnified on game day when I opened the sports section of the national newspaper to find a huge picture of our team manager, a local character prone to dressing in brightly colored dashiki robes and posturing himself as a part-time witch doctor. The bold headline in the newspaper read "We'll stop Bullets," and in the text the manager pronounced: "Martin Luther King, Jr. had a dream, and as team manager I have a dream that Bata may be unbeaten now, but we are sure of getting a victory against Bata. . . . We are trying to ease the pressure. It's unfortunate that we didn't start well but we have the best players in the country, very talented players." The odd MLK references and misplaced confidence enhanced my sense that strangeness defined Malawian soccer culture.

Later, when the team arrived at the field, I was perplexed when I realized the starting team was warming up with a twined rag ball of the sort kids use in rural villages rather than our usual panel-stitched models. Here we were preparing for one of the biggest games of the year, playing in front a full stadium in the big city against the nation's favorite team, with boots polished and uniforms sparkling, and the team had pulled out a dirty ball of plastic wrappers sewn with twine. It would have been comical, were it not for the pallid hush that came over the settling crowd and the nervous eyes of the Bata Bullets players.

When the referee blew his whistle for captains, the rag ball was brought to the middle of a tight circle of my team's players. Our team manager, decked out in a dotted orange dashiki, made a long, slow walk from the sideline to the huddle. With each step he took, the crowd jostled in a flurry of prompting elbows and ominous whispers.

After a brief silence, the huddle broke. One player grabbed the mysterious ball and sprinted toward our bench. Placing the ball at the intersection of the midfield line and the sideline, the player darted away to make room for the team manager. Solemnly, the manager hovered over the ball, raising his arms and lowering his head. The whole stadium strained, trying to hear the incantation they seemed sure he was reciting.

Then, with a shrill primal yell, the manager dropped his hands. The stadium softened, fans taken off the edges of their seats with audible relief. Either a curse had been put on the game, or a lot of people believed a curse had been put on the game. In some ways, it didn't matter which. The game was a lively, surprisingly competitive 1–0 loss.

I learned immediately after the game that my teammates—a relatively educated crew of players, most of whom had some affiliation with the national university—had created the whole pregame ritual as a way to "psych out" the crowd and the Bata Bullets players. It was all a clever cultural drama, creatively highlighting diversity within as well as between Malawian teams. It was also a lesson to me to be wary of making assumptions about cultural differences that at first just seem strange.

Noticing, and then overcoming, feelings of strangeness is essential to understanding what culture is, what it is not, and how it can shape the social meanings of soccer. The very notion of culture, it turns out, is contested and questioned by the social scientists who pay it the most attention.[2] Do countries really have a national culture when massively diverse peoples exist within all artificially demarcated boundary lines? Isn't it demeaning to assume any two people share a set of values and meanings simply because of where they were born, or because they come from a certain type of community? Is it fair to reduce culture to visible practices, employing what a colleague of mine calls the "food, festivals, and fabrics" version of the concept?

The more questions you ask about culture, the more you realize the concept is less of a tangible map and more of an intangible concept. We know culture is learned and shared, we know it is not written in our genes, and we know it is like water to a fish—a ubiquitous presence that is easy to take for granted, but impossible to live without. We just don't know exactly how it seeps into any individual mind, or into any particular human activity.

Despite the slipperiness of the culture concept, the study of culture has only grown as globalization has highlighted its importance. If we want to understand the diverse manifestations of a global form such as soccer, we have to consider culture. Fortunately, cultural anthropologists and other social scientists have offered useful tools for cultural analysis. My favorite such tool comes from a catchy, well-known, and deceptively simple anthropological dictum: make the strange familiar, and the familiar strange. The idea is to access cultural understandings by taking feelings like the strangeness that gnawed at me in Malawi and work to understand how they are embedded with values, meanings, and beliefs about how things "should" work. And, simultaneously, take things that feel comfortably familiar and work to consider how strange those might seem to people whose social experiences are oriented by a different set of cultural understandings.

This interpretive work requires cross-cultural comparisons, which are useful to social science not just for revealing differences but also for identifying universals. When we can identify universal characteristics of people and communities we get clues as to the fundamentals of human nature. When we find significant variations across peoples and communities, we get important insights into where social and cultural forces matter most. And there are always both: the universal along with the culturally particular and the strange along with the familiar.

With such tools, the strangeness of my Malawian soccer experiences starts to feel more familiar—and some of my American soccer experiences start to seem strange. My sense that Malawians lacked tactical awareness was in part my own failure to recognize their superiority in the types of small-sided situations more familiar to the types of street soccer I never played in the United States. And why, anyway, is so little of contemporary American youth soccer unstructured and unorganized? The fluidity of player age in Malawi was partially about a less rigid emphasis on chronological age generally, and made me curious about the U.S. emphasis on strict birth-year requirements in youth soccer that ignore how people physically mature at very different chronological ages.[3] My fascination with *juju*, what I perceived to be a primitive form of sports psychology, blinded me to the wide variation in how seriously Malawians themselves took black magic. And it led me to wonder about the prevalence of superstition and unscientific "mind games" played on every American team I know.

My experiences in Malawi sparked an ongoing fascination with global soccer cultures, and what differences across and similarities between societies reveal about the game. I've come to think that cultural analyses of soccer in different parts of the world can even help us understand culture itself. This chapter begins with a brief overview of social science concepts that inform an understanding of soccer as a global phenomenon. Research and theory on globalization is particularly relevant here, given that soccer is a rare mass cultural form that has spread across the entirety of the globe and offers us insight into the process of cultural diffusion.

The bulk of the chapter provides examples of comparative cultural analysis through three case studies of national soccer cultures in England, Brazil, and South Africa. Each of these countries has hosted soccer's highest-profile event (the men's World Cup), each offers a different continental perspective on the game, and each is discussed here to suggest examples of how culture works. England, with its claim as the home of soccer, highlights the ways particular cultural values and traditions circumscribe the social identities that intersect with the game. Brazil, arguably the iconic soul of soccer, combines a massive national interest in the game and a deceptive *jogo bonito* brand to illustrate the complex tensions embedded in soccer cultures. South Africa, as the first men's World Cup host in the global south, represents the ways in which culture and power intertwine to determine who gets to play and what the game means to a society. These case studies are necessarily brief and selective in their use of social history, but in sum make the case for why culture matters in soccer—and why soccer matters for understanding culture.

The Glocal Game?

Though the exact historical origins of soccer are subject to some dispute, most agree that the modern form of the game has a home culture: soccer was codified in England and spread globally by the British Empire. British sailors brought the game to Brazil; British colonists brought the game to South Africa; British immigrants brought the game to the United States; British missionaries brought the game to many other corners of the world. The game caught on quickly in diverse locales in part because of its elegant simplicity. There is a comforting familiarity to dividing into two teams and trying to kick a ball across a line. But the simplicity of that premise, and the basic themes that follow, also allows for elaborate variations. The question then becomes: what are the cultural themes, and what are the cultural variations?

One strain of social science analyzing cultural themes and variations centers on an ongoing debate about the degree to which globalization leads to cultural homogenization.[4] Are cultural practices such as soccer subject to the phenomenon the sociologist George Ritzer called "the McDonaldization of Society"—where a global emphasis on efficiency, calculability, predictability, and control makes for the standardizing of everything from food to education to sports?[5] While some sport sociologists think the general answer here is yes, they also emphasize that global forces always interact with local influences to create hybridized cultural forms. In the twenty-first century, the superficial elements of soccer can look remarkably similar whether in Malawi, Michigan, or Manchester, but the more cultural elements are embedded in local stories, symbols, and traditions that mash global similarities into a particular time and place. Sports, in this view of globalization, are both "grobal" and "glocal."[6]

As an example, think about the relatively recent creation of professional soccer clubs with the corporate moniker of Red Bull in diverse global settings including Salzburg, Austria; New York; Sao Paulo, Brazil; Leipzig, Germany; and (briefly) Sogakope, Ghana. These clubs have clear superficial similarities: there is an obvious theme to how each Red Bull soccer club looks on TV. But that global homogeneity coexists with heterogeneous local incarnations. Among the Red Bull teams, the New York version is largely just another corporate American sports franchise, the Leipzig version is seen as affront to the community-based meaning of a soccer club traditional to Germany, and the Ghanaian club was designed to be a youth development project focused on mining for raw talent. Further, if we spent time with the players and fans of each team, we would undoubtedly find many more subtle themes and variations in motivations, backgrounds, emotions, expectations, and other more psychological nuances to the experience of soccer.

Our psychological experiences of soccer also have themes and variations across global settings, and these too help illuminate how culture works. As cultural psychologists phrase it, human development is a process involving "one mind, many mentalities," with our shared hardware shaped by genes and evolution only becoming useful when expressed through software written by socialization.[7] Cultural psychologists think of research across cultural settings as looking for both the global hardware of the human mind (the universals) and local mentalities shaped by socialization (the variations). In the balance between the two we find culture.

Comparing human experiences across cultural settings is useful enough to social science analysis to have its own data repository hosted by Yale University called the Human Relations Area Files (HRAF). The HRAF compiles cross-cultural research, much of it from cultural anthropologists undertaking ethnographic studies of relatively distinct and disconnected communities, so researchers can ask meta questions about human universals and variations—including questions about games and sport.

It turns out that the human mind naturally likes a good game. Sport anthropologist Gary Chick has analyzed the HRAF database to find that games and sports of some type seem to be universal—showing up across early human history and diverse cultural settings.[8] Chick suggests this is in part because sports and games serve as "expressive models" that allow for learning and modeling skills, strategies, and human interactions that are useful for functioning. Many sports and games in early history, for example, model combat and tactical strategy in ways that are a lot less dangerous than actual warfare. There also, however, seem to be significant differences in how much emphasis different societies put on games of strategy, games of chance, and games of physical skill, and in the gendered nature of sport participation. Team combat sports in the historical and cross-cultural record, for example, are often wrapped up with valuing toughness and aggressiveness—and female participation is significantly greater in less patriarchal societies. It seems plausible to suggest that looking at how a society treats something like its women's soccer teams can tell us something more broadly about gender, culture, and opportunity—something I will discuss further in the case studies of soccer cultures in England, Brazil, and South Africa.

Other, more minute cross-cultural universals may be evident in the simple act of watching the World Cup. In one fun example from the 2018 men's World Cup, the *New York Times* noted a remarkable similarity in how players from around the world respond to missing a reasonable shot on goal.[9] No matter the national team or the cultural background, players raise their hands to their heads in a motion universally understood as a particular mix of disappointment, frustration, angst, and shame. But why, in a game where the hands and the head have little to do with most of the play, are the hands and the head involved at all? According to the *Times*: "It has nothing to do with soccer and everything to do with the human psyche." It cites psychologist Jessica Tracy from the University of British Columbia as interpreting the gesture as a universal sign that "you know you messed up. . . . It's going to tell others, 'I get it and I'm sorry, therefore you don't have to kick me out of the group, you don't have to kill me.'" Tracy has observed the same gestures in congenitally blind Olympic athletes—suggesting physical reactions to pride and shame are not traits we have to see to enact.[10] Other psychologists speculate the gesture may have evolutionary value as an instinct to protect the head—our most vulnerable appendage when we have angered others.

While there is a sense in which such behaviors have "nothing to do with soccer," the fact that their universality is most evident on soccer fields reinforces the argument that the game does have a contribution to make. Analyzing soccer as one social practice enacted across many cultural settings makes for a particular way of watching the game as we attend to the ways the universals and the variations, the global and the local, the familiar and the strange all combine to reveal understandings of human nature, human diversity, and the game itself. In the limited space available here it is impossible to do justice to the complexity of soccer cultures in nations as diverse as England, Brazil, and South Africa, let alone consider soccer's many other important cultural outposts. Yet given the richness of the game as a site for cultural analysis, these three brief case studies do still make it possible to learn something about how culture works.

England: Soccer Cultures as Identities

As the ancestral home of modern soccer, it only makes sense for England, and the United Kingdom more generally, to have soccer thoroughly integrated with national identity. That integration was on particularly vivid display when England hosted and won its one and only men's World Cup in 1966. The stadiums were aflutter with the Union Jack flag, a sea of blue, red, and white that expressed the type of pride and patriotism so often tied to global soccer. Strangely, however, that Union Jack flag did not exactly represent the team that won that World Cup. Due to the quirks of soccer history, the United Kingdom rarely ever competes in global soccer competitions. Instead, each of the "home nations" composing the United Kingdom (England, Northern Ireland, Scotland, and Wales) has its own national team—and in recent decades the only flag to be found at English national team games is the red cross on a white background known as the St. George's Cross.[11] If England wins another World Cup in the foreseeable future, the Union Jack will likely be scarce. This curious shift across a few decades from the Union Jack to the St. George's Cross suggests that while soccer may be thoroughly integrated with English national identity, that identity is fragmented.

To further complicate matters, the use of the St. George's Cross flag by English soccer fans has evolved in ways that jumble national identity with more local identity claims. As pointed out by sport sociologist Tom Gibbons, many of the St. George's Cross flags used by England fans are now commonly adorned with regional and local symbols—conveniently using one part of the flag quadrant created by its two intersecting lines to distinguish, for example, fans from Newcastle as distinct from fans from Brighton.[12] The representation of English identity further fragments into different layers and diverse combinations.[13]

Using soccer to navigate the complexity of identity has a long history in the English game. Though the British first codified the rules of soccer in 1863, those standardized rules did not involve using referees until the first English FA Cup in 1871, a national tournament that helped form and cement community identities during a period of industrialization, improved transportation, and increasing access to education.[14] The British were so enamored of their own local competitions that when FIFA was formed in 1904 (by Belgium, Denmark, France, the Netherlands, Spain, Sweden, and Switzerland), the home nations did not bother to join—though England, Scotland, Wales, and Northern Ireland did have international competitions against each other. The British nations also skipped the World Cup until 1950 and put in only halfhearted efforts in several World Cups thereafter. English soccer cultures, in other words, often valued the local over the global.

The emphasis on the local in English soccer shifted dramatically with the country's World Cup win at home in 1966. That is such an important event in modern English history that entire academic books have analyzed its impact—including John Hughson's fiftieth anniversary analysis *England and the 1966 World Cup: A Cultural History*.[15] Hughson argues that prior to the 1966 World Cup, the soccer powers in England were concerned primarily with the FA Cup as a national competition, situating English soccer cultures in regions and cities (as the homes of FA Cup teams) rather than in relation to international competitions. The 1966 World Cup win made English soccer more of an inter- rather than intranational affair.

Even in more recent eras when England is all-in on global competition, the English case illustrates the messy intersection of national identity and soccer cultures. In preparing to host the 2012 London Olympics, for example, English soccer authorities had to confront the fact that the International

Olympic Committee, like the United Nations, considers the United Kingdom one country. If the host country was going to compete in soccer, it needed to figure out a way to represent the United Kingdom beyond just England. This made for something of an identity crisis.[16] After much debate among officials, politicians, fans, and players about the plausibility of a unified British soccer team, differing conceptions of national identity reared their head. Perceiving an English power play, officials from Scotland, Wales, and Northern Ireland discouraged players from joining a unified team representing Great Britain. And, consequently, "Team GB" on the men's side ended up all-English except five players from Wales, and on the women's side ended up all-English except from two players from Scotland.[17] It turns out that while soccer is indeed central to English identity, it is also central to Scottish identity, Irish identity, and Welsh identity—places that each have different relationships to British identity and, in an era of Brexit, to European identity.

A more contemporary view of identity in English soccer cultures also prompts reflection on thornier social identities such as race/ethnicity, social class, and gender. Historically and stereotypically, soccer in England is associated with White working-class masculinity. In regard to race, the English men's national team featured its first black player only in 1978 when Viv Anderson appeared at age twenty-two, but Anderson himself describes a soccer culture in which racial abuse and the tossing of bananas to mock Black players was common.[18] In regard to class, the working-class roots of English soccer, with many teams originally created by and for factory workers, still shape the way English soccer is organized—Simon Kuper and Stefan Szymanski note that fully 85 percent of men's English national team players have working-class origins, and that the English talent development system is distinct in essentially forcing promising players to choose between soccer and education at age sixteen.[19] With regard to gender, the cultural boundaries were even codified: the English FA put a ban on women's soccer between 1921 and 1971 as a way of explicitly maintaining a masculine hegemony in the sport.[20]

The White, working-class, male social history of soccer in England is not, however, the definitive story of English soccer cultures. In one analysis of players in the English Premier League during the 2017–2018 season, the proportion of British players with Black, Asian, and Minority Ethnic (BAME—a category used politically in the United Kingdom) backgrounds had reached

33 percent—doubling from the 1992–1993 season.[21] The financial success of the English Premier League, not unrelated to the inclusion of more diverse players and an opening to infusions of international players, coaches, owners, and fans, has also worked to shift class dynamics, with working-class fan culture now just one segment of a crowd that often needs significant economic resources to afford ticket prices in upgraded stadiums. And the deep community infrastructure for soccer in England has also led to a rapid revitalization of women's football (which also had early robust periods prior to the 1921 ban[22]), with the English women's national team reaching the World Cup semifinals in both 2015 and 2019 and with the English "Women's Super League" supporting twelve fully professional teams (most affiliated with men's Premier League clubs) after only ten years of existence.

I had a chance to observe some of how English soccer cultures are, and are not, evolving firsthand on a Christmas week visit to London in 2019. The city itself is a dense mélange of peoples and identities; my scanning of English Premier League crowds on television had not prepared me for the incredible range of languages, ethnicities, races, gender identities, and religious symbols on the streets of London at the turn of the 2020s. But when I went to an English Premier League match in person at the new Tottenham stadium the most visible diversity in the crowd was in the form of abundant South Korean fans there to support national hero and Tottenham winger Son Heung-Min. Many of the Korean fans came ready with South Korean flags. These were some of the few visible markers of fan-generated symbolism in a stadium designed to accentuate advertising and banal sloganeering over grassroots fan culture ("the game is about glory" and "to dream is to do" were flashed regularly on the overwhelming number of electronic signboards).

During the game itself, a Chelsea defender from Germany (with a mother from Sierra Leone) experienced racial abuse from Tottenham fans, generating booming PA announcements emphasizing that "racist behavior among spectators is interfering with the game. Please remember in football there is no place for racism."[23] The exact nature of the incident was ultimately contested, but it drew a reasonable amount of media attention and reflection on the state of racism in English soccer. As the Chelsea manager noted, "I don't know if it [racism] is getting better or worse or not. We are much more aware that we have a protocol to report it, which is a positive step. Of course, in a perfect world that protocol isn't needed."[24] English soccer culture, in other words, continues to evolve. But that evolution is like any cultural identity: messy, contested, and imperfect.

Though the atmosphere at the gleaming new Tottenham stadium, modeled on American NFL stadiums for their ability to create a mass-marketing spectacle, was antiseptic, I also attended lower-budget games at Watford FC's Vicarage Road and Charlton Athletic's stadium, The Valley. While each had many fewer fans and video screens than Tottenham, each also had more palpable energy, a wider range of songs in the fan repertoire, and more of a community feeling. But none had particularly visible diversity among the fans (though the players and the stadium staff were a very different story). In his aptly titled 2014 social history of English football, *The Game of Our Lives: The Meaning and Making of English Football*, sociologist and writer David Goldblatt notes that the global infusion of players, owners, managers, and fans to English professional soccer has so far done little to change the complexion of local supporters.[25] Goldblatt cites Premier League statistics suggesting that between 1997 and 2007 crowds went from 98.8 percent describing themselves as "white British" to 95 percent, while female fans during that same time went from 12 to 15 percent. The most notable demographic change Goldblatt cites is that fans are getting older, often because younger fans can no longer afford tickets.

What, then, does this very brief and selective consideration of English soccer suggest through the lenses of social science? On the difference side of the equation, English soccer is strange in the extent to which it prioritized the local over the global in its soccer history and the fragmented version of national identity its national team portrays. English soccer was also particularly stubborn in situating the game as primarily for the White male working class—though that positioning is being actively challenged. English soccer starts to look more familiar in the way it provides space for negotiating relatively universal social issues such as racism, sexism, and class inequality. It is also familiar in its centrality to the messy, dynamic, and universal process of constructing communal identities at both local and national levels. Overall, the English case shows us culture, and soccer cultures, as a repository for the many types of identities created through the experiences of people in social worlds that shape, constrain, and enable human development. The English also did us the favor of exporting soccer to places as culturally distinct as Brazil and South Africa—allowing further exploration of what the universals and the variations of soccer cultures really are.

Brazil: Soccer Cultures as Tensions and Negotiations

Like many Americans of my generation, the first men's World Cup I followed closely was the first World Cup hosted in the United States—the 1994 tournament won by Brazil for its fourth of five championships. The image of Brazil as the pure heart and soul of soccer, effectively promoted by both Brazilian players and multinational corporations such as Nike, was deeply embedded in my then unworldly mind. There is something undeniably ebullient about the image of Brazilian soccer, from the iconic canary-yellow uniforms to the imaginative ball skills highlighted in video clips often set to jaunty samba music. So, when the U.S. team played Brazil in the first knockout round of the 1994 World Cup, I watched with romantic expectations of *jogo bonito* and *futebol arte*. Instead, I got one of my first lessons in the complex tensions of culture and the risks of oversimplifying people's internalization of cultural tropes.

The U.S.-Brazil game was both colorful and competitive. It was the first-ever knockout round appearance by a U.S. men's team at the World Cup, it was the Fourth of July, and there were eighty-four thousand sun-bathed spectators at Stanford Stadium in California. The game was scoreless through most of the first half, and at least some of the U.S. players looked in their league. I was particularly impressed with Tab Ramos, who was then playing at Real Betis in Spain and had a touch on the ball that matched most any of the Brazilians. It seemed the Brazilians noticed that too. In one of the most cynical and violent moves in the history of the World Cup, the Brazilian Leonardo took the measure of Ramos during a tussle near the sideline and threw a savage elbow that literally broke Ramos's head. Leonardo was immediately red-carded, and Ramos was immediately taken by ambulance to the hospital. And in that moment, the United States lost any chance of winning the game—eventually conceding a lone goal in the seventy-fourth minute. Though Ramos himself was magnanimously forgiving of Leonardo, my own belief that Brazilian soccer represented some kind of noble aesthetic ideal was as thoroughly fractured as Ramos's skull.[26]

Brazilian soccer does indeed have a *jogo bonito* soul, but that soul is not pure. It, like both human cultures and the human psyche, is full of tensions and contradictions. The most visible tension to soccer fans is between styles of play: the joyful artistry and trickery popularly associated with Brazilian players and teams (*futebol arte*), versus the pragmatic efficiency Brazilian teams often adopt to win games and titles (*futebol resultado*)—such as that

1994 World Cup title, won on penalties after a desultory 0–0 draw with Italy. Even on the women's side, Brazilian soccer culture seems ambivalent in the classical psychoanalytic sense of strong but contradictory impulses. On the one hand, Brazil's six-time world player of the year, Marta, plays with an artistic verve that personifies *jogo bonito*. On the other hand, the Brazilian women's team has often employed pragmatic-bordering-on-cynical tactics that enable a notable disciplinary record: they led the 2019 World Cup in yellow cards with eleven in four games (compared, for example, to England's three in seven games).

It is tempting to try to connect an on-field style of play with local cultural dynamics. This is a position famously articulated by Uruguayan writer Eduardo Galeano, who explained that "a style of play is a way of being that reveals the unique profile of each community and affirms its right to be different. Tell me how you play and I'll tell you who you are."[27] In writing about soccer and globalization, however, political scientist Scott Waalkes warns against making that connection too quickly.[28] Yes, Waalkes notes, Brazilian legend Pelé himself has claimed that "the Brazilian style of play also reflects our national character: full of joy, improvisation, and our willingness, for better and for worse, to ignore established rules and conventions."[29] But at high levels of the modern game, there are many ways in which tactics and playing styles are becoming more similar across the globe. Globalization and an emphasis on efficiency is, according to Waalkes, raising concerns about McDonaldization.

Galeano himself recognized this concern; his famous quote goes on to say that "for many years soccer has been played in different styles, expressions of the personality of each people, and the preservation of that diversity is more necessary today than ever before. These are days of obligatory uniformity in soccer and everything else. Never has the world been so unequal in the opportunities it offers and so equalizing in the habits it imposes: in this end of the century world, whoever doesn't die of hunger dies of boredom."[30]

This concern about homogenization was shared by another Brazilian soccer legend, the aptly named Socrates, who diagnosed the problem in an interview with Alex Bellos as one of modernity and professionalization: "We've become an urban country. . . . Before, there were no limits for playing—you could play on the streets or wherever. Now it's difficult to find space. This means that whatever type of relationship you have these days with sport involves some kind of standardization."[31] Bellos, whose book *Futebol: Soccer the Brazilian Way* offers a thoughtful English-language analysis of Brazilian soccer culture, furthers the diagnosis: "The cliché about Brazil, that its happy football comes from childhood games played with unrestrained abandon, is false. The barefooted tykes kicking footballs on Rio's beaches are not doing so at liberty—they are members of 'escolinhas,' Beach Soccer training clubs, which operate along the seafront. In São Paulo, children do not learn to play on patches of common land—because there is no common land any more. They learn in society football or futsal escolinhas. The freedom that let Brazilians reinvent the game decades ago is long gone."

The tensions of modernity and changes in Brazilian culture were also illuminated by events around the 2014 World Cup. When Brazil was selected to host in 2007, after previously hosting in 1950, the economy was on rocket fuel and there was a sense that the country was fully emerging as a global power. But that all changed in 2013 as the economy started to cool and social issues around politics, inequality, and corruption captured Brazil's popular imagination. As preparations (and costs) for the World Cup accelerated in 2013, soccer became a canvas for protest and dissent. The 2013 Confederations Cup, a quasi-regular and usually staid trial run for World Cup hosts involving only eight teams and lower stakes, turned into an excuse for mass street marches.

The protests, which began with thousands in the streets and ended with millions, were not exactly about soccer or the World Cup—most accounts agree that the trigger was an ill-considered rise in bus fares, perceived as a slap in the face from political elites to the poor and working class.[32] But it quickly became clear that a high-profile soccer tournament offered the impetus and visibility for addressing significant social concerns. Protesters directed most of their ire at the Brazilian powers that be, but also made sure soccer officials knew they were on watch—chanting, "I give up on the World Cup. I want money for education and health"[33] and carrying signs saying "Fifa—you pay the bill."[34] In this way, soccer became a stage for Brazilians to work out sociopolitical issues, and in doing so illustrated one way soccer reflects and refracts larger cultural tensions.

Sociologists have noted that soccer itself can serve multiple roles in its effect on people's sociopolitical engagement. In one early (1969) effort by an American sociologist to interpret the cultural role of soccer in Brazil, Janet Lever drew on the famous Marxist metaphor to argue that soccer often served as an "opium of the Brazilian people."[35] Using a structural-functionalist perspective, a sociological tradition focused on showing how social institutions work to maintain a rough equilibrium, Lever found that Brazilian soccer mostly served to reinforce class distinctions, allowing wealthy social clubs to portray exclusivity and giving poor players the delusion of social mobility.

Brazilian anthropologist Roberto DaMatta attends to a very different dimension of the game, suggesting that soccer is important in Brazil in part because it is a "drama of social justice."[36] Taking a more interpretive approach, DaMatta argues against the idea that "football is the opiate of the people" because that makes the game something that is somehow against society. DaMatta instead suggests that "we think of football in Brazil and of sport in general *as an activity of society* and not as *an activity in opposition or in competition with society*. As a social activity, sport is society itself expressing itself through a certain perspective, through rules, relations, objects, gestures, ideologies, etc., allowing for the opening of a particular social space, the space of sport and of the 'game.'"[37]

DaMatta further suggests we see Brazilian soccer as a drama that informs us about Brazilian society without necessarily making judgments about functionality, using examples including politics: "The good football player and the wise politician know that the golden rule of the Brazilian social world consists precisely in knowing how to emerge well from any situation; in knowing how to survive difficult situations with great dissimulation and elegance so that others will think that the player had an easy enough task."[38]

What, then, would such sociologists see in Brazil's experiences hosting the 2014 World Cup? In the case of the mass protests in the run-up to the tournament, the 2013 Confederations Cup seems to provide a vivid example of soccer as a drama of social justice. The tournament, which the Brazilian team ended up winning emphatically with a 3–0 victory over Spain in the final, was largely upstaged by tensions in Brazilian society between grassroots activists and police, between rich and poor, between politicians and citizens, and between FIFA as an international governing body and local needs. The Brazilian star Neymar, the player of the tournament in 2013, explicitly connected his play with the protests, proclaiming "I'm Brazilian and I love my country. I have a family and friends who live in Brazil. For that reason, I want a Brazil which is more just, safer, healthier and more honest.... The only way I can represent and defend Brazil is on the pitch, playing football. From now on, I will enter the field inspired by this movement."[39]

While the protests succeeded in vividly dramatizing the inequalities that permeate everything from bus fares to World Cup budgets, they also faded in between the 2013 Confederations Cup and the 2014 World Cup. Though most of that had to do with other dynamics in Brazilian society beyond football, it was significant that FIFA and the Brazilian government were able to do just enough to enforce an orderly tournament—to seemingly serve up the world's greatest football tournament as "opium for the masses." The 2014 World Cup saw only relatively minor protests, and perhaps that explains some of how the team itself lost its inspiration—ignominiously crashing out of the tournament with a shocking 7–1 loss to Germany.

The Brazil case again offers examples of both the strange and the familiar. Brazil is rightly famous for its distinctive ability to produce players and teams that bring aesthetic joy to soccer. But, that joy combines with a brutal cynicism that creates a particular cultural mix. Brazilian soccer is also famous for producing its players and teams through a culture of street and beach soccer that is both iconic and at-risk; with globalization has come an emphasis on regimenting Brazilian soccer in a way that makes it sadly familiar. What is also familiar in the Brazilian case, however, is a tension between soccer as a functionalist distraction and soccer as a space for dramatic social activism. Soccer around the world can sometimes maintain order and keep people happy, but it can also sometimes give people a way to express dissent, to engage in collective action, and to question authority. This tension is worked out in local ways in Brazilian soccer cultures, but the existence of tensions within soccer cultures is a global phenomenon. Tensions are also part of how culture writ large works, through dynamic processes of negotiation among people and between social forces. So, the next question in our social science analysis of soccer cultures is where in those negotiations the power lies.

South Africa: Soccer Cultures as Power

When South Africa hosted the men's World Cup in 2010, there was little hope that the national team—*Bafana Bafana*—would be a serious competitor in the tournament, but there was a sense that South Africa had already won. When, in 2004, FIFA awarded South Africa the right to be the first World Cup host on the continent of Africa, the iconic South African leader Nelson Mandela wept tears of joy and told an audience at FIFA headquarters in Zurich "I feel like a young man of fifteen."[40] In South Africa itself there were massive street celebrations, and a recognition that this entrée onto the most prominent stage of world soccer was both a symbol of South Africa's emergence from its apartheid past and a validation of how much soccer means to the people of South Africa. For many, the 2010 World Cup was about the power of the game.

Mandela himself saw power in the ability of soccer to unify people: "The 2010 FIFA World Cup is much more than a game: it symbolises the power of football, which can bring people together from all over, whatever their language, colour, political beliefs or religious faith."[41] It is always worth being careful about oversimplifying this phenomenon. As described elsewhere in this book, there are as many examples of soccer rivalries tearing people apart as there are of the game bringing people together. But, who am I to disagree with Nelson Mandela?

In the case of South Africa, and with the guidance of Mandela as a master politician, there are many ways in which the 2010 World Cup did in fact put the power of soccer on display. Though there was widespread fear and pessimism in the run-up to 2010 about South Africa's ability to meet the requirements for a twenty-first-century mega-event, the tournament largely went off without a hitch: beautiful stadiums, rich stories, and wholehearted fans confirmed what is possible for a continent too often stereotyped as dangerous and pitiable. And yes, as I experienced in person while in South Africa during the tournament, there were moments of incredible unity. I also argue later in this book, when discussing the social impacts of soccer, that there are clear limits to how much good events such as the World Cup actually do and there are legitimate questions about whether hosting was good for South Africa in the longer term. But the tournament itself was indeed powerful.

Power, however, is another complicated concept in social science. Beyond the power to bring people together around a shared interest, there is another type of power that is everywhere in soccer cultures but has been particularly stark in South Africa. This is the type of power that sociologists and critical theorists since Max Weber and Karl Marx see circulating through society to shape opportunities, rights, and human experience. This type of power, though lacking a consistent definition, refers to the conscious and unconscious ways that participants in a social world wield influence over themselves and others. Recognizing, as in the cases of England and Brazil, that soccer cultures work through multiple identities and embody dynamic tensions, the case of South Africa can help us recognize how culture often involves power bringing identities into tension.

The apartheid policies of South Africa were an appallingly blunt example of wielding influence based on racial identity—and that type of power filtered into South African sport. Throughout its modern history sport in South Africa has been racialized—with the prime examples being the idea of rugby as a "White sport" and soccer as a "Black sport." This contrast is also a massive oversimplification, as there is a robust tradition in South Africa of both Black rugby and White soccer, but it is true enough to convey the real ways that segregationists and the apartheid government used sport to divide by race. As South African sociologist Lloyd Hill has argued, for well over one hundred years South African "sport has helped to 'codify' the relationship between key social categories, notably those of race, class and gender."[42] Explicitly, sports clubs and national sports associations often had racially exclusive rules that enforced privileges for White teams and marginalization for Black teams. Implicitly, Hill argues that "success at rugby also helped to forge a generic sense of white nationalism, which would underpin the subsequent development of Afrikaner nationalism.... Success in a relatively small transnational field, defined by amateurism and the shared white class habitus of the southern dominions, therefore bolstered rugby's status as the code of choice in the unified—but racially exclusive—post–1910 field of 'national sports.'"[43] Soccer, on the other hand, created spaces for Black populations to engage in a much larger global game and to build community amid displacement during large-scale migration to urban areas for work and education.

In the second half of the twentieth century, during the period when apartheid was most active, social historian Chris Bolsmann has shown how soccer continued to serve as a pawn in power games related to racial politics.[44] In the 1950s and 1960s, the support of White soccer authorities for apartheid (including through the creation of separate national leagues and governing associations for White and Black players) led to increasing attention to how South Africa was represented internationally. When FIFA suspended South Africa from international soccer in 1964 due to apartheid policies, White administrators tried to create faux "multinational" and "multiracial" soccer competitions—mostly by proposing competitions between all-White and all-Black teams—as a way of simultaneously gaining readmission to FIFA and maintaining White supremacy. But it did not work, and rather than sacrifice power White South African authorities largely sacrificed the game.

Only with the end of apartheid in 1994 did the official segregation of South African soccer end. Relatively soon thereafter, the integration of South Africa and South African soccer was brilliantly symbolized in its hosting and winning the 1996 African Cup of Nations. When the White team captain,

Neil Tovey, shared the hoisting of the tournament trophy with Nelson Mandela after winning the final thanks to two goals by Black striker Mark Williams, it was a moment of effusive joy for the majority Black population.
Though the 1995 Rugby World Cup victory by a majority-White Springboks
team gets more attention globally (at least in part due to the well-known
movie *Invictus*), it was the soccer team that showed the power of sport in
post-apartheid South Africa to represent the entire nation.

The racial power dynamics of South African soccer also intersect with
gender and sexuality power dynamics. As sociologist Cynthia Fabrizio Pelak
has pointed out when interpreting the history of "women and gender in South
African soccer," even a casual observer visiting rural South Africa is likely to
notice the near ubiquity of boys playing late afternoon soccer matches on
improvised fields while "young girls spend their last hours of daylight hauling
water and making preparations for the evening meal."[45] Pelak also notes that
despite obstacles, South African women have found ways to participate—
first by creating interracial teams and leagues before the end of apartheid.
The end of apartheid in the early 1990s coincided with significant global
growth of the women's game, and significantly accelerated opportunities
for Black women to compete. At points, this led to White women retreating
to the relatively exclusive space of indoor soccer while Black women came
to dominate the outdoor game. However, as of the 2019 Women's World
Cup, the South African women's national team was more racially represen-
tative of the national population than South African national teams in
other sports.

The growing access of Black women to soccer in recent South African history has brought other challenging power dynamics to the fore, such as the
sometimes perceived threat of women's players to norms of gender and sexuality. In one tragic 2008 case that garnered international attention before the
2010 men's World Cup, South Africa women's national team player Eudy
Simelane was attacked, gang-raped, and killed in her township community
after leaving a local pub. Simelane had challenged local expectations by living openly as a lesbian, and her courage may have prompted her attack—two
of her four attackers became the first men in South Africa to be convicted of
"corrective" rape. As *South Africa History Online* explains in its article on
Simelane: "The concept of 'correctional rape' involves the idea that raping an
LGBTQI+ identifying woman will 'cure' her of her sexuality. This violently
homophobic practice has been a plague on South Africa's LGBTQI+

community, particularly the black lesbian community in townships."[46] Though this type of violence is not specific to soccer, nor to South Africa, in the case of Eudy Simelane it seems to have been an appalling assertion of power in reaction to the public identity Simelane had claimed in part through the game.

As a final example of the power circulating through and around South African soccer, the nation itself has used soccer as a claim on political power. Several scholars see the 2010 World Cup in just this light—as an effort by South Africa to claim political gains both for and within Africa. For example, Sifiso Mxolisi Ndlovu has argued that the 2010 World Cup was a form of "cultural diplomacy" for South Africa, helping it to assert its leadership in a pan-African vision for an "African Renaissance."[47] Ashwin Desai and Goolam Vahed qualify that this effort at "soft power" served to politically obscure and distract from South Africa's own internal problems with xenophobia and inequality.[48]

All these types of power were there during the 2010 men's World Cup, with dynamics of race, gender, sexuality, politics, class, and more circulating just below the surface of what ultimately proved to be a magnificent month of soccer. As the first World Cup to be hosted in Africa, there was significant anxiety in the global media before the tournament—worries about crime, corruption, inexperience, and the relatively low standing of the South African team made for regular pessimism about the tournament's success. But, as Peter Alegi and Chris Bolsmann wrote in reflection after the tournament, all that faded with the very first game: "When Siphiwe Tshabalala scored to give South Africa the lead against Mexico in the opening game, lingering doubts and fears magically dissipated as millions of South Africans united behind the team. At that moment, the country experienced what no other event, with the exception of the first democratic elections in 1994, had ever achieved: a unified nation, collectively imagining the impossible."[49]

That power was real, but it was also ephemeral. Since 2010, South African soccer culture has continued to evolve—though the promised World Cup boost to the quality of its men's national team and its economy never quite materialized. The men's team has failed to qualify for the World Cup since 2010, and even failed several times to qualify for the biennial Africa Cup of Nations. The women's team has done better, in its 2019 qualification for its first Women's World Cup and in creating a national league, but it is still struggling for true professional opportunities.[50] And while the South African men's Premier League is arguably the most professional league in sub-Saharan Africa, the most popular league in the country by the metric of fan interest may well be the English Premier League—according to one digital media survey, as many South Africans regularly watch the EPL as do fans in England.[51]

Putting all the expressions of power and identity together, the South African case is strange in the extent to which its apartheid history made the power dynamics embedded in soccer cultures so explicit. Racial power dynamics of more subtle types are, however, a sadly familiar global phenomenon. South African soccer is not unique in struggling with race, though it is distinctive in how visible it makes those struggles. South Africa's soccer cultures are distinctively plural—characterized by long periods of racial segregation, and tentative promises that the power of the game might offer something better. But South Africa also offers hope that soccer's promises can be fulfilled. Soccer in South Africa has sometimes brought diverse peoples together. It has provided a forum for women to claim opportunities and justice, and it has projected a positive image of Africa to the world. Cultures are universally infused with power relationships, but the South African case shows how that power can both unify and divide, and how soccer cultures can either be part of the problem or part of the solution.

The Lessons of Soccer Cultures

These selective examples from soccer cultures in England, Brazil, and South Africa reinforce the idea that culture itself is a slippery concept. There is no one unified web of meanings that explains soccer or society in any particular nation-state. But there are dimensions of culture toward which social science lenses can usefully direct our attention. Soccer cultures in England are embedded with identities related to class, race, gender, and more—changing the meaning of the game depending on who is playing when and who is watching how. Soccer cultures in Brazil are characterized by social tensions reflected in the game—tensions between aesthetic joy and utilitarian cynicism, between opium for the masses and dramas of social justice. Soccer cultures in South Africa are replete with power dynamics—balancing the hopeful power of sport to unify with the darker history of soccer as a tool for segregation, discrimination, and violence. Each of these processes, visible to greater or lesser degrees, are parts of soccer cultures all over the world. And each helps us see soccer as a deeply cultural form.

The implication here for thinking fans is to move beyond superficial differences in playing styles and exotic rituals to recognize soccer cultures as meaning systems learned through personal experiences of a shared social history. Yes, there are some small but observable differences between how English teams tend to play and how Brazilian teams tend to play. But those differences can easily fall into stereotypes of, for example, the English as all long-ball bluster and the Brazilians as all buoyant trickery. Our minds like shortcuts, and stereotypes about playing styles and culture provide easy ones. But a deeper understanding of culture involves recognizing that culture is almost always "glocal" and it is enacted by people operating with shared mental hardware. We are all immersed in hybrid cultures, some of which seem strange and some of which seem familiar. And our cultural socialization is counterbalanced by more universal aspects of human nature. There is both great diversity and great similarity in global soccer cultures, and each is worth recognizing.

The differences in soccer cultures between England, Brazil, and South Africa, or between Malawi and the United States, or between any set of nations, are most often related to social history, socialization, and social organization. There we see significant variation in how soccer relates to identities and hierarchies of stratification—gender, race, class, and sexuality. We also see variations in political meanings, from the use of soccer to foment political movements to the self-contradictory idea that soccer should be apolitical. And we see variations in how power circulates through the game, creating opportunities for some depending again on identities and politics. We see soccer as a game that is infused with cultural dynamics both on and off the field.

The similarities in soccer cultures around the world depend upon shared characteristics of the human mind and the universal pleasures of the game. Soccer helps us understand culture precisely because it can be found virtually anywhere you go. My first intense cross-cultural experience with soccer in Malawi was only possible because many Malawians loved the game as much as I did. I had to learn to recognize that culture is neither exotic nor all-powerful, learning that was made possible by a lifetime of experiences with the diversity of the game. I've also learned that when we start to think of soccer as a deeply cultural game—when we can disentangle both the familiar and the strange—we open possibilities to one of the best things about being a thinking fan: more authentic engagement with the actual places and people who play.

A street advertisement in Ghana promoting the future through soccer talent.
Photo by Alan A. Lew from Flickr.com with a Creative Commons license.

CHAPTER 4

Players

Talent Development Versus Human Development

WHAT DOES IT TAKE TO MAKE A GREAT SOCCER PLAYER, or a great anything? This general question is at the center of a robust self-improvement industry, a large sector of the business world, a significant portion of educational endeavors, substantial government policy making, many researchers studying talent development—and pub conversations among soccer enthusiasts all over the world. One particularly fun version of the question is to imagine what you'd do if you suddenly became a soccer sheik. What if you had nearly unlimited funds, a decade or two to develop players, and dreams of soccer glory? For the Qatari royal family preparing to host the 2022 World Cup, this question was much more than a fun hypothetical. And the answers highlight how talent development is a *very* social science—an endeavor dependent upon remembering that soccer players are people rather than things, making human complexity a key variable in any talent development equation.

The Qatari effort to make great soccer players began in the early part of the aughts when the immensely wealthy Qatari royal family (and particularly the soccer-mad Sheikh Jassim bin Hamad al-Thani) decided to make soccer a key part of a plan to "modernize" Qatar. As relayed in multiple journalistic reports, including a 2014 series in the *New York Times* and an excellent 2018 book by Sebastian Abbot titled *The Away Game*, the goal was to use the global game to put Qatar at the center of the global stage.[1] Winning the right to host the 2022 World Cup was the most famous manifestation of that goal, but that right was built on years of strategic investments in soccer. With seemingly unlimited funds from natural gas and oil revenue, and the seemingly unlimited ambitions that come with such wealth, the Qataris undertook something like a soccer social scientist's fever dream: a massive natural experiment in developing soccer talent.

As the 2022 men's World Cup host, the Qatari national team is an automatic qualifier for the finals—the first host to have never previously qualified for a World Cup finals. Qatar, in fact, has little significant soccer history. Around the time Qatar was awarded hosting rights in 2010, its men's national team was at an all-time worst global ranking of 114th—a few spots behind the Central African Republic, and just ahead of Suriname and Ethiopia. To add to the challenge, Qatar only has about 300,000 eligible citizens (though the country's total population is around 1.8 million, most of those are "guest workers"). This means it has needed to create a competitive World Cup team relying solely on players from a population the size of that living in Lincoln, Nebraska (2018 population estimate of 287,401), or one-seventh of the medium-sized metropolitan area where I live (the Portland, Oregon, metropolitan area had a 2017 population estimate of 2,453,168). Note, however, that neither Lincoln nor the Portland metropolitan area has ever managed to produce a men's player capable of making the U.S. World Cup team.[2]

So, as the *New York Times* series on Qatar's soccer experiment phrased it, "What is a royal family with unlimited resources to do?"[3]

First, Qatar started by building world-class facilities and identifying local talent with the most soccer potential. In 2003 it created the Aspire Zone, a "sports city" in the capital of Doha that includes state-of-the-art sports fields, gyms, labs, and any other buildings that might contribute to sports excellence, along with a talent development center called the Aspire Academy. While Qatar has a wide range of ambitions for the Aspire Zone and Aspire Academy, including improving the health and physical fitness of its previously sedentary citizenry and training elite athletes in a variety of sports, the most prominent goal has always been developing World Cup talent.

Second, Qatar started buying sports expertise. Aspire spent significant sums to complement its world-class facilities with top-level coaches, scouts, and sport scientists from around the world.

Third, recognizing that the available talent in its small population would not be enough, Qatar started a global search for raw soccer talent. In 2005 Qatar "looked for a way to support developing countries in combination with helping local Aspire talents in their development" and came up with

"Aspire Football Dreams"—a massive hunt for gifted thirteen-year-old soccer players off the radar of the world's top clubs and youth programs.[4] Football Dreams mostly focused on sub-Saharan Africa, adding attention later to Asia and Latin America, sending talent scouts led by Spaniard Joseph Colomer (a former FC Barcelona youth director) to organize open trials across remote parts of the continent. In *The Away Game*, Sebastian Abbot evocatively describes Colomer's hardscrabble scouting trips in locales ranging from the remote Niger River delta to small towns in semirural Senegal.[5]

The core idea of the Football Dreams project is enticing because of how perfectly it integrates different ways of optimizing soccer talent. From a technocratic perspective, the project played an impressive numbers game: according to the Aspire website, Football Dreams "screened" 3.5 million kids between 2007 and 2014 in 17 countries, offering 18–20 academy scholarships each year. Any student of statistics has to appreciate the possibility of such a massively large sample size finding the right outliers—players with the rare combinations of physical and psychological traits that make for true greatness. Placing those outliers in world-class facilities with tutelage by global experts only furthers the project's technocratic appeal.

But there are also more romantic and humanistic charms to Football Dreams. Any soccer fan who travels through the developing world, and particularly sub-Saharan Africa, has to wonder how many of the barefoot soccer phenoms playing on the side of most any road might by the next Messi or Marta if only they were ever "discovered." And the Aspire website itself emphasizes that Football Dreams started as a "CSR" (corporate social responsibility) initiative intended to help low-resource countries and low-opportunity youth in their own quests for soccer glory.

So, what were the results of this provocative natural experiment in talent development? Like much intriguing research involving a great number of variables, the results are decidedly mixed. The Qatari national team has gotten noticeably better—winning the 2019 Asian Football Confederation championship over quality teams including Japan, South Korea, Iran, and Australia. As of April 2020, it had risen to a respectable fifty-fifth in the FIFA world rankings, just behind former European champion Greece and ahead of recent World Cup qualifiers such as Côte d'Ivoire and Ecuador. The injection of world-class facilities, expertise, and global talent could yet help Qatar be competitive in the 2022 World Cup.[6]

If the goal of Football Dreams was to develop elite global talents, on the other hand, the program simply has not worked. Though a few of the alumni recruited from around the world have had modest professional soccer success, it is fair to say that none of the top 0.004 percent of athletes skimmed off by Aspire (figuring 120 academy spots from screening 3.5 million 13-year-olds) is mentioned today in the same breath with Messi or other truly elite talents.[7]

This failure to cultivate elite players, despite massive resources, highlights a central tension in talent development: even with the best technocratic efforts, most players won't make it to the top of the talent pyramid. The pyramid metaphor here is both common and intentional, used in discussing talent development precisely because it is a design feature in most systems where few players succeed. In *The Away Game*, Abbot cites estimates that "only around 1 percent of the 10,000 kids in the entire English academy system end up making a living in the game."[8] In an ideal world the other 9,900 kids leverage their soccer experiences into other opportunities for education, jobs, and successful lives. But we don't live in an ideal world. As just one example, Abbot notes that while Aspire Academy claimed to value education as much as soccer, "only one of the Football Dreams players from the first class actually received a high school diploma. The number was zero in the second class. The situation didn't improve much in the future either, as only 10 percent of the kids ended up getting a diploma while they were at the academy."[9]

The question then becomes: What does it mean to succeed in the game of talent development? Is it about producing great teams at the club and national level? Is it about producing transcendent talents of the Messi and Marta ilk that earn the types of awards and remuneration that meet a commercial standard for success? Or is it about facilitating the development of human potential, even if that potential ends up best expressed off the playing field? The argument in this chapter is that most talent development systems focus primarily on producing great teams and elite players at the expense of broader human potential. That is a moral problem because it means talent development systems prioritize the success of the few at the expense of the many. But it may also be a soccer problem—dehumanizing players in ways that limit the potential of the game.

Social science lenses can help us better understand the meanings and methods of talent development by offering examples from an extensive academic literature, and by framing case studies of different global models. The theory and research discussed in the first part of this chapter will focus on a soccer version of classic nature and nurture questions. How much of elite soccer talent depends on natural genetic gifts? How much depends on the nurturance of particular traits and training? And how much depends on access, opportunities, and luck? A discussion of these ideas will segue to more extensive case studies of talent development approaches in Holland, Ghana, and Iceland. The intention of these case studies, in the spirit of the comparative cultural analysis employed in the last chapter, is to contrast ideal types of talent development, with Holland representing a more technocratic model, Ghana representing a more romantic model, and Iceland representing a more humanistic model.

While most all such approaches to talent development integrate the science of performance in some form, that science gives only an illusion of precision. We might like to believe that with the right combination of resources and expertise we could design the perfect talent development system, perfect players, and a perfect team. But the evidence from Qatar and elsewhere suggests otherwise. We can indeed learn lessons from research about talent development and this chapter will discuss several. But the research ultimately shows that talent development is a very human phenomenon, with all the imperfections that implies. As such, and by using social science as a guide, talent development becomes partially about the science of performance and partially about expressing personal, cultural, and social values. The values underlying this chapter hold that human development is more important than talent development, but I will ultimately suggest that within soccer, it just might be possible to combine both.

Nature, Nurture, Access, and Luck

If you ask the Internet what it takes to succeed in sports, at least in the form of inspirational quotes from sports stars, you quickly learn that it is all about attitude. You learn from Argentine great Diego Maradona that "When people succeed, it is because of hard work. Luck has nothing to do with success." The U.S. women's star Carli Lloyd tells us, "I love when people tell me I can't do something. That's what keeps me going. . . . If you have a dream, that dream is attainable." Current best player on the planet Lionel Messi assures us, "If football has taught me anything it is that you can overcome anything if, and only if, you love something enough."[10]

As a psychologist, I should love this rhetoric. It tracks perfectly with the popularity of positive psychology, which has been influential in American culture for promoting "non-cognitive skills" such as grit and optimism as the secret sauce that ensures success across domains. Positive psychologists such as Martin Seligman and Angela Duckworth have promoted these types of attitudes as keys to success in domains ranging from the military to charter schools serving low-income youth.[11] But when I put on my sociological lenses, and look at the empirical evidence, the rhetoric makes me nervous.

The "attitude is everything" idea in soccer dovetails closely with what sport sociologists Jay Coakley and Robert Hughes call "the Sport Ethic." The Sport Ethic is a set of values often embedded in contemporary sport culture that has four main norms: (1) putting a commitment to sport above everything else; (2) seeing competitive distinction as the only positive outcome; (3) taking risks without regard to things like pain; and (4) "refusing to accept limits in the pursuit of possibilities."[12] Think here of the types of inspirational slogans popular for youth soccer T-shirts: "Pain is temporary but pride is forever" or "Our blood, our sweat, your tears." The Sport Ethic is pervasive in ways athletes talk about their success. But Coakley and Hughes also suggest it is dangerous. They say an overcommitment to these norms helps explain phenomena ranging from the use of performance-enhancing drugs to psychological burnout.[13] Believing that anything is possible with the right attitude and the right level of commitment can be highly motivating for athletes, but it also must inevitably confront a less inspiring reality.

Take, for example, Lionel Messi—who is quoted claiming that success is mostly about loving something enough. It does seem clear that in his youth, Messi loved soccer. Videos of his early days in Argentina, portraying a mop-haired dervish bubbling around much bigger players with the ball elasticized at his feet, convey a clear sense of a passionate savant. And Messi's small stature was something he needed to overcome—though it is an obstacle soccer accommodates better than most sports. Research cited by Sebastian Abbot suggests that "28 percent of men have the height and weight combination that could fit in with professional soccer players, even as athletes' bodies have become more specialized over time. That's over five times the number they found could play in the NBA."[14] Lionel Messi, for all his physical gifts, would have never had a chance in the NBA even if basketball had turned out to be his true passion. Yet it is still worth noting that 72 percent of us don't have bodies that fit professional soccer no matter how much we love the game.

Messi does also have clear physical gifts. His ability to accelerate and maintain balance are capacities few people could develop no matter how hard they worked or how big they dreamed. As Ray Hudson, the BeIn Sports commentator famously obsessed with Messi's play and with creating new ways to describe it, once phrased it: "He abides in a magnetic spectrum of genius with the ball, where his divine connection of eyes to brain to feet cannot be measured with a stopwatch or a number. Like that once in a lifetime moment when you see your first love, across a crowded room. There are some things that can't be measured, thank God. And all we can do is look in disbelief at Messi's pure footballing magic."[15]

In more pedestrian language, while about a quarter of us have body dimensions that *could* allow us to be elite soccer players, most of us do not have the other physical and genetic gifts that matter to talent development. We are not fast enough, quick enough, or kinesthetically balanced enough to truly excel. We were not gifted with a "divine connection of eyes to brain to feet" that cannot be measured.

So how can we explain such gifts? The foundation is certainly genes. One study of British twins, relying on the important technique from behavioral genetics of comparing identical twins (who share 100 percent of their genetic material) with fraternal twins (who share, on average, 50 percent of their genetic material) to calculate the relative contribution of nature and nurture to development, estimated that the genetic heritability of "athlete status" is 66 percent.[16] For sake of comparison, our major personality traits seem to have 40–60 percent heritability,[17] whereas heritability rates for major depression seems to be more in the 30–40 percent range.[18]

The importance of genetic gifts does not, however, mean that talent development is as simple as identifying the right genetic profile. For one thing, despite significant effort from sport scientists and entrepreneurs promoting genetic testing for "sports genes," there is no specific set of genes that can successfully predict athletic excellence. The genes that do contribute to athletic excellence are too many, and as with virtually all of our psychological and behavioral traits, they work only through complex interactions that are not yet possible to reliably predict.

As sport scientist and geneticist Collin Moran explains, "There is no "talent" gene, but many 'talent' versions of many genes, which collectively help determine sporting talent. While we now understand a great deal about the genetic predisposition to sporting talent, there is more left undiscovered and genetic testing to identify future talent remains science fiction. Genes alone will not take you all the way—this is where the training, nutrition, psychology, strategy and technique all come in. All are necessary; none are sufficient."[19]

The necessary-but-not-sufficient framing of genetic gifts is also where we can start thinking about how nature interacts with nurture, access, and luck. This is, however, a huge area of research that quickly becomes overwhelming to distill. In one 2016 literature review,[20] sport science scholars looking at differences between elite and sub-elite sports talent identified key factors that could be organized into three areas with specifically delineated sub-factors in each: the performer (including genetics, anthropometric and physiologi- cal factors, psychological skills and motivational orientations, psychological factors, personality traits, and birthdate), the environment (including birth- place, support from parents, family, siblings, and coaches, and athlete sup- port programs), and practice, training, and play (including the volume of sport-specific practice and training and early specialization versus sampling and unstructured play). They note there are likely other factors that do not yet have enough clear evidence, including socioeconomic status; cross- cultural variations; recovery, rest, and sleep; emotional regulation; and even childhood emotional trauma.[21] Talent development, in other words, is really complicated.

That multiplicity of factors may be worth delving into for those with some specific investment in talent development—like the Football Dreams scouts searching for the "next Messi" in rural Africa. But for our purposes here, we can use just one factor as an example of further complexity within the com- plexity. The role of sport-specific practice time has gotten significant atten- tion due to the "10,000-hour rule" popularized by Malcom Gladwell in his 2008 book *Outliers: The Story of Success*.[22] That "rule" is based on famous research undertaken by psychologist K. Anders Ericsson assessing expert performance in music.[23] The idea was that distinctions between great and not-so-great orchestral musicians seemed to be heavily dependent on "delib- erate practice," with the performers needing an average of 10,000 hours to achieve elite status. There has since been much research and debate on how broadly applicable this finding might be. Ericsson himself has emphasized that 10,000 hours should not be thought of as a definitive rule, but also emphasizes that specific types of deliberate practice—particularly when expert instruction challenges athletes to consistently work at tasks just beyond their initial capacity—are a key differentiator of sports performance.[24] Other sport-specific research has, however, found a wide range of total hours required for true expertise and has raised questions about the merits of deliberate practice in contrast to unstructured play.[25]

It may also be the case that in some organized soccer contexts the "10,000-hour rule" has been distorted to suggest that young athletes should specialize at early ages in order to get a head start on becoming elite.[26] While it is obvious that elite athletes in all sports do need to practice a lot, for most sports (including soccer) it also clear that playing a variety of sports and playing soccer just for fun are significant predictors of long-term success. In just one soccer-related example from research, two separate studies compared elite German players (including national team players) with non-elite players on both the men's and women's sides.[27] The researchers found that the elite players were more likely have engaged in "non-organised leisure football play making" during childhood, played more of other sports besides soccer during adolescence, and rarely had enough specialized training to achieve 10,000 hours of deliberate practice.

The research on elite German players also found that there was no one specific pattern of training that had "explanatory power to explain success differences in German elite football at the individual athlete level."[28] There is, in other words, no set of controlled variables that optimizes talent development. This means we have to allow for and attend to uncontrolled variables. We have to move away from the idea of an indomitable attitude, a magical sports gene, an optimal number of training hours, or any other individual factor as a panacea. We need to recognize the roles of access and luck.

All the many factors that matter to talent development, such as those Moran summarized by listing "genetic gifts, training, nutrition, psychology, strategy and technique," matter only when given opportunity. And opportunities to develop talent are often a matter of access and luck. Even Lionel Messi, the man who "abides in a magnetic spectrum of genius," had the need for some very tangible intervention in order for his talents to be expressed. While Messi was always on the small side physically, and always successful with the ball at his feet, he was also diagnosed around age eight with a hormone deficiency that stunted his growth. His parents started giving him injections at an expense reported to be over $900 per month.[29] While Messi was from a working-class family, they had access to health care and enough money to cover the treatments until Lionel's soccer talents enticed professional clubs to take on the cost. Argentine clubs River Plate and Newell's Old Boys were apparently unwilling to cover the expense, so Lionel and his family moved to Barcelona, where FC Barcelona assumed the cost of the continued human growth hormone treatments. Messi was talented, but he was also lucky.

During my time working in places such as Malawi, Tanzania, Angola, and South Africa, I've had conversations with coaches from soccer academies who say one of the first things they look for in scouting young teenage talent is whether they are "stunted" physically. This stunting is usually not from the type of medical condition Messi experienced, but from a lack of nutrition and medical care. It is, however, tragically common and it means the soccer academies usually do not consider the players further—no matter their gifts, their determination, and their dreams. If players have not had access to nutrition and health care, they are out of luck.

It is also impossible to discuss the role of access without considering global women's soccer. As noted in chapter 1, one of the reasons the United States has been so successful in women's soccer is because of its head start in supporting women's opportunities to play soccer. Other countries where soccer had more historical popularity among men saw the women's game as a threat to be explicitly forbidden. As historians Brenda Elsey and Joshua Nadel document in their book *Futbolera: A History of Women and Sports in Latin America*, Brazil outlawed women's soccer (and a variety of other sports) in 1941, with legal provisions stating "women were strictly forbidden from playing a variety of team sports, including 'football, rugby, polo, and water polo, because they are violent sports and not adaptable to the female body.'"[30] As noted in the last chapter the English FA also banned women from playing in English team grounds starting in 1921,[31] while the German FA banned women from playing competitive soccer in 1955 with the claim that "In the fight for the ball, the feminine grace vanishes, body and soul will inevitably suffer harm."[32] Both England and Germany rescinded their bans in 1971, and the official prohibition in Brazil was rescinded in 1981, but the recovery of opportunities all over the world was slow and much talent went to waste.

Even within the United States, however, it is obvious that women's soccer does not provide equal access for prospective talents in diverse communities. Despite the historic success of legally mandating that women athletes have access to school sports opportunities (through the 1972 Title IX legislation), the U.S. soccer system is increasingly composed of expensive privatized clubs that depend upon players and families to pay significant fees. The expenses of the pay-to-play model limit the potential growth of the future talent pool. As just one demographic marker, while the 2018 census estimates that about 53 percent of American college students are non-Hispanic White,[33] NCAA data shows that in 2018 75 percent of female college soccer players were White.[34] Further, analyses by sociologist Jen McGovern and her student Esther Wellman found that players for the U.S. Women's National Team, U.S. Youth National Teams, and top-level college players are overwhelmingly from communities wealthier than average (in 70 to 80 percent of cases).[35] Similarly, a 2014 research brief from the Aspen Institute program "Project Play" found soccer participant households, when compared with baseball, football, and basketball, included the smallest number of poor kids (only 11 percent from families with less than $25,000 in annual income), and the greatest number of well-to-do kids (37 percent from families with more than $100,000 in annual income).[36] Barring a significant reinvestment in school sports, public recreation, or other mass-access opportunities, American soccer will continue to lose a significant portion of its potential talent pool—and a few scholarships are not enough to make a real difference.[37]

This particularly American problem of access also highlights the many ways talent development happens across soccer cultures. Because there is no one formula for successful talent development, culture, values, history, and place are all inextricably linked with talent development systems. Different places put different priorities on nature, nurture, luck, access, and the many variables in the unsolvable talent development equation, making talent development systems another rich site for comparative analysis. So, let's turn to such an analysis, using selective case studies that represent a spectrum of talent development examples. Each contrasts with the United States' historically school-based system and embeds key characteristics of more technocratic (Holland), romantic (Ghana), and humanistic (Iceland) models.

A Technocratic Approach: Holland

In the summer of 2010, around the same time as the Dutch national team reached the World Cup final, only losing to Spain in extra time, American journalist Michael Sokolove published an article in the *New York Times Magazine* about the famous Ajax Academy in Amsterdam.[38] Ajax is the most successful Dutch professional soccer club and has long been known around the world for cultivating young talent. That talent is part of a business model dependent on selling players from Ajax to the very richest clubs in the world—starting with Johan Cruyff to Barcelona, where his influence later shaped Barcelona's own famous academy, *La Masia*. Ajax, and Dutch soccer more generally, have become icons of talent development in Europe, emblems of how to systematically construct technically superior players for a good price.

Sokolove wrote about the Ajax model as a contrast to American approaches that have largely failed to create world-class men's players, and to other successful talent development approaches around the world:

> There are two ways to become a world-class soccer player. One is to spend hours and hours in pickup games—in parks, streets, alleyways—on imperfect surfaces that, if mastered, can give a competitor an advantage when he finally graduates to groomed fields. This is the Brazilian way and also the model in much of the rest of South America, Central America and the soccer hotbeds of Africa. It is like baseball in the Dominican Republic. Children play all the time and on their own.

> The other way is the Ajax method. Scientific training. Attention to detail. Time spent touching the ball rather than playing a mindless number of organized games.

Though I am suggesting in this chapter there are more than two ways to become a world-class soccer player, the point here is that the Ajax method is an archetype of technocracy. This approach is blunt in how it defines success and in thinking about players as products made through "scientific training." When, for example, Sokolove expressed surprise that youth players' total hours on the training field are strictly limited, an Ajax staffer told him "Of course, because they do not want to do anything to injure them or wear them out. They're capital. And what is the first thing a businessman does? He protects his capital."

The young players themselves seemed to understand their commodification. Because players (who start at the academy as young as seven years old) are ruthlessly culled every year for not fulfilling their talent development potential, those who remain through the years are socialized to be unsentimental. One put it bluntly: "You can't have real friends at Ajax." Another, asked if any of the abstract skills he was learning through football such as focus and perseverance might have benefits if he didn't make it in professional soccer, was equally direct: "No. We're training for football, not for anything else."

Perhaps most striking to me as an American academic was the recommendation to Sokolove from Huw Jennings, identified as "an architect of the English youth-development system" and an admirer of the Dutch approach. In diagnosing the problem with American talent development, Jennings believes "the N.C.A.A. [college sports] system is the fault line. I understand that it is good for a person's development to go to university, but it's not the way the world develops players." The technocratic approach, in its purest form, does not care about what "is good for a person"—only the player as a manufactured thing.

The manufacturing process in Holland starts with technical training to refine the basic techniques of the game. Perhaps the second most famous Dutch soccer institution aside from Ajax is "Coerver Coaching," a franchised skill development program that focuses on endless repetitions of minute ball skills to provide a foundation of "ball mastery." Its origin story involves the ultimate technocratic exercise: Dutch coach Wiel Coerver using video to analyze great players in slow motion and break down their movements into specific pieces that could be taught through methodical exercises.[39]

Though the program has evolved over the years, and evolves with player age to incorporate more team skills, it is most famous for asking players to work individually with a ball through a series of choreographed movements until after years of practice their feet, toes, ankles, and knees can perfectly coordinate rolling, dragging, feinting, cutting, and any other imaginable minutiae of technical soccer skill. I have memories of working with a ball in my front yard as a young player to mimic Coerver moves from videos shared by my coaches, then going to a three-week skills academy using a variant built on the same principles of the Coerver system. It was mind-numbing, exhausting, and incredibly effective. I'm not sure I would have ever learned to effectively strike a ball with my left foot if it hadn't been for that three-week technical training academy.

Coerver himself coauthored a book whose title translates to *The Textbook for the Ideal Soccer Player*, and was so certain of the superiority of his method that he had "a small rift" with other Dutch coaches and associations, though versions of his program are still popular supplements to club training in Holland and around the world.[40] And such technocratic systems for talent development are common in Dutch soccer. Ajax itself uses a coaching system based on the acronym TIPS (Technique, Intelligence, Personality, and Speed),[41] while the book *Dutch Soccer Secrets* describes other named and systematized programs such as the "Five-Phase Model" of Dutch talent development, the "Rene Meulensteen Method" for soccer technique, and the "Frans Hoek Method" for training goalkeepers.[42]

While focusing just on technocratic methods and systems can make the Dutch system seem to be an exemplar of sociologist Max Weber's warning that modern society is moving toward a world of "specialists without spirit, sensualists without heart," there are certainly humanistic dimensions of Dutch talent development. When, for example, the editor of an esteemed Dutch football training magazine was asked by the authors of *Dutch Soccer Secrets* for insight into the country's soccer success he explained that "What is special in the Netherlands is that most amateur clubs are much more than just soccer clubs. They organize a lot of other, non-sporting activities. So, the club is more than just a place where people learn to play soccer."[43] And the availability of widespread community clubs with deep roots and local social networks is a key to providing opportunities for talent to be identified in the first place. The fact that Holland is a small place that tends to invest in communal institutions means it does relatively well with access.

In recent years, the Dutch have also somewhat ironically realized that a key foundation for refined technical training is acquiring the joy of "street soccer" in unstructured settings. Extracting friends and fun from the soccer talent manufacturing process turns out to be counterproductive. So, in fine technocratic form, the Dutch soccer system is trying to find ways to organize youth soccer in order to replicate the types of street soccer lost to modernization. According to at least one account, to make the Dutch talent development model work, "it is fundamentally about replicating as much as possible street football which was the breeding ground of all great players before economic advances took kids off the streets. Indeed in Holland they are going even further. Soon they will bring in junior football without referees, with no sideline coaching and with parents restricted to standing behind a rope 30 meters from the playing area. Again it's about mimicking street football where there are no referees, no coaches and no parents. And no league tables."[44]

That account is, interestingly, from an Australian commentary—since Australia in recent years has invested heavily in the Dutch talent development model as something that can be readily imported to improve Australia's global soccer success. Similarly, as of the end of 2019, the U.S. Soccer Federation put its talent development fate on the men's side largely in the hands of technocrats from the Low Countries: Dutch American Earnie Stewart is the U.S. Men's sporting director, Dutchman Nico Romeijin is U.S. Soccer's chief sport development officer, and Belgian Barry Pauwels is the U.S. director of coach education.

Both American and Australian soccer fans are placing bets on whether the Dutch approach can be directly exported or whether the technical thoroughness of the system depends upon it operating in a particular cultural milieu. My money, and my understanding of cultural pluralism, says that even the most technocratic system needs deeper roots in culture and place.[45] The technocratic approach seems to work in Holland because it has, among other facilitative social forces, a national infrastructure of community clubs to help identify potential academy players, a cultural history with the game that makes soccer stardom a prominent aspiration, and widespread technical expertise in soccer. More abstractly, according to David Winner's cultural history of soccer in Holland, Dutch soccer values a type of "neurotic genius" that also permeates Dutch architecture, geography, and social movements.[46] Add the fact that the technocratic approach to talent development doesn't sound that fun, and it's worth considering how places with different soccer cultures employ other approaches.[47]

A Romantic Approach: Ghana

U.S. soccer fans may remember Ghana as the team that eliminated the United States men's team from both the 2006 and 2010 World Cups. Or they may recognize Ghana as one of the biggest producers of talent for Major League Soccer—in 2019 Ghanaian-born players were only outnumbered in the MLS foreign legion by French-, Colombian-, Brazilian-, and Argentinian-born talent.[48] Ghanaian players are also among the top exports in the 31 European professional leagues, behind only Brazil, Argentina, and Nigeria (each of which has a population between 16 million and 180 million more than Ghana's 27.5 million).[49] Or U.S. fans might remember that Ghana was the birthplace of the most hyped talent that the U.S. failed to develop: Freddy Adu, the youngest American ever to play professionally in a U.S. league when he signed with DC United at age fourteen after spending the first eight years of his life in Tema, Ghana. So, what is it that makes the relatively small and relatively poor West African nation of Ghana one of the best men's programs in the world, and one of soccer's top talent producers?

The short answer, and one reason I use Ghana as an example of a romantic approach to talent development, is that Ghanaians love the game. The street soccer that the Dutch federation is trying to re-create using top-down managerial dictates is still a passionate part of the daily ritual for a huge number of Ghanaian boys. And soccer in Ghana is woven into the ideals of the nation. As the first African country to gain independence from colonial rule, early Ghanaian leaders such as Kwame Nkrumah saw soccer as a way to simultaneously build national unity, to mobilize "the youth of the nation around a common identity," and gain global status.[50] The men's national team's nickname of the Black Stars derives from that heady time and from Marcus Garvey's Black Star shipping line, which offered former slaves passage back across the Atlantic with the romantic dream of creating new lives in an independent African state.

As a model of talent development, this means that Ghanaian players spend a disproportionate portion of their childhood playing the game and developing skills in unstructured settings where the primary goal is fun. In one ambitious research study comparing the developmental trajectories of elite boys soccer players from Brazil, England, France, Portugal, Mexico, and Ghana, they found that Ghanaian players were by far the last to start in supervised training (at an average age of 9.5 compared with around at 6 in England and Sweden).[51] Even in street and beach soccer mecca Brazil, which had the next latest average starting age, players start supervised training nearly 2 years younger than in Ghana. Likewise, the elite Ghanaian boys were by far the last group to start playing in formal youth soccer leagues, at over 11 years old. The only statistical findings where Ghana is not an outlier is the overall number of hours in soccer by the time of reaching the under-16 age group and the age at which players started in soccer academies. Ghanaian players, on average, start in academies just short of 13 years old, which is very similar to the average for youth players in Brazil, France, Mexico, and Sweden (England and Portugal start players in academies at significantly younger ages).

These researchers also looked at the number of other sports kids played besides soccer, and found a significant range—from an average of 4 other sports for English youth, to an average of only 1.40 other sports for Brazilian youth (Ghanaians were much closer to the Brazilian numbers, at an average of 1.91 other sports). These researchers then suggest that talent development pathways can best be categorized into three types: early specialization (where players start receiving specialized training at a very young age in one primary sport), early diversification (where players start with a wide range of organized sports, only gradually transitioning into specialized training in one sport), and early engagement (where players start by engaging the game in unstructured settings, only later undertaking organized training).

This scheme for different talent development patterns doesn't exactly trace onto the scheme I'm using in making these arguments, but if we force the analogy, the early specialization pathway is most akin to the technocratic model, the early diversification pathway is most akin to the humanistic model, and the early engagement pathway is most akin to the romantic model. It is worth noting here that early specialization in any sport has been a major topic of debate in U.S. youth sports in recent years, as the increasing privatization of the sport system encourages talented players to make exclusive year-round commitments to club teams and private coaching at younger ages. The data is clear that U.S. athletes in all sports are specializing more and at earlier ages. But the social science is equally clear that this trend is a problem. Athletes of most types gain significant long-term health and performance benefits from using their younger years to develop a range of physical skills, and they gain psychological benefits from not overcommitting to one sport before having a chance to explore other interests and identities.[52]

At younger ages in Ghana, there is little pressure for most players to commit to year-round club teams or private coaching because those opportunities simply aren't available. Until right around, or just after, puberty, Ghanaian players mostly develop their skills with their friends and their motivation to play at younger ages is largely intrinsic and self-generated—the type of motivation sport psychologists tend to prefer over extrinsic motivation (playing because of external rewards, validation, or expectation) because intrinsic motivation seems to have significant long-term benefits for persistence and enjoyment.

Then, for the very best players with access to the right opportunities, the academies take over and the romance often ends. The passion of kids on the streets playing for little but joy shifts to passionate dreams of a promised land: wealth and fame in the English Premier League, the German Bundesliga, Spain's La Liga, Italy's Serie A, or France's Ligue 1. Or even, in a strange twist on the usual soccer global order, an American college soccer scholarship.[53]

Elite talent development academies in Ghana, and across sub-Saharan Africa, come in many different forms but share a goal of sending players to greener pastures. Scholars Paul Darby, James Esson, and Christian Ungruhe, who have undertaken extensive research on the academy system in Ghana, offer a typology of African soccer academies that includes local professional academies, "Afro-European" academies partnering with European professional teams, sponsored charitable academies, and improvised academies run by a range of both entrepreneurs and hucksters.[54] While each type can range widely in quality and sincerity, all define success at least in part by developing talent in a way that allows that talent to leave (ideally for a significant price).

The academy system is where the romantic model of talent development reaches its denouement. And like many romantic stories, that point only rarely means everyone lives happily ever after. Even the best academies are built on the assumption that many more players will fail than will succeed. Those failures can come in many forms, including exploitative agents and clubs that treat young players—and particularly young players from developing parts of the world such as Ghana—as disposable property. That type of failure has been well addressed elsewhere by more geopolitical analysis.[55]

But there are also failures that derive from basic principles of developmental psychology and the fact that talent development depends heavily upon the vagaries of physical maturation. *The Away Game*, in following Qatar's Football Dreams project and its taking players from African countries including Ghana to the Aspire Academy, comes to its own denouement when the reader learns that most of the players were likely much older than they claimed when trying out at "thirteen years old." In some cases it seems the players may have been as much as four to five years older than claimed— which clearly provides an advantage when playing against real thirteen-year-olds. This is sometimes a matter of blatant misrepresentation, where players and coaches know that subtracting years from young talent's biographies makes them seem like they have more potential for the future. But it is also partially related to less nefarious factors, such as a generally more flexible attitude toward age in many African countries (where in some cases, until recent decades, it was rare to have a birth formally documented) and the fact that people really do mature at different ages.

Maturational differences are another reason talent development is such an inexact science; it is impossible to know when youth players have reached their physical peak. Players that seem precocious are often early to mature and players that mature late are often weeded out of competitive systems. The ages around thirteen years old are where maturational differences are most pronounced, and they are also the ages where talent development academies most intensively select and de-select players. Many savvy academies are now trying to combat these "relative age effects" by grouping players through "bio-banding" (i.e., physical size and maturation) rather than birthdate.[56] In a place such as Ghana, age is less concrete and physical stature at younger ages can shape later destinies. I suspect, for example, that one reason Ghanaian-born Freddy Adu never fulfilled his young potential is due to the simple fact of his early maturation. He peaked around age fourteen, when other players were just starting to get better.

Ultimately, then, the approach in a place such as Ghana presents a talent development model that relies less on scientific methods and more on a type of alchemy. It starts with a large pool of potential players who develop skills and passion through street soccer, then funnels the most talented of those players into intensive academies geared toward polishing a few into high-value professionals. When it works, the results can seem magical. Watching Ghana eliminate the U.S. Men's National Team from both the 2006 and the 2010 World Cups was a testament to how players, forged first through their own passions and then only secondarily through intensive training, can best bigger and wealthier opponents. But the process only really works when luck ensures the right players end up in the right place at the right time.

In this way the romantic model ultimately combines some magical successes with a lot of broken hearts. The academies in places such as Ghana accommodate only a tiny minority of interested players, and the number of big-money contracts on offer is even smaller still.[57] The Ghanaian talent development system is admirable in kindling passion for the game, and some of its academies do impressive work to stoke that passion into bright talents. But the system also accentuates the role of chance in talent development and raises concerns about what happens to the unlucky majority. Those concerns may be best addressed with other talent development systems that combine the romantic appeal of producing magical players with a humanistic attention to producing good people.

A Humanistic Approach: Iceland

In August 1997 the Icelandic men's national team was ranked 88th in the world by FIFA, a few spots behind soccer non-powers such as Lebanon, Cyprus, and Uzbekistan. After a brief blip of success, things got worse: by 2010 the men's team was ranked 112th. These statistics might be unremarkable for a nation with a population of only around 350,000 people, ranking it around 180th by population for the countries of the world. But during the decade following 2010, Iceland's team made a remarkable rise, advancing to the final eight of the European Championships in 2016, qualifying for the 2018 World Cup finals in Russia, and reaching a world ranking of 18th during 2018. This is an astonishing success for a country, like Qatar, with a player pool the size of a small American city (comparable to the greater Flint, Michigan, area).

But something else was not going very well in Iceland in 1997. In an article by journalist Emma Young, an Icelandic psychologist named Gudberg Jónsson explained that "Icelandic teens were among the heaviest-drinking youths in Europe."[58] His colleague Harvey Milkman noted, "You couldn't walk the streets in downtown Reykjavik on a Friday night because it felt unsafe. . . . There were hordes of teenagers getting in-your-face drunk." But this too has changed dramatically. According to Young: "Today, Iceland tops the European table for the cleanest-living teens. The percentage of 15- and 16-year-olds who had been drunk in the previous month plummeted from 42 percent in 1998 to 5 percent in 2016. The percentage who have ever used cannabis is down from 17 percent to 7 percent. Those smoking cigarettes every day fell from 23 percent to just 3 percent."

How might these two trajectories possibly be related, and what do they have to do with talent development? The answer starts with social scientists in Iceland in the 1990s, concerned about teen substance use, finding a constellation of protective factors made a big difference: spending time with parents, feeling cared about at school, not being outdoors in the late evening, and participating in organized activities—especially sport—three or four times a week. The research became one piece motivating a new national plan called "Youth in Iceland." Among its many components was increased state funding for organized sport (along with other youth activity programs).

This approached dovetailed seamlessly with what scholars Frode Telseth and Vidar Halldorsson frame as a distinctively "Nordic" approach to soccer success.[59] The approach is first characterized by the "Nordic welfare model" where the public sector makes significant investments in human welfare, including support for voluntary sport organizations that promote "sport for all" and children's sport. Second, they argue, Nordic sport is founded on an amateur ideology where sport is seen as a good in and of itself. Success in elite sport is justified, from this way of thinking, only in its "ability to attract more children to sporting activities."[60]

In practice, this philosophy manifested in several practical efforts that served both human development and talent development. Telseth and Halldorsson present it in multiple parts, including the construction of indoor football halls in communities across Iceland, which allowed for year-round participation, which coincided with broad-based coach education ("Iceland now has the highest number of UEFA-accredited coaches in Europe per participant"), improved professional opportunities for players, an improved Icelandic league, increased opportunities for players to migrate to and from Iceland, and more specialists in "coaching, physiology, physiotherapy, psychology and training."[61]

Importantly, however, the increase in professionalism has been gradual. As Telseth and Halldorsson explain, "One of the key reasons for the achievements of the Scandinavian countries in sports is that the sport system is a blend of 'democratic' and 'competitive' fostering, in other words, a combination of amateurism and professionalism. Thus, despite the increased professionalism in Icelandic football it was, and remains, in this developmental stage and lacks many of the methods and structures that are in place in professional sport. . . . There are, for instance, no high-tech laboratories in

Icelandic sports, no hidden technological innovations, hardly any systematic talent identification programs and no genetic searches for potential talent, and little emphasis on early sport specialization."[62]

I happened to be in Iceland in the summer of 2016 when the men's national
team had its most famous moment, beating a heavily favored England team
in the round of sixteen at the European championships in France. I watched
the game in a public square in Akureyri, the largest town in Iceland outside
of the Reykjavik area at just nineteen thousand people. It was a fun day, and
the locals were in good spirits. But I was most struck by the relative lack of
irrational exuberance. There was no dancing in the streets and no lighting
bonfires, just a matter-of-fact sense that global sport success was a natural
outgrowth of Icelandic communities and Icelandic character. It was the same
sense I got when attending a game in the top Icelandic men's division, where
the crowd leaned their bikes against the fence and acted as interested in ami-
able socializing as in football fanaticism. And I got the same sense again
when poking my head into several of the giant indoor football halls that dotted the Icelandic countryside, where players of all ages waited patiently for
their turn on the artificial turf.

In a 2017 book titled *Sport in Iceland: How Small Nations Achieve International Success*, the Icelandic sociologist Halldorsson attributes the country's
relative success to a combination of infrastructure and good policy (facilitated by a small, relatively wealthy, and relatively homogeneous population),
a culture of determination and comradery (a mentality toward sport he calls
"the Icelandic madness"), and a simple valuing of play.[63] Though all these are
important, for purposes of thinking about a humanistic model of talent
development, it is this last factor that seems most important to emphasize.
Halldorsson notes that in prior generations Icelanders thought of sport as
largely "a waste of time." But due to an intersection of local and international
trends, community sport clubs became a productive place for children with
positive socialization effects.[64]

In the current iteration of Icelandic talent development international success is essentially a by-product of humanistic goals. Or, at the least, humanistic
goals are the by-product of international success. In both the technocratic
and romantic models of talent development, the systems depend upon mass
failure: commodification and limited opportunities mean the few that succeed necessarily do so at the expense of the many who tried. But the Icelan-

dic example suggests there may be another way: using soccer as an engaging community activity for everyone, a very few of whom may well go on to international success.

It is, however, worth noting that Telseth and Halldorsson's analysis of the Nordic model contrasts Iceland's success in the most recent decade with Norway's relative success in the 1990s. They argue that both relied on a constructive mix of amateur ideals and sport-for-all with burgeoning professionalism. But Norway's fortunes since have declined precipitously (the men's team has not qualified for the World Cup since consecutive efforts in 1994 and 1998, while the women's team has gone from World Cup champions in 1995 and Olympic champions in 2000 to World Cup mediocrity and a failure to qualify for the three most recent Olympic Games). Thus, Telseth and Halldorsson warn, "Iceland could share Norway's fate if it loses its most important asset, its heart and soul, to a more professional, commercial and idolized sports culture. If that happens, Iceland risks vanishing from the top-level international football scene as quickly as they appeared on it."[65]

The Lessons of Talent Development

So, if you were a Qatari sheik with virtually unlimited funds to spend in hopes of developing elite soccer talent, what would you do? Would you, as happened historically for U.S. women, invest in school sports and mandate opportunities for all as a way of increasing the talent pool? Or would you, as today's U.S. Soccer Federation seems to have done, put your hopes in a technocratic model embodied by the Dutch talent development approach made famous by the Ajax Academy? Would you, as Qatar attempted, engage a romantic global talent search in places such as Ghana, looking for unpolished gems around the age of thirteen to enroll in intensive academies designed to turn raw potential into high-value professionals? Or would you, as it may by now be obvious is my preference, invest in a more humanistic, community-based sport-for-all model as a way of simultaneously improving youth well-being and expanding the national talent pool in places such as Iceland that have limited histories of success?

Or, what if the question were less hypothetical and more personal: given what we know about talent development, how would you approach developing your own talent or that of your children? You could start by instilling grit and optimism, which would fit well with the popular rhetoric and "sports ethic" of soccer stars who believe success is all about attitude. But you'd have to confront the vagaries of physical ability and maturation, recognizing that basic genetic gifts mean only a small number of us have the potential for true greatness in soccer, and understanding that there is no firm science for identifying that number nor for understanding at what point in development that potential will come to fruition. To further complicate the matter, you would also have to consider where your real opportunities, and opportunity costs, lie. Will you get access to resources, expertise, competition, and all the other factors outside yourself necessary to fulfill your potential? If you do everything right, putting in just the right number of hours of deliberate practice, and still fail (remembering that failure is a feature rather than a bug of the elite soccer academy system), will you have regrets? And finally, to put it all together: do you feel lucky?

While this may all make intentional efforts at talent development seem futile, the fact that it is not an exact science is also precisely what makes talent development such a rich topic to view through social science lenses. Talent can't be produced in a laboratory; it has to be produced by people. Talent development happens when governments decide girls and women should be encouraged to play; it happens when kids with physical challenges (like Lionel Messi) are given access to quality health care; it happens when social groups and entire societies (like Iceland) decide to invest in the general well-being of youth. And it happens in different ways at different times and places, reflecting and refracting the cultural pluralism that offers diverse pathways to success.

Thinking about talent development through such social science lenses could ultimately have significant benefits for both people and soccer success. Approaching talent development from a more humanistic perspective could, as just one example, allow young athletes to engage in healthy identity exploration and to become more well-rounded people. This might, in turn, provide a stronger psychological base from which to approach competition, to work with and relate to teammates, to avoid burnout, and to make more significant long-term contributions to the game, like shifting to coaching and administration after the inevitable early end of a playing lifetime.

Soccer players are not, in the words of critical theorist John Hoberman, "mortal engines" to be manufactured and tuned for high performance.[66] Instead, we are all imperfect mixtures of natural gifts and limitations, nurtured skills and flaws, opportunists and victims of fate. We can and should seek to understand each component of that mix. But if we want to try to optimize talent development, or optimize any aspect of soccer performance, we have to first remember that players are people too.

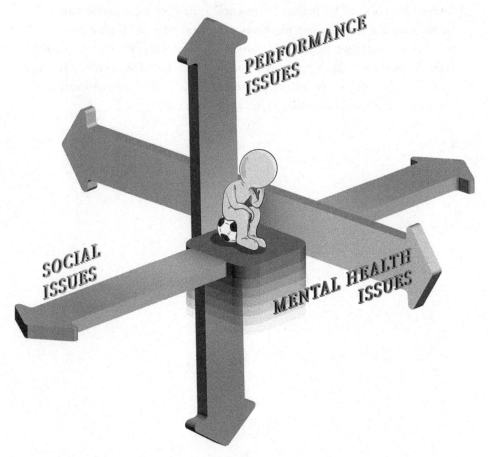

This octant represents three dimensions of psychological issues confronting individual players, including performance issues, mental health issues, issues imposed by the social context of competitive sport, and (most often) combinations thereof. Image by a_t___art.

CHAPTER 5

Performances

Mental Skills, People Skills, and the Psychology in Soccer

B RAZIL'S EXPERIENCE OF THE 2014 World Cup is perhaps best characterized by tears. There were the tears shed by protestors gassed by police
for having the temerity to use a soccer tournament to air political dissatisfaction. There were the tears streaming down star player Neymar's face, over-
whelmed with a patriotic fervor during the pregame playing of the national
anthem. There were the tears of captain Thiago Silva when Brazil's round of
sixteen game against Chile went to a penalty shootout and he was too ridden
with anxiety to take a kick. And, of course, there were the tears of the entire
nation when Germany humiliated Brazil 7–1 in one of the most memorable
World Cup semifinals of all time. Brazil in 2014 put the raw psyche of soccer
on vivid display and reminded fans around the world that the game is as
much about psychology as it is about physical skills.

The psychology on display in the 2014 World Cup drew much commentary from fans, the media, and psychologists themselves. As the tournament
progressed, all of the above could see the expressions on Brazilian faces evoke
a shifting panoply of emotions: angst, ardor, anger, anguish, and more than a
bit of anxiety. The slow-motion panning of faces during national anthems, a
television shot that has become standard stage-setting for World Cup games,
became a Rorschach test for the nation. And the nation was concerned.

Former Brazil captain Carlos Alberto conveyed his concern more directly
than most: "The team is crying when they're singing the anthem, when they
get hurt, when they shoot penalties! Come on . . . Stop crying! Enough! They
say it's the pressure from playing at home. But they should have been prepared for this."[1] Some Brazilian psychologists agreed. The president of the

São Paulo Association of Sport Psychology, João Ricardo Cozac, explained with a bit more nuance: "You can cry, it is a way of venting emotion. But, before an important and decisive moment, seeing the goalkeeper and the captain crying, and the coach, instead of calming and motivating, standing on the edge of the field complaining about the refereeing and cursing opponents demonstrates a lack of emotional control that is most dangerous."[2]

What, then, would it mean for a team to be psychologically prepared for the type of pressure Brazil faced in 2014? After the explosion of tears Brazil's manager, Luiz Felipe Scolari, did make the effort of calling on psychologist Regina Brandão, who had done some psychological profiling work with the team prior to the tournament.[3] Brandão apparently built on the psychological profiling to help players employ various relaxation techniques (standards in the sport psychology tool kit) as ways of managing their feelings of massive pressure. Unfortunately, taking as evidence the dramatic 7–1 semifinal humiliation Brazil suffered against Germany, it seems to have been too little, too late.

In any sport context, psychology is, of course, only one of many factors determining results and performance quality. In Brazil's loss, Neymar, who fractured a vertebra in his spine during the quarterfinal, took no part. Silva had picked up a second yellow card in the same quarterfinal game and was suspended for the semifinal. Germany was ruthless and showed its quality by going on to win the final.

But even if psychology was not the primary cause of Brazil's debacle, it was certainly a primary effect. The loss produced an outpouring of emotion: an iconic cover of Brazil's *Metro* newspaper was simply a horizontal rectangle of a deep-black night sky above the stadium scoreboard, *Correio Braziliense* led with the headline of "A Shame for Eternity," while *O Globo*'s cover consisted of three psychologically loaded words: *Vergonha, Vexame, Humilhação* (Shame, Grief, Humiliation).[4]

The moment was so ripe for psychological interpretation that distant commentators chimed in with their own theories of the Brazilian meltdown.[5] Andrew Lane, a professor of sport psychology at the University of Wolverhampton in the UK, posited that the game was about Bandura's self-efficacy theory, observing that "Brazil's confidence deteriorated on a moment by moment basis due to their failing performance."[6] Author and "stress expert" Angela Patmore argued that the Brazilian team put too much emphasis on needing to just relax, and not enough on how to cope with adversity: "Rather than stress management, beleaguered sportsmen need traditional psychological training designed to increase their mental resilience."[7] Gavin Brent Sullivan, from the Centre for Psychology, Behaviour and Achievement at Coventry University, focused less on the performance and more on the broader emotional experience of collective shame: "The loss was not just humiliating because another team inflicted the defeat on the Brazilian team and, by implication, Brazilian supporters; as odd as it sounds, it is also the Brazilian team's active rather than passive contribution to the historically bad result by failing to mount sufficient resistance that means it is appropriate to talk of collective humiliation and shame."[8]

The profusion of psychological explanations and angles for Brazil's 2014 performance highlights something important about applying psychology to soccer: it is, as with talent development, an inexact science. There are no magical psychological techniques that guarantee players can manage intense pressure and anxiety. There is no one definitive psychological theory to explain how soccer plays with our individual and collective emotions. The human mind, and human experience, is just too complicated. But, like any social science, psychology offers a range of techniques and theoretical perspectives that have the potential to improve performance and inform our experiences of the game—especially when applied modestly and thoughtfully. The goal of what follows is to make just such applications.

In this chapter, we'll focus particularly on the psychology embedded in soccer performance, beginning with an overview of how sport psychology works in concept and in practice. How, for example, does sport psychology think about anxiety and arousal, particularly in the "critical moments" that come so often in a game where one goal can make all the difference? We'll then look at a particular type of critical moment that turns out to be a rich object for psychology: the penalty kick. Given that any reasonably competent player can execute the physical skills of putting a ball past a goalkeeper from twelve yards away, how might psychology make the difference in a moment of distilled pressure? Finally, so as not to forget our sociological lenses, we'll conclude with a consideration of how other pressures of soccer can undermine a psychologically healthy self-concept. Players often have a finely tuned performance mindset, but that sometimes comes with losing a sense of self beyond the game. Understanding the significance of that sense of self, learning to recognize the person behind the performance, offers thinking fans the chance to genuinely understand why all the emotions evoked by soccer matter.

Sport Psychology in Concept and in Practice

When I've talked about sport psychology with soccer players, and athletes of all types, the topic tends to make them wary. First, psychology often evokes thoughts of mental illness and related problems—and athletes are often socialized to avoid any signs of weakness, believing that all challenges can be overcome with hard work and discipline. Second, psychological interventions sometimes connote quackery and a tendency to overpromise when in fact sport psychology, like most forms of psychology and many types of health care, has no miracle cures. Third, most soccer players share with the general population a reasonable confusion about just what sport psychology is (and what it's not).

Much of the confusion about sport psychology distills to the fact that it is not just one thing. The type of sport psychology that might be engaged by the Brazilian national team, or by any soccer player looking for a mental edge, would be technically referred to as "mental skills coaching" and focuses largely on sport performance rather than mental health. This version of sport psychology tends to focus on a set repertoire of mental skills that include imagery, goal setting, self-talk, and arousal management (psyching up or calming down) and is often practiced by consultants or life coaches instead of by licensed psychologists.

Licensed psychologists and related mental health professionals, on the other hand, often work with athletes and soccer players dealing less with performance issues and more with personal distress. This version of sport psychology is more like any type of mental health work dealing with depression, anxiety disorders, eating disorders, and other clinical syndromes—but with an appreciation for the particular ways sports cultures can impact mental health. Part of that impact is the shame many elite athletes feel in admitting to mental health distress, but these stigmas may be slowly changing. In recent years, players such as U.S. icon Landon Donovan and England international Danny Rose have gone public with experiences of depression, and U.S. women's legend Abby Wambach has publicly confronted substance abuse related to anxiety.

Persistent stigmas have, however, made it hard to get good data about rates of mental health challenges among elite athletes. It may be the case that intensive sport participation either selects for or builds a certain type of psychological resilience. Or it may be that the pressures and restrictions of intensive sport participation, along with the fear of admitting weakness, make athletes more vulnerable to mental health distress. But whatever the general pattern, elite soccer players and athletes of all types are only human—meaning that as many as 50 percent will likely struggle with some types of mental health challenges at some point in their lives.[9]

The mental health challenges faced by athletes intersect in complicated ways with the performance issues that are often addressed through mental skills coaching. To conceptualize those potential intersections, the American Psychological Association division devoted to "Sport, Exercise, and Performance Psychology" provides a four-quadrant graphical representation, placing "mental health issues" on the x-axis of the two-by-two grid, and "performance issues" on the y-axis. Though merely conceptual, the helpful idea here is that some athletes may be dealing primarily with performance issues that are unrelated to mental health (calling mostly for mental skills coaching) while some athletes may be dealing primarily with mental health issues that are largely unrelated to performance (calling mostly for licensed mental health care). Likewise, some athletes may have neither performance issues nor mental health issues and some may have both—the former requiring no intervention, and the latter requiring more careful consideration.

This useful conceptual framework could benefit from a third dimension—a z-axis that represents the social concerns embedded in sports that can bring either or both of performance issues and mental health issues to the fore (as illustrated in figure 5 at the start of this chapter). As one example, many elite youth soccer players now experience social pressure to specialize intensively in the sport at a very young age. This intensive early specialization is furthered by the structures of the sport, with under-twelve players now competing for youth national team spots and in national "development" leagues. Sport sociologists such as Jay Coakley have long pointed to these social forces as a recipe for "burnout."[10] Though we will return to this discussion of burnout in more depth later in the chapter, for conceptual purposes the idea here is that burnout for soccer players can be primarily a performance issue (as with an inability to cope with stress), primarily a mental health issue (as when feeling demotivated by depression), primarily a social context issue (as per the social pressure toward early specialization and identity foreclosure), or—more likely—some combination thereof.

We will concern ourselves primarily with the psychology of performance issues and mental skills because they are most distinctive to soccer and its place in the sports world. Mental health issues along with social issues that impact performance deserve a more thorough treatment than can be provided here, though they are woven briefly into discussions of identity and burnout. And they are always important to keep in mind with any discussion of psychology and soccer. Mental skills can genuinely improve performance, but the psychology of peak performance is rarely just about mental skills.

Mental Skills Coaching

Though soccer players and other serious athletes are often wary of sport psychology as a general practice, they rarely need convincing about the importance of mental skills. When I ask athletes to estimate the percentage of day-to-day performance that is due to psychological factors rather than physical readiness, the difference between a good game and a bad game, they usually estimate something in the 50 to 90 percent range. As Yogi Berra proclaimed in one of his fabled sports malapropisms, "Ninety percent of this game is half-mental." But if you ask those same players the percentage of training time that they spend preparing physically and the percentage of time they spend preparing psychologically, it is usually somewhere in the 90 to 95 percent physical range. That logical inconsistency has been the basis of many claims that sport psychology should be a foundational part of modern training environments.

These claims have been around for a long time, but the uptake of sport psychology has been slow. Many top club teams do now have entire departments and staff devoted to "sport science," and that work does often include psychology, but it is still rare to see a sport psychology consultant or mental skills coach have a prominent full-time place on a training staff. Likewise, when World Cup teams involve sport psychology it often receives media attention primarily as a sideshow. In 2016, for example, Mexico coach Juan Carlos Osorio brought on Imanol Ibarrondo as the team's "mental coach." According to the *New York Times*, Osorio had to defend the decision "amid fierce criticism from the unrelenting Mexican news media, as standard practice in modern sports. 'The United States is a top country in the world and all the athletes have mental help,' Osorio said. 'What is wrong with that?'"[11]

Perhaps the most prominent example of successful mental coaching in U.S. soccer, as with most of U.S. soccer's successes, comes from the women's national team. While the U.S. team won the first Women's World Cup in 1991 with a dominating performance that established the squad's physical and athletic talent, by the time of the second Women's World Cup in 1995 the United States seemed to need something more. After a draw with China in the group stage, the U.S. team lost to eventual champion Norway in the semi-finals. The Norwegians rubbed it in, crawling around the field joined hand to ankle in a "train" celebration to which the U.S. players took offense. Norwegian captain Linda Medalen later explained, "It's fun to beat the Americans because they get so upset, make so much noise, when they lose. . . . This is a problem. Never be weak."[12]

The U.S. team seemed to agree, and with the first Olympic women's soccer competition coming up on home soil during the 1996 Atlanta Olympics, they took a pitch for mental skills coaching from Dr. Colleen Hacker, a former college coach and professor of kinesiology at Pacific Lutheran University. In an Olympic Channel retrospective Hacker explains there was some hesitation among the players: "I think there was a little bit: who is she, and what's this about? And I said, if I can help make a 3–5 percent difference, just a 3–5 percent difference, would you be interested? Every hand in the room went up in the air. And so I didn't go in with illusions of I have some magic potion. It really was going to be about hard work and learning techniques and strategies that would help them deal with the weight of the Olympic Games being in the United States and being a gold medal favorite."[13]

What were those techniques and strategies? As Hacker said, there was no "magic potion." It was team building, coping skills for dealing with adversity, exercises for cultivating self-confidence, and other standard fare that wouldn't seem out of place at a self-help seminar or a life coaching session. But Hacker built relationships with the players, helping them rehearse according to their individual roles and needs and creating imagery videos and scripts for the players to continue practicing off the field.

This kind of individualization is another key principle to sport psychology work. Mia Hamm is widely considered the greatest U.S. attacking player of all time, but at points in her career she famously struggled with a lack of self-confidence that also served as a motivation to make sure she worked hard enough to avoid failure. Hope Solo is widely considered the greatest U.S. goalkeeper of all time, but at points in her career she famously struggled with an excess of self-confidence that made her both a bane to coaches and a dominant force in her penalty box.

There is, in other words, no one optimal psychological profile for elite performance. In one study involving 588 soccer players from Germany, France, and the Czech Republic, researchers compared higher-level and lower-level players, finding significant differences in physical traits such as reaction times, but few overall differences in psychological characteristics.[14] Reviews of research across other sports find some average differences, with elite athletes demonstrating higher levels of traits such as self-confidence and the ability to manage anxiety along with more use of mental skills techniques such as self-talk and imagery.[15] But in much of this research, it is hard to disentangle cause and effect. Elite athletes may, on average, be more confident because they have had more success. And they may use more mental skills because they've had more access to mental skills training.

Average differences between elite and non-elite players also obscure the self-evident fact that there is great psychological variability within any particular group of players. The distinct personalities and characters among players are part of what make fandom fun; some prefer Cristiano Ronaldo while others prefer Lionel Messi, some prefer Megan Rapinoe while others prefer Alex Morgan. Each of these different personalities bring different psychological needs and dynamics. What is typical is the range of psychological characteristics, rather than any one psychological type, across elite athletes.

For applying sport psychology to produce elite performance, the first step of mental skills coaching is an individualized assessment. What are a particular player's strengths and weaknesses? This assessment then segues to building an action plan or intervention focused on developing specific mental skills that can help an athlete minimize weaknesses and maximize strengths. The next step of mental skills coaching is to make the process recursive by assessing the success of the intervention and adjusting as necessary. In addition, many sport psychology consultants will offer pre- and post-competition sessions to develop specific strategies for major events like the many consultants hired around World Cup time.

What, then, are the mental skills that psychologists think help with elite performance? The menu tends to be consistent and relatively simple. One example comes from a potentially surprising source: the U.S. military. According to the American Psychological Association, the military was once the largest employer of people with applied sport psychology training through its Comprehensive Soldier Fitness—Performance and Resilience Enhancement Program.[16] In its diagram of mental skills foundations, the program identified five basic mental skills that are standard to the sport psychology tool kit: building confidence, attention control, energy management, goal setting, and imagery.[17] Each of these skills involves empirically supported techniques, such as self-talk scripts and relaxation strategies, that a skilled practitioner can make feel personal and transformative. But they are ultimately somewhat formulaic and the details are available in other writings and workbooks.[18]

Here it seems more useful to consider the psychological dynamics within soccer that make mental skills training necessary. Take, for example, anxiety. The emotions that led the Brazilian team to their flowing tears during the 2014 World Cup, and the emotions that drove the U.S. women's team to lose confidence before the 1995 World Cup, related to the pressure to perform from a perceived threat to one's physical or psychological self. Anxiety involves both our body and our mind, with bodily (or "somatic") responses including muscle tension and inefficiencies in physical movements along with mental (or "cognitive") responses including a difficulty in making decisions and a narrowed attentional focus.

Anxiety is not necessarily a bad thing. As sport psychology consultant Mark Nesti explains in a chapter from the book *Soccer Science*, high-level professional players often said "they like to feel anxious because it was a sign that they cared about the outcome and that they were ready to perform well. They explained that they had performed poorly in the past when they had no or little pre-event anxiety or when they had too much."[19] Or, as former U.S. women's captain Julie Foudy described when asked about the best piece of advice she ever received: "From Dr. Colleen Hacker, who worked with our national team for many years, when I asked her what to do about the pre-game nerves . . . she said, 'Butterflies are great; just teach them to fly in formation.'"[20]

The idea from sport psychology, then, is to find the right level of anxiety and arousal for optimal performance. The classic theory here is called "drive theory," positing that the greater an athlete's level of physical and psychological arousal the better their performance. I think of this as a sort of old-school American football coach theory: use yelling and threatening to get athletes banging heads and running through walls. And this may actually work for certain very basic physical tasks, like an American football lineman who mostly needs to hit an opponent hard. But most sports, including soccer, involve more nuance. This nuance can be expressed, in part, with what sport psychology theorists call "the inverted-U hypothesis," suggesting that the relationship between arousal and performance is curvilinear. Too little arousal leads to demotivation, too much leads to debilitating stress, but a moderate amount can be just right to ensure we perform. Other theorists have elaborated on and individualized this theory to suggest the ideal is to identify a "zone of optimal functioning" where particular levels of arousal and anxiety lead to optimal performance of a specific sport task while accounting for individual differences.

This all means that the task for a mental skills coach helping a player to manage anxiety is to find their zone of optimal functioning. There are specific survey tools in sport psychology to help with the identification process, and then there are specific strategies from the sport psychology tool kit that can get a player into that zone.[21] Examples here include imagery training, in which a player simulates situations that cause anxiety or arousal and mentally practices managing those situations successfully; using self-talk scripts to reduce perceived threats (often involving brief phrases that players themselves find either motivating or relaxing); and teaching relaxation techniques such as deep breathing that allow players to manage anxiety.

Though I can't be sure, I suspect techniques like imagery, self-talk, and relaxation are exactly the types of tools Dr. Colleen Hacker brought to the U.S. Women's National Team in 1995 after its painful World Cup defeat. While none of these approaches are magical, by most accounts they seem to have achieved the goal of offering a 3–4 percent boost to the team's already elite performance. In the 1996 Olympics, after about a year of mental skills coaching, the U.S. women played on home soil in Atlanta wanting to prove a point in the first women's Olympic soccer competition. The United States again played Norway in the semifinals and again fell behind 1–0. As Mia Hamm explained when reflecting on the difference between the team's experience at the 1995 World Cup and at the 1996 Olympics, "We had all the right pieces going into '95, but we didn't have that final piece when things started to kind-of crack."[22] This time, however, they were brimming with the resilience that can come from good mental skills coaching. As Hacker recalled: "I don't think there was an athlete that didn't think we were going to do anything other than win. People in the stands maybe weren't so sure. But I honestly believe there was a collective belief that we would find a way."[23] Indeed, in the seventy-sixth minute Michelle Akers confidently finished a penalty kick to send the game to extra time, where Shannon MacMillan scored a golden goal in the one-hundredth minute to ensure a U.S. place in the final. The Americans went on to win the gold medal.

Would better mental skills coaching have also helped the Brazilian men in the 2014 World Cup? We'll never know because sport psychology, like soccer itself, is an inexact science. But we do know that sport psychology offers useful insights into managing parts of the game, such as anxiety, that are also part of the human experience off the soccer field. Most of us will never step onto the field at a World Cup or an Olympic Games, but all of us sometimes have to manage anxiety in productive ways and perform under pressure. Luckily, soccer and sport psychology offer an example of distilled performance under pressure that has lessons for us all.

Psychologizing the Penalty Kick

One of my all-time favorite soccer books is an entire volume about one of the briefest and rarest moments in the game: *Twelve Yards: The Art and Psychology of the Perfect Penalty Kick* by English journalist Ben Lyttleton.[24] The book itself is a rollicking journey through history, science, personalities, culture, highlights, data analytics, tactics, interviews, aesthetics, and intuition. It demonstrates the extent to which minute parts of the game can comprise vast parts of human experience. According to Lyttleton, however, the book was motivated in part by something less grand: the fact that historically the English national team has been famously, heartbreakingly bad at penalty kicks. The first chapter of the book, in fact, is titled "The English Disease" and Lyttleton cites statistics showing that of all the men's national teams participating in a minimum of five penalty shootouts at major soccer championships, England had indeed been the worst—at the time of his writing, it had won only 14 percent of its shootouts, compared to 83 percent for Germany.

As Lyttleton wrote: "I'm fed up with England losing on penalties now. I'd rather England lost in normal time, or extra time. I wanted to find out why England kept losing, and to see how they could improve their chances of success."[25] To the delight of many English fans, Lyttleton did not have to wait long after writing his book to see things change: in the 2018 World Cup the English suddenly and surprisingly became world-beaters at penalties, advancing to the semifinals after their first-ever World Cup penalty shootout win over Colombia in the round of 16. The game itself had ended regulation 1–1 because of a Harry Kane penalty kick, and Kane was the tournament's leading scorer based in large part on two other penalty goals.

Though Lyttleton himself attributed much of England's 2018 penalty success to the intentional practice and strategic approaches of coach Gareth Southgate, the English media also gave credit to a sport psychology consultant hired by the English FA named Pippa Grange.[26] Grange called herself a "culture performance coach" and considered much of her task to be helping the English players support each other while managing the pressure and anxiety that comes with representing England's soccer obsession on the world stage. As another sport performance consultant, Andy Barton, explained to *The Guardian*, the English players used to "talk about the dread of taking a penalty, as if it's the worst thing you could possibly do. We create this narrative in our heads and live it."[27] But the presence of Grange, along with the efforts of the coach and the youthful innocence of the players, seemed to shift that dread. As Barton saw it during the 2018 World Cup, "They're playing with freedom; there's no fear of failure. Fear is essentially made up because it is a projection into the future, where you have created a narrative of something badly going wrong. We all do it, and we get very good at creating the negative [future] rather than the positive one."

Fear and anxiety clearly influence penalty kicks through multiple routes. Lyttleton, for example, cites research by Norwegian sport psychologist Geir Jordet (the world authority on the psychology of penalty kicks) suggesting that high-profile players suffer from status anxiety when taking penalties.[28] Jordet finds that players struggle with penalties after winning major individual honors, such as South America's Footballer of the Year or the European associations' Team of the Year. Previous winners, over-anxious to protect their status, only converted 59 percent of their penalties. In contrast, the conversion rate was 74 percent for players who have never won awards, and 89 percent for players who would go on to win awards but had not yet at the time of the recorded penalty shootouts. As expectations rise, penalty performance seems to fall.

The decrease in performance with an increase in pressure and expectations has a name shared by both popular culture and psychological research: choking. Sports of all types provide a rich natural laboratory for studying choking because they often distill moments of intense pressure into one brief physical act—such as a golf putt, a basketball free throw, or a soccer penalty kick. In their review of choking research and interventions, Peter Gröpel and Christopher Mesagno emphasize that choking happens only when both skills and motivations are high.[29] Novice players who miss a penalty kick because of a lack of skill do not "choke." But Roberto Baggio, who famously botched his decisive penalty in the 1994 World Cup final while he was reigning World Player of the Year, did.

The major theories of choking suggest that it is fundamentally and paradoxically a problem of too much skill and motivation. Anxiety, when not appropriately channeled, can cause us to overthink and under-trust our training. In their research review Gröpel and Mesagno suggest two major theories of choking, both of which revolve around misplaced attention: one is distraction, where pressure causes us to think too much about "task-irrelevant cues" (such as the hecklers in the crowd or the worries in our head), and the other is an excessive self-focus, where players hijack their own well-trained motor movements by thinking too much about how to execute the task at hand (such where to place your feet when kicking a ball twelve yards).

While both distraction and excessive self-focus can help explain why we sometimes fail to perform under pressure, the general idea here is that we often just care too much.[30] Players think about how badly they want to score their penalty rather than just shooting the penalty. Players who have trained their bodies exceptionally well to execute physical skills override that training with the bad kind of self-talk, the kind that makes us overthink what we know how to do. Psychologists call this phenomenon the "automatic execution model," where well-learned or "automatic" skills can be overridden by too much attention.[31] The theorist behind this model, social psychologist Roy Baumeister, has found that even well-intentioned praise ("you've got this penalty, no problem, we believe in you . . .") can cause us to think too much and trust our physical training too little.[32]

Psychologist Sian Beilock identifies a similar phenomenon in what she calls "explicit monitoring," which is consciously directing our cognitive attention to physical skill performance. In one well-known study, Beilock and colleagues asked both novice and experienced soccer players to do a classic dribbling drill by slaloming through cones as quickly as possible.[33] For one group of participants, the players were instructed to attend carefully to the part of the foot they were using to dribble the ball, putting conscious attention (or "explicit monitoring") onto their soccer performance. For another group, the players were instructed to listen to a recorded series of words and note when they heard a target word (which happened to be "thorn"), removing conscious attention from their soccer performance and putting it on an irrelevant task. The expert players, when dribbling with their dominant foot, performed significantly better when attending to irrelevant words. The task stopped them from explicit monitoring. The novice players performed significantly better when attending to their soccer performance. Their lack of trained skills meant explicit monitoring was actually helpful. Once a skill is well learned, in other words, we benefit from letting go of conscious control and trusting our bodies to do their thing.

So, if one of the main problems for elite soccer players is trying too hard and paying too much attention, what tools might sport psychology offer as a counter? The recent popularity of mindfulness as a method for general psychological well-being has started being applied in sport contexts and does seem to hold some promise.[34] Though, like all sport psychology techniques, mindfulness is no magic potion. Instead, we can return to our specific example of penalty kicks to extract from the most minute moment of soccer performance towards broader principles of elite performance.

Though Geir Jordet and other researchers have identified a wide range of interventions and strategies that make for (more) successful penalty kicks, in my reading of the literature there are three small tips that stand out as the most significant psychologically. As summarized by Lyttleton, the top players all easily have the physical skill to beat a goalkeeper one-on-one from twelve yards away, so "For these guys, it comes down to pure psychology. The fascination of the shootout is that it puts psychology in pole position."[35]

The first tip is to simply take a bit of time to manage anxiety and physiological arousal. Jordet and colleagues have found dramatic differences in penalty success related to the length of time shooters take after the referee blows the whistle to allow a penalty to be taken and the time it takes players to actually strike the ball.[36] In analyzing video of penalty shootouts from the World Cup, European Championships, and UEFA Champions League, they found that players who took less than a second to strike the ball scored about 58 percent of the time while players who took longer scored about 80 percent of the time. They explain this as a case of "self-regulatory breakdown" where "performers, under high levels of threat and emotional distress, sometimes primarily focus on obtaining relief and escape from the unpleasant states."[37] The researchers even cite the playing autobiography of 2018 England manager Gareth Southgate in their explanation. When discussing his own experience of a penalty shootout, Southgate explained, "All I wanted was the ball: put it on the spot, get it over and done with." He famously missed a penalty in the 1996 European Championship that *The Telegraph* ranked as the second most agonizing miss in England history.[38] He should have slowed down for a second.

As Jordet explained to Lyttleton, the idea really is just to take only a second to ensure the player is not acting out of anxiety: "Waiting for five to ten seconds can bring on a series of new psychological challenges that the player needs to cope with, such as thinking too much about the mechanics of the performance. My advice would be to make sure that players don't rush by simply asking them to take an extra breath, lasting for half a second or a second, and not necessarily more."[39] So, for all the complicated psychology involved in choking, one of the basic lessons is as simple as what I try to tell my eight-year-old son once or twice each week: "Before you do that, take a nice deep breath."

The second tip involves a slightly different type of self-regulation: facing the challenge with a sense of self-efficacy. Jordet finds the one of the most typical avoidance strategies for players unable to cope with pressure is to turn their back to the goalkeeper after placing the ball on the penalty spot. As he explained to Lyttleton, "You can't turn your back forever, at some point you have to turn around and face the stress full on."[40] The idea here is that facing the penalty with a sense of confidence is one small marker of a broader mindset that is a core tenant of sport psychology: performance generally benefits from trusting in one's training and one's abilities. This is not quite as simple as the power of positive thinking—excess confidence that is not founded in reality is a recipe for failure. In fact, psychology as a field has generally disavowed the excesses of the "self-esteem movement" in placing feeling good about oneself before tangible achievement. Very high levels of self-esteem are as likely to predict a dangerous narcissism as they are to predict excellent performance. But in the context of a penalty kick, or any other skill domain where the basic task is well within one's competencies, embodying a trust in one's self by standing tall behind the ball seems to enable performance.

The third tip relates to the alternative many psychologists propose to unqualified self-esteem: self-compassion and an ability to tolerate failure. In an "expert statement on the psychological preparation for football penalty shootouts" produced for the British Association of Sport and Exercise Sciences by Mark Wilson, Greg Wood, and Geir Jordet, they suggest teams and players should intentionally practice "what if?" plans "for each individual to deal with his/her missed kick and for the group to support those players who do miss."[41] The idea here comes back to something we regularly hear from good coaches: we all fail sometimes, so the question is how do we cope with that failure. People tend to cope best through self-compassion, or the ability to maintain a healthy core sense of self in the face of failure and adversity by owning our imperfections and accepting that many things are out of our control.

It is also important to note here that in a penalty shootout, the group has a significant responsibility to support individual players. Coping is not only an individual skill. Jordet and colleagues suggest that coaches are well advised to emphasize to players that they recognize "mistakes under pressure *will* occur and rather than focusing solely on reducing individual errors, the coach should focus on having individual and team coping strategies in place in the event of personal and team failure. Being proactive in recognizing, accounting for, and supporting mistakes has the potential to reduce ego-threat and the possibility of 'choking' under pressure."[42] When players miss, in other words, their teammates should make a show of accepting them back into the team to reinforce collective support for each individual. Conversely, other research suggests that celebrating robustly as a team after a successful penalty can induce an "emotional contagion" that can enhance one's own team's performance and be detrimental to opponents.[43] We do better when our whole team relishes our success while that team also accepts the reality that we will sometimes fail.

Overall, while sport psychology tends to emphasize the mental skills that individuals can hone to enhance performance, this last idea that our psychology is also deeply embedded in our teams as a social context reinforces the importance of considering performance through multiple lenses. As the example of penalty kicks illustrates, individual psychology clearly matters. When we feel as though our status is on the line, when we perceive the weight of others' expectations, when we pay too much attention to environmental distractions, and when we overthink well-learned tasks, our psychology can override our physical skills. Training ourselves to manage anxiety with something as simple as a deep breath, or giving ourselves the boost in confidence that comes from facing our fears, are just a few of the many mental skills that can boost performance. But these experiences of performance anxiety fundamentally come from social pressures and are best managed through social support. Players often try too hard, and care too much, because soccer has become psychologically linked to who they are as a person.

Soccer and the Self

Landon Donovan, arguably the best men's player ever produced by the United States, seemed to live a charmed soccer life. A star at an early age, Donovan was one of the first players to be given a chance to join U.S. Soccer's full-time residency program for under-seventeen players in Bradenton, Florida. He then led the U.S. team at the 1999 U-17 World Cup and won the Golden Ball as the best player at the tournament—essentially designating him as the best seventeen-year-old in the world. In the same year he joined German Bundesliga club Bayer Leverkusen, becoming one of the first major American players to skip college and go straight to a major European professional club. By the end of his career, Donovan had played in three World Cups, scored one of the most famous goals in U.S. World Cup history (the goal against Algeria in 2010 that provoked the primal fan reaction described in chapter 2), and became such an icon of Major League Soccer in the United States that the league's most valuable player award is now named in his honor. That short gloss of Donovan's career, however, does not do justice to the much more complicated human dimensions of Donovan's story—nor to the complicated psychology of investing one's entire self into a game.

Donovan's stint at Bayer Leverkusen was largely a failure; he quickly became homesick and spent most of his six-year contract "on loan" with the San Jose Earthquakes near his family in California. In his mid-twenties he had a brief failed marriage to an actress, and in 2013 he took a break from professional soccer to backpack through Southeast Asia, citing mental exhaustion and the need for a sabbatical.[44] Though he initially retired at the end of the 2014 MLS season he seemed irresolute, coming out of retirement in 2016 to rejoin the LA Galaxy, coming out of retirement again in 2018 to play with Club León in the top Mexican league, and one more time in 2019 to play with the San Diego Sockers in the Major Arena Soccer League. In 2013, after his sabbatical, Donovan took the rare step for a professional athlete of admitting to struggles with depression, and opened a small window onto the reality of a less-than-charmed soccer life—a life where being a great soccer player existed in tension with being a thoughtful, sensitive, and unsettled person.

I've never had the chance to meet Donovan, and I use his experience as an example here primarily because he is one of the few elite soccer players to be open about his mental health challenges. We don't know Donovan's whole story, and his experiences with depression may well have nothing to do with soccer. But we do know that the pathway to becoming an elite soccer player that Donovan trod, and the pathway of many young athletes, is not one psychologists recommend for a healthy self-concept. One of the foundational theories of lifespan development, Erik Erikson's psychosocial stage theory, suggests that the core task in our social development is to develop a balanced sense of ego identity. And that this task is never more salient than during adolescent identity exploration. The challenge for many elite soccer players is that they rarely have the opportunity to explore dimensions of identity— or other domains of selfhood—beyond athletic domains. With pressure in the youth sports system to specialize at earlier and earlier ages, good soccer players find themselves "choosing" to commit their young lives to soccer at ten or twelve years old, a process sport sociologist Jay Coakley calls "identity constriction."[45] Who would trust themselves at twelve years old to make commitments that may canalize the rest of their lives?

Developmental psychologists call the early commitment without exploration trajectory "identity foreclosure" and worry about its effects on healthy development through the lifespan. In one summary exploring identity foreclosure in sport, Brewer and Petipas note research finding that individuals with a highly invested athletic identity more often have difficulty thinking in mature ways about careers beyond sport, are more likely to consume alcohol and performance-enhancing drugs, and have trouble adjusting to injuries or the end of one's career.[46] There is also some evidence that identity foreclosure in sport is a risk factor in burnout, with highly invested athletes eventually feeling overdependent on the fickle nature of sport success.

The risks of heavy investment in sports at an early age, and the risks of early success, are evident in many stories of young soccer prodigies, including Landon Donovan. The fact that Donovan was celebrated by much of the soccer world for his early precocity set him up for a fall in his first foray into European soccer, where his lack of immediate adolescent success in Germany seems to have left long-term scars. Freddy Adu, discussed in chapter 4 as an example of the challenges of talent development, is a more extreme example, having debuted for DC United at the age of fourteen only to fade nearly entirely from high-level soccer by age twenty-four. The latest example in U.S. soccer comes from the women's side, with thirteen-year-old Olivia Moultrie being celebrated for signing a "six-figure deal" with Nike in 2019 and leaving school to train with the Portland Thorns.[47]

There seems to be a cultural fascination in soccer with an idea of "the earlier the better" for elite players, a fascination that is embedded in soccer's talent development system. This all has psychological costs. Being named the best player in the world at age seventeen or being the youngest player to earn a professional contract comes with a type of identity constriction that is imposed by social pressures and by the structures of youth soccer. From this perspective, the psychological experience of soccer players becomes as much about sociology as it is about psychology, performance, and mental health.

A sociological perspective offers a critical counterpoint to performance-oriented sport psychology. It can be tempting to think of phenomena such as burnout exclusively in psychological terms. From a psychological perspective, burnout is based on failures in stress management and limited coping skills, and so the solution lies in mental skills training for anxiety of the type described elsewhere in this chapter. But this form of sport psychology ignores the broader social forces that shape athlete experiences regarding burnout.

Sport sociologists such as Jay Coakley have offered a dramatic warning to sport psychologists, calling the prescription of individual mental skills to cope with broader social problems tantamount to "psychodoping." As Coakley defined it, "Psychodoping consists of using psychological techniques to help athletes adjust to conditions of dependency and powerlessness, and to discourage them from asking critical questions about why they participate in sport and how sport participation is tied to the rest of their lives."[48] In this way of thinking mental skills training may, as with drug doping, improve sport performance only by putting broader personal health at risk.

The alternative to a sport psychology focused only on performance at the expense of health is to attend more carefully to soccer players as multidimensional people embedded in multilayered social systems. Thus, rather than just teaching players to address experiences such as burnout by learning techniques to manage stress, Coakley suggests an "empowerment model." The idea is to provide athletes the autonomy to engage in identity exploration outside of sport, to empower them to ask critical questions about how their experiences are socially organized, and to not expect them to adhere to the rigid expectations of elite soccer, where players must sacrifice themselves and their entire sense of self to the game.[49]

My read of Landon Donovan's time away from soccer, and his speaking out to destigmatize discussions of mental health, is as a claim for some of this type of self-empowerment. Donovan's key refrain in explaining his path to the media was "I have to live the life I want to live."[50] Because the pressures and structures of high-level soccer only provide limited opportunities for such autonomy, it is a credit to athletes like Donovan that they have the psychological strength to make that claim. Psychological skills in soccer are, in other words, not just about arousal management, self-confidence, imagery, and the like. Psychological skills are about the ability to assert one's self as a person defined by more than performance on the soccer field.

The Performance and the Person

In many ways it is a testament to the psychological attributes of elite soccer players that we don't see more emotional breakdowns of the type experienced by Brazil's men in 2014. Imagine having to perform your job live in front of tens of thousands of spectators—many of whom feel emotionally dependent on your success, while others actively want you to fail. Imagine knowing that millions more people are watching you on television, many of whom are compatriots watching with some sense that your performance is a marker of your communal value. Imagine that any emotions you display will be analyzed and replayed for what they might say about your community, about your psyche, and, as has been the goal of this chapter, to explain something about human psychology more broadly.

Imagining the psychological experiences of elite players raises two major questions that underlie this analysis. First, what exactly is it that allows the vast majority of players to still perform, and allows an elite few to perform exceptionally well? The truth is that while psychology offers many rich insights into sports performance, it does not offer any single "magic potion." There does not seem to be one psychological profile for elite performance, though there are mental skills such as arousal management, imagery, self-talk, and goal setting that can genuinely help. There also does not seem to be one recipe for sport psychology practice, though when appropriately targeted—carefully considering differences between mental health issues, performance issues, and social concerns—psychological consultation can make a significant positive impact on performance. Players perform best when they are empowered to execute the physical skills of the game in ways that integrate body, mind, and self.

Second, what does the psychology of elite sport performance illuminate about broader psychological issues such as coping with anxiety and developing a healthy self-concept? In regard to coping with anxiety, penalty shoot-outs offer a distilled example of needing to perform under pressure, and there is good evidence that learning to manage that pressure through basic relaxation techniques, self-compassion, and social connectedness can help both penalty takers and anyone else who might be impacted by anxiety. In regard to developing a healthy self-concept, watching elite soccer players cope with burnout and identity constriction helps remind us that a deep immersion in a unidimensional self-concept from a young age may have short-term benefits to player development while causing long-term problems in personal development. Soccer thus reminds us that while psychology can help explain performance, our performance should not define our psychology.

In this light, all the tears shed around the Brazilian men's national team in the 2014 World Cup, and all the intense emotions prompted by soccer the world over, become illustrative of the delicate relationship between performance and people.[51] Soccer is just a game but it contains deeply human emotions, from the stirrings of a national anthem, to the intense anxiety of a penalty shootout, to the cries of sadness after a painful loss and the tears of joy after an important win. Performance, more than just physical actions, is both an antecedent and consequence of our emotional engagement.

With that in mind, it is worth noting that not all Brazilians thought the tears of their players in 2014 were inappropriate. The legendary Brazilian columnist Juca Kfouri reportedly said that the tears in 2014, and particularly those around the quarterfinal victory against Chile, were indicative of something well beyond psychological weakness: "So what if Thiago Silva and Neymar cried during the national anthem? So what if Júlio César wept after flying like a bird and saving two penalties? My God, who does not cry after witnessing such a miracle?"[52] The intense emotions embedded in soccer performance, in other words, are not always a problem to be solved. Sometimes they are a vital part of the experience.

Argentine legend Diego Maradona soaked in the adulation of fans at a 2018 FIFA World Cup game in Russia despite a histrionic display in his VIP box. Xinhua/ Alamy Stock Photo.

CHAPTER 6

Impacts

Players, Games, and the Greater Good

JOURNALIST AND WRITER SIMON KUPER had a job that seems designed to make soccer fans jealous: getting paid to watch the most important global soccer games and writing stories about the biggest world stars. Imagine being paid to spend time with Megan Rapinoe, David Beckham, Marta, and Diego Maradona, paid to learn what they are really like off the field and away from the television cameras. Imagine gaining insight into people who are global icons, along with practicing amateur psychology with players who sell products with their mere image and command huge crowds for a slight chance at their autograph. Imagine having all that and ending up mostly with a question that perhaps more soccer fans should ask: Is soccer really any good for people?

The introduction to Kuper's 2011 book *Soccer Men*, a series of profiles of soccer's elite men's players from Andrés Iniesta to Zinedine Zidane, is essentially a disquisition on the disappointments of actually talking to the best players in the world.[1] Even beyond the fact that athletes are often socialized to use vapid sports clichés and avoid critical thinking, Kuper suggests most elite players just don't offer much: "I have never thought that most soccer players have anything special to say. I know a colleague who believes that only by speaking to a real live player can you access truths about the game. This man is forever texting players, and saying things like, 'If you speak to Franz Beckenbauer, he'll tell you that . . .' I reject that idea. I do believe that you can access truths about the game by speaking to Arsène Wenger, if he feels like telling you, which he probably doesn't. I don't believe you can access them by speaking to Wayne Rooney."[2]

Why not? Given the exceptional talents of elite soccer players, why might they not offer exceptional insights into their experiences? Kuper speculates it may have to do with something like the identity foreclosure discussed in relation to performance psychology, in which "Few of the game's superstars have broad life experience outside soccer. From their early teens, when they typically start the move into top-class soccer, they are actively discouraged from developing interests outside the game. One friend of mine, who had a mostly successful playing career, says it's not that players are stupid. Rather, they're blinkered."[3]

But Kuper also recognizes the compulsion to believe otherwise. He notes that many soccer journalists talk to each other about the stars they have interviewed: "We ask, 'What was he like?' in part because we are looking for the secret of the man's success. We want to believe that great players become great in part because of the men [sic] they are. They cannot just be good at kicking a ball. We assume their characters must also be conducive to great achievement. Surely, there are personality traits that unite the firecracker Maradona with the brooding Zidane and the homeboy Messi. In other words: Are superstars exceptional people?"[4]

This last question is one where my own experiences with soccer and the tools of social science intersect. In its broadest sense, it is the classic question of whether sports build character. Have all the years I've spent playing soccer made me a better person? The answer from research is one that wouldn't surprise Kuper: a qualified no. In one massive study of moral character and moral reasoning with a database of around ninety thousand people, researchers from the University of Idaho found an inverse relationship between moral reasoning and immersion in competitive sports. Athletes generally score lower on moral reasoning than non-athletes, and the longer one is involved in sports the worse their moral reasoning scores.[5] The qualification is that sports *can* build character in the right context, but that context is usually not found in elite soccer competitions.[6] Examples of elite athletes willingly violating basic rules when navigating between competitive advantage and moral purity are not hard to come by. Think here of U.S. goalkeeper Briana Scurry in the 1999 Women's World Cup leaving the goal line far too early to save the penalty kick that won the Americans the tournament,[7] or of Uruguay striker Luis Suarez in the 2010 World Cup using his hand to save a sure Ghana goal that would have been the difference in the quarterfinal.[8] As Uruguay coach Oscar Tabarez argued in defending another of Suarez's transgressions, "This is a World Cup. This is not about cheap morality."[9]

But the question of what soccer does to players begets a larger question of what the game itself does to people and communities. Even beyond time playing the game, I want to believe that my love for soccer translates into some kind of greater good. Promoters of the World Cup, marketing consultants for professional teams, and others falling under the rubric of what sport sociologists call "sport evangelists" certainly believe it does. World Cup bids are sold with astonishing claims of economic and social benefits to host countries, public subsidies for soccer stadiums profiting wealthy team owners are justified with obscure formulas predicting community value, charitable projects promote the power of soccer to solve complex social problems, and youth programs proclaim miraculous powers of sport for personal transformation. With just a bit of critical thinking, to say nothing of accumulating evidence from social science research, most of us know not to accept such claims at only face value. Yet the claims of soccer's positive social impact persist with remarkable consistency, challenging us to think carefully about how soccer does and does not actually do good in the world.

This chapter, along with the next chapter on soccer as a tool for international development initiatives, takes as a premise one of the key themes underlying this book more generally. I believe soccer *can* have a positive social impact and contribute to the greater good, but whether it does or not depends on the context in which it takes place. Soccer, as an empty cultural form given meaning socially, is just as likely to have a negative impact on people and communities—particularly when claims for its essential goodness are accepted uncritically.[10] The purpose of these next two chapters is to use social science, along with examples and case studies, to critically engage claims around the social impact of soccer. Here we will pay particular attention to the impact of the high-profile side of soccer, focusing on star players and global mega-events; in the next chapter, we will focus on lower-profile grassroots initiatives that use soccer as a tool for community-level development.

The more I've used social science lenses to understand these ways that soccer might have social impact, the more I've shared Kuper's sense of disappointment in the game. But I've also come to recognize that the evangelical fervor prompted by a global love of the game is too robust to be put off by a little critical inquiry. In fact, some such inquiry might just be the best way to justify a love of soccer and to understand how the game can indeed do some social good.

The Halo Effect

If we agree with journalists like Simon Kuper, as well as social scientists researching sport and character, that players, on average, are not special beyond their abilities on the field, why do we so often expect otherwise? The best answer I know of from psychology is the "halo effect"—a widespread phenomenon where people tend to expect that people with one noteworthy positive trait will also have other unrelated positive traits. It is as if exceptional soccer players, or great actors or rich business moguls or people blessed with stunning good looks, have a halo over their heads that glows across all their endeavors. But as social scientists—and many thinking fans—know, they don't.

The halo effect is a persistent cognitive bias that makes some sense psychologically because the human mind loves a shortcut. When solving problems or making decisions, there is too much raw information in the world for us to make perfectly rational calculations. So, we instinctively use past experience and probabilities in ways that are remarkably patterned. This is part of the explanation for stereotypes. When the mind tries to evaluate everyone on their own individual merits it brings on information overload, so we default to lazy shortcuts telling us that Manchester United fans are corporate sellouts or Latinx players are hot-tempered. Our minds can easily recall anecdotal examples for such stereotypes and we over rely on those examples to make problematic generalizations.

Within the broad tendency of the mind to use shortcuts, there are many specific cognitive biases identified and named by scholars working in a tradition founded by Nobel laureate psychologists Daniel Kahnemen and Amos Tversky.[11] We are, for example, more likely to fear things that are regularly sensationalized in the media (the "availability heuristic"), we are more likely to believe evidence that supports pre-existing beliefs ("confirmation bias"), and we are more likely to assume people who are really good at soccer are also really good at other domains of life (the "halo effect").

The halo effect has significant implications for branding, since the glow of the halo can extend from an individual to a product or club. As such, it is not surprising that much research on the halo effect comes from business scholars. In one soccer-specific example, German business professor Gerd Nufer surveyed groups of soccer fans and non-fans to ask their impressions of clubs VfB Stuttgart and FC Bayern Munich.[12] While fans obviously had better general impressions of the clubs compared with non-fans, Nufer sees the halo effect in his finding that fans also rated the teams' coaches and management more competent, and had more positive impressions of the teams' stadiums and jerseys. He connects these effects to the social identity formed by soccer fandom (as discussed in chapter 2), and suggests that it helps explain why fans often excuse the bad behavior of their heroes. As an example, Nufer cites 2014 German World Cup winner Kevin Großkreutz, who had his contract terminated by VfB Stuttgart after a series of embarrassing incidents (including a trip to the hospital after a street fight during a night on the town drinking with underage junior players). The team's fans, presumably under the glow of Großkreutz's halo, nevertheless filed an online petition with over thirty thousand signatures to bring the player back to the club.

The idea that there is a halo effect around not just individual players but also our favorite teams raises the possibility that there is also a halo effect around a sport itself. The argument here is that for anyone who loves (or maybe even just likes) soccer, we are biased to assume that the game is more than just fun, entertaining, and engaging. We are biased to assume that it also has a positive social impact. Like any cognitive bias, there may be some plausible reasons for this assumption. Players, teams, and soccer itself have indeed done some good in the world. But if we are careful to make a rational analysis using our social science lenses, we have to recognize players, teams, and soccer itself are not always good. Players abuse their prestige and status; teams exploit workers and communities to position themselves for maximum profit; the game itself is just as likely to foment hatred as it is to bring people together.

These contradictions make soccer fertile ground for another of the human mind's most fundamental interests: storytelling. Scholars such as Jonathan Gottschall have argued that we have evolved to understand the world through stories—many of which are mythological with little basis in fact or reason.[13] Soccer is a rich site for such mythology.

Take, for example, Diego Maradona. Along with his inclusion in never-ending debates about the greatest player of all time, Maradona was still a fixture of soccer story-telling three decades past his prime playing days. In just the few years prior to his untimely death in 2020, he was the object of an HBO documentary by an Academy Award–winning filmmaker and a Netflix series on his foray into coaching in Mexico. Both are well worth watching, but they merely add to a long list of media and scholarship obsessed with what Argentine scholar Edwardo Archetti called the "Cult of Maradona."[14]

The magic Maradona conjured on the playing field lit a bright halo, yet most soccer fans knew him to be a deeply flawed man. Before his death he acknowledged that serious drug problems derailed his playing career. His death at the relatively early age of sixty followed years of struggles with significant health issues including obesity, his family life was a chronicle of instability, and his emotional volatility was on regular public display. One of the iconic images of the 2018 World Cup in Russia was from Argentina's final group stage game against Nigeria, during which Maradona's performance in his VIP box seats was covered nearly as closely as the game itself. Drunk, Maradona alternated between wild gesticulations in response to the game (including a double middle finger gesture to the crowd after Argentina scored its second goal in a dramatic 2-1 win) and alcohol-induced somnambulance. He ultimately required assistance to leave his seat, and medical attention before leaving the stadium to fly on a private jet from St. Petersburg to Moscow.

Yet, in the midst of that 2018 World Cup display, Getty Images captured a moment where Maradona leaned over the railing of his VIP box, eyes rolling back in his head, arms stretched wide in a crucifixion pose, with an adoring pack of fans simultaneously snapping close-up pictures and readying to catch their fallen/falling hero. The picture, in evoking simultaneous pity and worship, is indeed an iconic image of the idolatry that characterizes soccer storytelling.

Archetti argues that the way to understand the Cult of Maradona is to recognize how Maradona represents an archetype within Argentine society, the *pibe*. The word is most directly translated as slang for a youngish boy, but Archetti suggests it also invokes a complicated cultural idealization of playful mischievousness in certain children. It represents a combination of innocence and guile that can be both frustrating and admirable. As Archetti explains it:

> The meaning of *pibe* is related to a cluster of features that promote and limit the social construction of the stereotype. One such feature is the small body.... The image of typical *pibe* player is based on an exuberance of skill, cunning, individual creativity, artistic feeling and improvisation.... A third related feature is the kind of daily life *pibes* carry on. In the case of a *pibe*, a lot of disorder is expected. Chaotic behavior is the norm. There is a tendency to disregard boundaries, to play games even in private life (life is

experienced as a permanent game or gamble if necessary); additionally, there is a capacity to recompense, penalize or forgive others in an exaggerated way; to convey arbitrary judgments and choices; to display stupid and irrational heroism, and a capacity to "die" (by being imprisoned, a drug-addict or an alcoholic) and to be resurrected; and a special talent in critical games to make the unexpected move, ensuring victory for the team.[15]

Maradona certainly fit the definition, with his "hand of God" goal against England in the 1986 World Cup, an emblem of such "stupid and irrational heroism" that simultaneously solidified his legacy as a player (and also neatly complimented his second goal in the same game—the result of a transcendent run through nearly every English player for the "goal for the century"). But the point here is that few of even the most ardent Maradona fans would hold him up as an icon of soccer's positive social impact. Instead, he offers a particular cultural story that has had an impact on Argentine identity and on global soccer but one that is not based on his inherent goodness. Instead, according to Archetti, his impact is something more emotional. Maradona's "possession of the human gift of producing and giving joy lies behind his incomparable cult. Being the cause of individual feelings of joy and enabling a collective expression is Maradona's precious secret, a very simple one indeed."[16]

These "feelings of joy" evoked by soccer, when combined with the halo effect and our innate attraction to storytelling, may help explain why we are so apt to uncritically accept claims for the positive social impact of the game. We take cognitive shortcuts that allow us to transfer good feelings and positive impressions onto players and into individual games, tournaments, and team affiliations. But we also can see that research on such shortcuts is useful. It encourages us to be careful about an overreliance on emotional reasoning. In many cases, and here in the case of soccer, it is worth instead engaging in more rational and systematic analysis of what the social impact of players and games actually can, or should, look like.

The Mythology of Role Models

There is a periodic debate in the sports media about whether elite athletes should be role models. This was famously sparked in the United States several decades ago by basketball star Charles Barkley's claim that "I am not a role model. I'm not paid to be a role model. I'm paid to wreak havoc on the basketball court. Parents should be role models. Just because I dunk a basketball doesn't mean I should raise your kids."[17] This claim, and similar variants, updated for application to complicated soccer icons ranging from Cristiano Ronaldo to Hope Solo, fostered much debate and raises key questions about the social impact of elite athletes. What should we actually expect from soccer players, and do children actually model their lives on their sports heroes?

Role model debates in the sports world tend to rely heavily on moral instincts and less on systematic analysis or evidence. This is a problem I became acutely aware of some years back when working with one of my University of Portland students on a thesis project. At that time the student, Stephanie Cox (née Lopez), had a vested stake in the debate. She was on the verge of playing with the U.S. Women's National Team at the Women's World Cup in China, was at the end of a college soccer career that would earn her the Senior CLASS Award "presented each year to the outstanding senior NCAA Division I Student-Athlete of the Year in women's soccer," and was even identified in an article on ESPN.com as "soccer's unassuming role model."

Bright, earnest, and intellectually curious, Cox wanted to try to explore whether and how high-level athletes matter as role models. We both realized she had access to a pretty good sample through her participation with the U.S. Women's National Team and with her top-ranked college team. So, we looked at the somewhat limited existing scholarly literature on role models, surveyed her teammates with some standard personality inventories and open-ended questions about being a role model, and tried to use the tools of social science to systematically consider the notion of soccer players as role models. Cox did an excellent job with the project, but only had a semester before moving on to start her professional career. I later went back to the original survey data and put together a peer-reviewed research article— which is to say that Cox should get the credit for gathering the data and I should get the blame for the interpretations offered here.[18]

The first thing that we saw in both the media and academic discourse is that "role model" expectations are particularly high for women and players from marginalized groups. In the United States, this has been most notable in the way women's professional leagues have presented themselves. After the dramatic success of the 1999 Women's World Cup, for example, the original WUSA professional league was premised significantly on the idea of the players as role models: "With this league," claimed U.S. team captain Carla Overbeck, "there will be 200 role models who are very willing to make a positive impact on some child's life." When the league failed, USWNT star Julie

Foudy said, "I miss [WUSA] because young girls and boys in local communities where we were playing go to see strong, confident women as good role models on a weekly basis." After two failed professional women's leagues relied heavily on the idea of players as role models, the third iteration (the NWSL) has survived in part by shifting from a role model discourse to another idea, one that emphasizes the simple fact that it is fun and engaging to watch international-class soccer.

Still, it is worth asking why the emphasis on being role models tends to be so much more prominent in the women's game than the men's. Sociologists think it has to do with broader social inequalities, pointing out that the disproportionate popular emphasis on the responsibility of women and racial minorities to act as role models implicitly highlights individual behavior and obscures social forces as influences on success.[19] Framing Mia Hamm or Marta as a role model conveys a misleading message of bountiful opportunity, implying that success is possible for anyone with individual hard work, and that structural inequalities in opportunities, along with institutional discrimination, can be safely ignored.

And then there is the question of why we expect athletes to be good at anything besides their sport anyway. A significant part of this can be attributed the aforementioned halo effect, but it may also have to do with broader social changes and increasing attention to celebrity culture. The early concept of a role model posited by social theorist Robert Merton was focused on the concept as limited to very specific *roles*.[20] A teacher would be a role model for teaching, a business manager would be role model for management, and a soccer player would be a role model for playing the game. But over time, our society has broadened and diffused this concept to suggest that a role model should be an exemplar for a more comprehensive set of traits that make for a good life. It is no longer good enough for Kylian Mbappé or Alex Morgan to be really good goal-scorers. They now also have to be humanitarians, fashionistas, social analysts, businesspeople, moral exemplars, master communicators, and many other things that have little to do with putting the ball in the back of the net.

Sociologist Chris Rojek argues that these strange expectations have to do with our modern commodified culture of sport and celebrity, where "the leading Sports Stars, in common with the leading celebrities from celebrity culture, are adopted as role models by fans and their lives are followed as parables of normative behavior."[21] Why? Because as a society we have a need to tell ourselves the sensible story that the people to whom we give immense attention and wealth deserve it. We want to believe that Cristiano Ronaldo's wealth, fame, and awards are about more than his being a really good soccer player. But they're not.

The reality is that elite soccer players, and elite athletes of any type, are often relatively young people, still in the process of forming a self-concept, who have devoted themselves primarily to their sport—often at the expense of education, diverse relationships, and other life experiences. Of course, there are exceptions. Some athletes are broadly talented, exceptional people. But like any quasi-randomly selected group, some elite athletes are also terrible people. And most fall somewhere in the broad swath of a normal distribution between exceptional and terrible.

This tendency toward a bell curve centered on population averages is, in fact, exactly what Cox and I found in our surveys of USWNT and elite college players.[22] In standardized survey measures of traits we thought might dispose players toward being positive role models, such as "generativity," "empathy," and "helpfulness," the average scores of the players was no different from the average scores of non-athlete samples. Like any group of diverse individuals, some players were high on certain traits, low on others, and it all evened out when averaged together.

We also asked the players about their own role models growing up, and overwhelmingly the people identified were not athletes—it was people in their own family, such as sisters, brothers, mothers, aunts, uncles, and other people with whom they had direct interactions.[23] This fits other research on role models suggesting that people generally tend to model most of their behavior off people they interact with every day rather than people they primarily know through the media.[24]

We also asked the players to describe their own characteristics they thought most worthy of serving as a model for others, and most focused on what Rojek calls the "meritocratic ideal"—being hardworking, dedicated, tough, and positive. Most interesting to me was the fact that only two out of thirty-nine players mentioned anything to do with their sport skills, despite the fact they were public figures because of their athletic ability and were taking a survey specifically targeting soccer players.

Other research has looked more specifically at whether soccer "role models" even have an influence on promoting sports participation. Japanese scholar Hideaki Ishigami investigated Japanese junior high school girls' participation in sports, including soccer, after the 2011 FIFA Women's World Cup.[25] That 2011 World Cup provided a dramatic storyline for the Japanese— so much so that the slickly produced Amazon documentary series *This Is Football* used the Japan team as the focus of an episode titled "Belief." As the official summary explains: "In 2011, an earthquake and tsunami killed 16,000 people in Japan. A country was in mourning and in need of a light at the end of the tunnel. A flicker of belief would come from the unlikeliest of heroes. This film tells the story of the Japanese women's football team and their remarkable World Cup triumph just 3 months after the disaster. . . . In an unprecedented portrait of the women's game, 'Belief' examines the obstacles, prejudices and unwavering faith needed by these women to not only inspire future generations of sports-women, but also win the admiration of the watching world."[26]

The Japanese victory in 2011 does make for an inspiring story, and it was breathtaking to watch Japan outlast a physically imposing U.S. team for a 3–1 penalty shootout win in the World Cup final. Empirically, however, Ishigame found no evidence that the team inspired "future generations of sports-women." Statistically there was no significant increase in Japanese girls' sports participation in the years after the event. In fact, Ishigame notes, much research in diverse settings around the globe finds that greater investment in elite sport seems to have little effect on grassroots sports participation, in some cases even redirecting resources from mass participation to the talented few. There is, in other words, little evidence for any "trickle-down" effect that could associate with being inspired by distant high-profile role models.

Accepting that very few people actually make life decisions based on models provided by soccer players, and that it is unfair to expect soccer players to model traits beyond their abilities on the field, we are still left with the fact that people care about their favorite players' lives. Here we can make an important semantic distinction: rather than serving as role models, players may serve as icons who offer important symbolic representations of our values, our communities, and our expectations. Somewhere between the classical meaning of an icon, as a holy figure worthy of veneration, and the more contemporary meaning, as a superficial graphic representation for a computerized application, players have an impact by offering space for cultural stories and mythology. High-profile athletes and celebrities of all types, to return to the framing offered by Chris Rojek, offer parables that provide insight into people and society.

It is worth emphasizing here that the mythology of elite soccer players as role models is not entirely a bad thing. Women athletes in particular have done much to destabilize gender stereotypes, and everyone—soccer players and otherwise—can do with reminders about the importance of social and civic responsibility. But we'd do well to also remember, especially when thinking about how to contextualize our favorite players in our own lives, that the impact of players themselves is mostly about the joy they produce on the field. The rest is up to us.

Mega-Events and the Feel-Good Factor

If we accept that the simple secret of "giving joy" and telling cultural stories is the most we should expect of players, what of the games they play? Just as society's expectations of players doing good has broadened, so has the discourse around the impacts of leagues, stadiums, teams, and tournaments. Events such as the World Cup and the Olympics regularly claim massive contributions to the greater good, as do the politicians, soccer officials, businesspeople, consultants, and entrepreneurs who thrive in a world where mega-events and sports stadiums are assumed to be in the public interest. Sociologists, other scholars applying social science lenses, and thinking fans tend to be much more skeptical.

All World Cup hosting bid proposals have to include an extensive discussion of the "legacy" projected for their event, and the discussions tend to the grandiose. Qatar's effort at hosting the 2022 World Cup even includes a "Supreme Committee of Delivery & Legacy," abbreviated SC, to emphasize supremacy. For an example of legacy claims that we have had some time to evaluate, however, the 2010 World Cup in South Africa proves useful. As the first World Cup hosted by an African nation, and with sub-Saharan Africa as the Ur-site for international development efforts, the 2010 World Cup put a spotlight on the rhetoric and the reality of soccer for social impact.

In the official 2010 FIFA World Cup Legacy Framework, the three major categories of "Tangible Legacies" are "Physical Infrastructure," "Economic Outcomes," and "Greening Initiatives"; the two major categories of "Intangible Legacies" are "Social Impacts" and "Ecological Impacts."[27] Within those major categories are no less than thirty-six subcategories of prospective impacts ranging from the "inculcation of volunteering culture" to improved "waste management" to "football development programs." In a post-event audit of these legacies, the Republic of South Africa Sport and Recreation department, along with the Human Sciences Research Council, interviewed stakeholders and reviewed official documents to see how it all went.[28] Not surprisingly, those involved generally reported that it all went well. But even the report itself acknowledges the problem of self-report bias: "It is important to note that the overwhelming positive feedback received from interviewees may be attributed to the fact that many of the interviewees were selected on the basis of their senior positions and extensive involvement in planning and implementing various aspects of the World Cup. Therefore, it is likely that their perspective was framed by a belief in the value of their own work."[29]

When you ask people who are deeply invested in the idea that soccer has profound social impact to talk about those effects, they are happy to do so and easy to find. Fortunately, journalists and social scientists can provide more objective accounts—and with these the question of legacy becomes more complicated. As one relatively benign example, South African psychologists analyzed the range of experiences in South African society around the World Cup and made the fundamental point that the effects can be *either* positive or negative in any given domain.[30] Drawing on other research on the impact of sports mega-events, they note that while mega-events can have economic effects through new jobs, those jobs are often short-term contract work.[31] And while new sports facilities often glimmer during events themselves, those facilities are often underutilized after the major events end. Improvements in "social cohesion" can further exclude already marginalized populations. Boosts to national pride can create hostility toward visitors or immigrants, improvements to sports infrastructure can serve elite performers at the expense of the grassroots level—and the ambivalences go on.[32]

In the specific case of South Africa, the impact of the 2010 World Cup on the state of local soccer seems limited at best. As mentioned previously, the men's national team has not come particularly close to qualifying for any of the subsequent World Cups (though the women's team qualified for France 2019), the local professional league has maintained about the same standard—decent compared with most leagues in the region but unexceptional globally—and the grassroots game has not been noticeably enhanced. In one recent analysis, a group of sport management scholars noted that the longer-term legacy of the 2010 World Cup is "hotly contested."[33] There was significant investment in some infrastructure (investment which might have happened anyway), and the "excellent delivery of the event has also been touted as a resounding rebuttal of the prevailing Afro-pessimism discourse, which had found expression prior to the tournament in claims that the event would be poorly organized and that the visitor experience would be diminished by exposure to widespread criminality."[34] But at the community level there has been little long-term impact—despite a short-term blitz of public relations related to corporate social responsibility initiatives during the World Cup season (including FIFA's "20 Centres for 2010" initiative discussed later in this book).

Beyond impacts on local soccer cultures, social scientists have taken significant interest in the economic legacy claims of elite global soccer. There too, the impact seems negligible if not negative. While the political economy of using sports stadiums for civic development anywhere in the world is an important topic that is well discussed elsewhere, the example of South Africa is again illustrative.[35] Put simply, many of the stadiums built or refurbished for the 2010 World Cup proved to be boondoggles and white elephants, adding value to already wealthy areas (as with the Greenpoint stadium in Cape Town) and/or having no realistic use once the tournament ended (as with the Mbombela Stadium in Nelspruit).[36]

One of the projects claimed as a legacy of the 2010 World Cup highlights the particular absurdity of the World Cup stadium game. The Moses Mabhida Stadium is a beautiful structure in a gorgeous setting: in the vibrant city of Durban on the South African coast of the Indian Ocean. The stadium has an elegant feathered clamshell roof opening to an immense white flow of girders that arch from a wide pyramidal base into a graceful single stream over the center of the field. With the right view from the hills over Durban, the stadium foregrounds both downtown towers and the coastal beach in a striking juxtaposition of sport, urbanity, and nature. But if that view isn't just quite right, or at least not to FIFA standards, you can also see another perfectly good stadium immediately next door—Kings Park Stadium is a fifty-two-thousand-seat rugby stadium that opened in 1958, was renovated for the 1995 Rugby World Cup, and regularly draws tens of thousands of fans for Sharks rugby games.

For complicated reasons that mix local politics, FIFA politics, business interests, and more than a bit of magical thinking, officials decided to not repurpose Kings Park for the World Cup and instead to build a gleaming new monument to the overlords of modern soccer just a parking lot away. The magical thinking focused on ways two massive stadiums could be viable in Durban, assuming a huge new market for concert events, tours, and a massive influx of new crowds to local professional soccer games—despite knowing that the top-division soccer teams in Durban only draw a few thousand fans on average. To their credit, Durban officials have been creative in finding ways to keep the stadium somewhat viable—offering a "sky car" ride up the stadium arch, along with a restaurant, an events venue, and a health club. According to local news sites, combining that income with occasional mega-church services and a very few high-profile sports events means the stadium only loses the equivalent of a few million dollars each year.[37] But the absurdity of two massive stadiums immediately next to each other in a relatively small market continues to symbolize the perverse impact of hosting mega events. South African sociologist Ashwin Desai explains it as an example of the "magical thinking" that often comes with popular sport:

> The case of South Africa demonstrates clearly how, contrary to what Max Weber expected, modernity can coexist with forms of charismatic leadership and magical thinking. In fact, modern state bureaucracies often feed off, use and encourage traditional forms of leadership, identity and mystical thinking to pacify dissatisfied social groups. But it is difficult in the long run to make a case for reliance on mega-events, secured by the Father of the Nation, and purported to somehow enrich all with the dividends of patriotism and act as the driver of sustained economic development. Moses Mabhida stadium is a living example of how we were duped into believing that the World Cup would turn the country around and fire up the economy. One is reminded of George Steiner's memorable phrase: "maximum impact and instant obsolescence."[38]

If the tangible legacy of mega-events is so easy to critique—with crumbs for the masses and massive profits for FIFA, a few construction companies, marketers, and security consultants—why are they still such tempting investments? This question might be better to ask a psychologist than an economist, though economists have gathered data that helps to make the point. In their book *Soccernomics*, the economist Stefan Szymanski and journalist Simon Kuper review data on the impact of major soccer tournaments to reinforce the general finding that the economic impact of hosting is minor if not negative. They emphasize that many of the consultant estimates for all the jobs and spending generated by mega-events look impressive until you realize that economic activity still has to come from somewhere: "Once you start thinking of people as having alternatives rather than just standing around waiting for the stadium to arrive, the economics begin to look less appealing. For every dollar going in, there is probably a dollar going out somewhere else."[39]

After demonstrating the limited economic impact of major soccer tournaments, Kuper and Szymanski use other data to instead support a psychological impact.[40] While cities and countries seem no better off financially a year after hosting a World Cup or European Championship, people in those places report themselves to be happier. As they explain, "A World Cup is the sort of common project that otherwise barely exists in modern societies. We've seen that the mere fact of following a team in the World Cup deters some very isolated people from committing suicide. If playing in a tournament creates social cohesion, hosting one creates even more. The inhabitants of the host country—and especially the men—come to feel more connected to everyone else around them. Moreover, hosting can boost the nation's self-esteem, and so makes people feel better about themselves. In the end, the best reason for hosting a World Cup is that it's fun."[41]

Kuper and Szymanski suggest "fun" is debatable as an economic rationale for hosting a very costly major soccer tournament—particularly in places where all the money required could be used for more pressing community needs. But it is a reason that many social scientists recognize as a major part of how soccer and other sports can have a social impact, labeling it the "feel-good factor."[42] In the right context, soccer can make us feel good about our teams, about the places we live, about the leadership in those places, and about many other related things lit by the halo of soccer's glow. As such, building on the argument that we should be wary of the halo effect for individual players, there is also reason to be wary of the halo effect around the game itself. The good feeling that comes from soccer can easily distract us from the social problems it can create, reinforce, or obscure.[43] But it still feels good.

Winners and Losers

When we consider whether soccer has an overall positive social impact—whether the elite game does good in the world—we tend to mostly hear from the winners. Journalists like Simon Kuper write books about the most successful players and managers. Scholars analyze the impact of champions such as Diego Maradona and high-profile "role models" such as the U.S. and Japanese World Cup–winning women's teams. Researchers auditing the legacy claims of World Cup events talk mostly to functionaries who were successful in winning funding and infrastructure projects. As Winston Churchill may (or may not) have said, "History is written by the victors."[44] Yet, one of the defining characteristics of competitive sport—and perhaps of the social impact of the soccer—is that not everyone wins.

There may be, for example, no more well-intentioned effort to use soccer for social impact than the Homeless World Cup. The event is a charitable effort to "deliver an inspirational week-long street football tournament" for players who "have faced homelessness and social marginalization."[45] It is an attempt to skip intermediaries like star players and mega-events so that the game itself can make a positive social impact. And, indeed, research based on self-report data—when those who have benefited are telling the story— tends to find that the Homeless World Cup has some positive effects.[46] The people that have good experiences at the event report enjoying the soccer and taking the opportunity to build social connections that might be helpful in the future. In at least one case, however, researchers Jonathan Magee and Ruth Jeanes embedded themselves with a Homeless World Cup team and observed the longer run of participant experiences.[47] They found that the players did appreciate the opportunity to train for the event and adopt healthy habits. But the games themselves were not so salubrious.

After the team Magee and Jeanes followed lost their first two games 1–10 and 0–9 the team's goalkeeper was angry: "Here is what I thought, I was like, Why am I doing this? To experience that? I was made a fool. This is supposed to be a good thing, making me feel better about myself, so I can sort myself out. Well it isn't. It's making me feel like crap. I thought I'd been doing really well in practice but then the teams here are like professionals, you seen how they back-heeled past me and laughed. It was just humiliating and I did not want to put myself through that again."[48]

Another player reflected on a wider sense of failure provoked by the team's games: "I don't know why I thought I'd be any good at this, it's pretty obvious I'm not very good at much that's why I'm in the situation I'm in. I'm always fucking up. I don't know why I thought this would be any different to what usually happens. Everyone can see that we are failing here as we are losing all the time so is that what we are, a bunch of losers?"[49]

Though these reflections may be on the extreme negative side of the soc-cer and social impact equation, they offer a reminder that many of the posi-tive stories told about the good of the game are also on an extreme. The game itself does little without accounting for context. The social impact of soccer is in the space it provides for stories and feelings that can lead to positive and negative effects. Players can model pro- and antisocial values, stadiums and mega-events can bring people together while also accelerating inequality, the game can give the winners a boost while highlighting for the losers their deepest flaws.

Sport sociologist Peter Donnelly has labeled this contradictory nature as "the Janus-face of sport," referring to the Roman god Janus, who is depicted as having two faces that look simultaneously in opposite directions.[50] Donnelly warns against accepting generic claims for the positive social impact of sport: "The claims of numerous 'sport evangelists' about the essential nature of 'sport for good,' appear to willfully ignore the more negative aspects of sport. Sport may be used to accomplish all of the claims made above, but it may also be used to promote ideological conformity, nationalism, militarism, consumerism, and inequitable attitudes about gender, race, and disability."[51]

Yet many of us still have a powerful impulse to assume the positive impact of sport overrides its more negative face. And there are good psychological reasons for this. We unconsciously perceive a halo around the players and games we love, using a widespread cognitive shortcut to imagine that talents and gifts in one domain—such as sport—easily transfer to other domains—such as life. We are hardwired to think about the world in stories, and soccer provides a tempting space for telling cultural stories with happy endings. We are attracted to things that make us feel good—when a player exhibits skills and attitudes that we find inspiring, when a World Cup makes us feel like we are part of a vibrant community, when playing the game invigorates our bodies and minds.

These positive social impacts of soccer, the positive stories and feelings it can conjure in the right context, are real and important. It is good to have fun, joy, and other positive emotions in our lives.[52] In recent years some soccer scholars have even started working groups and conferences on "football as medicine." As they explain it in the book *Football as Medicine: Prescribing Football for Global Health Promotion*, when used in the right ways soccer is healthy and fun—offering empirically documented benefits for physical fitness and emotional well-being.[53] But, again, the key is for it to be used in the right ways. Medicine, when not used properly, can be dangerous.

What, then, might social science suggest is the right prescription for high-level soccer to have a positive social impact? And how might a "thinking fan" navigate their own biases to be better or more thoughtful stewards of the game? Most generally we should be careful about the stories we tell about the game. We should put reasonable expectations on star players by recognizing that most are regular people who happen to be really good at soccer. We can feel the joy of watching Maradona play when he was at his best, but we shouldn't take his life as a model of how to live. We can appreciate the inspiring story of the 2011 Japanese Women's World Cup champions but shouldn't assume that inspiration will transfer into mass opportunities for Japanese children. To me, the most promising way of leveraging soccer celebrity for social impact is to use the fame and wealth of elite players to amplify the voices of experts on social issues and to contribute financially to critical social causes. Here initiatives such as Common Goal—which asks star players and coaches to contribute at least 1 percent of their salaries to soccer-related charities run by grassroots organizations and global experts—seem best able to take advantage of the halo over our favorite players.[54]

Likewise, we should recognize that glitzy stadiums and mega-events such as the World Cup often offer fun ways of generating communal pride in the short term, but also display a long term trend toward redistributing wealth and power from the poor and marginalized to the rich and powerful. FIFA marketing relies on the halo over the game to claim grand social impacts, but as the case of South Africa makes clear, those claims are often nothing more than hollow emotional appeals. There were some examples of local impacts from the 2010 World Cup—such as a Football Foundation of South Africa program in Gansbaai, Western Cape, described by researcher David Bek and colleagues—but those programs usually "did not emerge directly from the formal planning process driving FIFA 2010. . . . Instead, it evolved from the bottom-up but did benefit greatly from synergies created by the impending World Cup."[55] For soccer mega-events to have real impact, the process has to integrate communities at the grassroots level rather than just making proclamations from on high.

Even though the essence of high-level soccer is its competitive nature, we seem to have a hard time remembering that the stories of the game inevitably involve both winners and losers. It's important to not always rely on the victors to write the stories. We need voices other than those of soccer's brightest stars and its biggest games. For the game to have a positive social impact we need to think more critically about what we hear from the top down and engage more proactively with voices from the grassroots up.

A pickup soccer game among boys in the Kilimanjaro region of Tanzania, both a common sight and a trope of youth in the developing world. Author photo.

CHAPTER 7

Initiatives

Soccer for Development and Peace

T HE TROPE OF IMPOVERISHED BAREFOOT KIDS passionately engaged in dusty games of pickup soccer amid mud and stick houses has become a clichéd image of childhood in the global south. A version of the image, a picture shot in Angola, was the cover for the May 24, 2010 issue of *Sports Illustrated* in the run-up to the first-ever World Cup on the African continent. Like most tropes, the image offers both grains of truth and assumptions to be approached with caution. The pervasiveness of children playing soccer for fun in the streets and on dirt fields in places like Angola, sights that are rare in the global north, is real and evocative. In my own travels through sub-Saharan Africa, Central America, and Southeast Asia, seeing children joyously kicking a ball with friends (but without adult supervision) has been a common theme. It always makes me feel emotionally connected through a shared love for the game. It reminds me of the potential that opportunities to play and learn can unleash. But those images and scenes also trigger my inner social scientist, reminding me of more complicated questions about what a game can actually do so far away from the bright lights and big stars of elite soccer. What might soccer really offer to people and communities on the wrong side of massive global inequality?[1]

My best chance to address those questions as a social scientist happened to take place in Angola just as the country was emerging from a twenty-seven-year civil war. It was, at the time, rated by the United Nations Children's Fund (UNICEF) as the worst place in the world to be a child.[2] I was there to do research in conjunction with volunteering for an international nongovernmental organization (NGO) using sports and play to facilitate child development in refugee camps, a small initiative in the midst of a large international development industry that saw Angola as a prime target. Outside the capital of Luanda—a city where oil and diamond money made for a surprisingly vibrant and expensive safe zone insulated from persistent conflict—education, health care, jobs, and roads were all in short supply. My daily drive from the city to refugee camps on the outskirts of Luanda took me past a dystopian mix of landscapes: from gleaming new office buildings for oil companies, government ministries, and aid agencies to red-dirt hillsides packed with tiny scrap-wood huts, bisected by small canals full of trash and debris. Amid the intense inequality, whether at the gleaming new national stadium or in the dirt alleys of the most godforsaken refugee communities, there was one striking constant: soccer. Kids played constantly, young men organized semiformal leagues, and nearly everyone had a favorite team from elsewhere in the world—in a nod to Angola's Lusophone culture, the Brazilian national team and Sporting Lisbon were particularly popular. It is nearly impossible to spend time in a place like Angola and not hope the power of the game can do some real good.

For my research work, after several months of familiarizing myself with the communities and working on coach training and youth programs, I spent several weeks undertaking surveys and learning about the daily lives of children. One day, as a group of Angolan assistants and I surveyed kids in an open-air, tin-roofed school block, one of the assistants pulled me aside and said, "There's a kid here I think you'll find interesting to talk to yourself." He introduced a boy I've called "Diego" in other academic writing who distinguished himself from the crowd by a lack of functioning legs.[3] I never learned with any certainty why Diego's legs had no musculature, serving merely as stick-like props to balance his torso as he propelled himself about using his fists as levers, but the most plausible speculation was that he had been afflicted by polio.

Interviewing Diego about his daily life was emotionally conflicting. Many of my research questions were about sports and play, and I didn't want to make Diego feel bad about his disability. But for the sake of research protocol I asked, "How many days a week do you usually play sports and physical games?" And, I added quickly to lighten the blow, "It's okay if it's zero."

Diego looked at me with uncertainty, sensing that I had a particular expectation. Tentatively, he replied (in Portuguese): "I play soccer every day." Now it was my turn to be uncertain. "Every day?" I probably did not mean to say it out loud, but how could a boy with no functioning legs play soccer every day?

"Well," Diego tried again, "I guess there were a few days where I had a cold and couldn't play. So, almost every day?"

As it turns out, Diego and friends in this particularly desolate refugee community on the deep outskirts of Luanda had a daily "kick-about" on the bare patch of dirt that served as both local schoolyard and soccer field. Diego used his hands to bat the ball when the other kids used their feet to kick, but he was nimble enough at dragging his legs on their thickly scabbed knees to keep up. Later, while undertaking a more in-depth case study of Diego's life inspired by that first research interview, I asked his friends whether Diego's participation in the game ever caused problems.

"Kind of," his friends told me. "We sometimes disagree about what should happen when the ball hits his [non-functioning] legs. Some of us think that's just like a handball for the rest of us. But mostly we just play."

Diego thus became my most vivid case study of the psychological adaptability of children in difficult circumstances, while also serving as an example of the promise and peril of using soccer to play the international development game. Diego did indeed love the opportunity to play soccer. The game fulfilled an important emotional need. But he didn't really need me or any outside organization to create that opportunity. Instead, any rational analysis of his basic needs would have to emphasize the inequalities facing his community: the lack of health care, physical safety, education, and material opportunities. I do still think soccer can have a place among such daunting needs—it feels both inaccurate and cruel to say children such as Diego should focus only on "the basics." But a more inclusive concept of human development in contexts of extreme poverty does require modesty and humility.

Modesty and humility, unfortunately, have not always been part of the recent explosion of domestic and international initiatives exploring the good the game can do at a grassroots level, under the broad label of sports for development and peace (often abbreviated as SDP). A 2011 *Sports Illustrated* feature article on the growing popularity of SDP was headlined "Sports Saves the World."[4] The impulse to grandiosity is somewhat understandable: the combination of sport's massive global popularity, the needs and potential of children in the world's poorest countries, and the belief that opportunities and joy should be more justly shared can easily trigger immense humanitarian instincts.[5] But that exuberance and emotional appeal comes with significant risks for oversimplification.

Balancing emotional appeals with a need for rational thinking returns us to a core idea underlying the very social science of soccer: the game as a whole evokes a delicate balance between our emotional and rational selves. People like me hope sincerely that shared emotional connections can play some small part in overcoming global inequalities, but we also have to confront rational understandings of what something like soccer can actually do. So we social scientists have increasingly been attending to ways in which the zeal of soccer fans and SDP practitioners can be balanced with more rational analysis.

This chapter attempts such balance through a case study approach that also integrates academic perspectives on SDP. The case studies here focus on specific soccer for development and peace-related initiatives: FIFA's 20 Centres for 2010 program affiliated with the World Cup in South Africa; Grassroot Soccer programs to combat HIV; the One World Play Project's "ultra-durable ball to bring the transformative power of play to the hundreds of millions of youth who don't even have something as simple as a ball"; and women's soccer teams to promote gender empowerment in Zanzibar as described in several documentary films. These examples all rely on the global emotional resonance of soccer, but each employs a slightly different rationale for how soccer can contribute to international development. While I haven't worked with any of these programs directly, I'm intrigued by the different ways each mixes a love of soccer with humanitarian goals. The results suggest a few potential best practices, but also offer key ideas for ways both emotion and reason might make soccer more than a game.

The Peril and the Potential of Soccer for Development

The "official social responsibility campaign" of the 2010 World Cup was a SDP initiative with the clever name of "20 Centres for 2010" and a worthwhile goal of creating youth centers across the African continent that mixed soccer, education, and development. The marketing for the initiative was impressive. As I wrote in 2014 when reflecting on the legacy of the 2010 World Cup,[6] the logos for the 20 Centres for 2010 program were everywhere at the official venues in South Africa, taking a prominent place next to the brand marks of official corporate sponsors as if to say, "Look, we are not just shilling for multinationals; we are also doing good in the world." Unfortunately, in contrast to the polished promotional campaign, something was missing: the actual youth centers.

At the time of the 2010 World Cup only one of the 20 Centres *for* 2010 (italics mine) had actually been completed: a center in Khayelitsha township of Cape Town that provided a scenic backdrop for promotional events. There were perhaps four more centers completed within a month of the tournament ending, at least according to one of the few media sources to follow up on FIFA's promotional campaign.[7] But it is still hard to confirm the actual numbers and completion dates both because FIFA never publicized the actual "20 Centres" as much as the concept, and because they were spread out across the entire continent of Africa. FIFA does have a final report, available as a difficult-to-find web resource, indicating that by early 2018 twenty centers were indeed being operated by nongovernmental organization partners.[8] Many of the links for "more information" about each center, however, were no longer operational.[9]

While a few available pictures suggest that each individual center could offer a nice community space, with a miniature turf field (often 40 meters by 20 meters) and an accompanying small building with meeting spaces and offices, it is noteworthy that none seems to have a full-sized soccer field. In other words, as a legacy of a World Cup cycle that took in an estimated $3.89 billion in revenue and $2.17 billion in profit, from which FIFA, a nonprofit organization, took $631 million to supplement its reserves, all of Africa was gifted 20 miniature fields—approximately 1 for every 50 million people on the continent.[10] It seems to be a textbook definition of a token gesture.

This tokenism is one of the biggest problems with both the promotion of the FIFA 20 Centres for 2010 program and many other efforts to use soccer for development. International development is an immensely complicated enterprise that has been working for decades to redress global inequality with mixed success. Yet, soccer-for-development initiatives often say or imply that just a field and a ball can "save the world"—often justifying their efforts through the good feelings that come "if the game can just make one child smile."

While no one would object to the idea of making children smile, there are several problems with this emotional justification for soccer as part of international development. First, it assumes kids in developing communities would not play or smile without outside help. As Diego's story at the start of this chapter suggests, that is a problematic assumption. In fact, one of the few scholarly accounts of the 20 Centres for 2010 initiative found that within a few short years the small turf field FIFA laid in Johannesburg's Alexandra township seemed less used (and less accessible) for soccer than neighboring dirt streets.[11] Second, and more subtly, the notion that soccer is important to development because it makes people happy may encourage us to focus on the individual feelings of poverty and underdevelopment without taking seriously the broader social and structural forces that maintain inequality. If the smiles of kids such as Diego implicitly allow us to feel okay about the material poverty in his community, little will ever change.

As scholars have started paying more attention to SDP endeavors, they often comment on this tension between the individual and societal levels of international development. David Black, for example, is a Canadian scholar of international development who has written several cautiously critical analyses of SDP emphasizing that the endeavor does have the advantage of being "latecomers to the 'development enterprise,' with the opportunity to learn from some of the dangers and missteps that have befallen more 'mainstream' development practitioners through the chequered post-Second World War history of this enterprise."[12] One of Black's key cautions to SDP practitioners is to be aware that international development works best when "bottom-up" grassroots community endeavors combine with "top-down" political policy that addresses structural inequalities. It is nice to play a fun game of soccer with kids, but for that game to be meaningful it has to also relate to some kind of opening for broader policies offering opportunities and resources, such as for education, health, and recreational spaces. The 20 Centres for 2010 program was trying to provide those types of openings, but the scale of it was just too small to make a meaningful impact.

Black thinks this relates to the unease many have at thinking of sports as political. He writes: "No serious sport studies scholar would any longer defend the 'myth of autonomy'—the idea that sport is apolitical, 'above' or autonomous from politics. Nevertheless, it is very hard to develop the sort of contextualized understanding of the communities in and with which one is working that is necessary for successful and sustainable development interventions. This challenge may be compounded for many sportspeople, convinced as they are of the transcendent power of sport and often having been relatively disengaged from mainstream politics."[13]

If soccer is going to do some good in the world, in other words, it cannot depend solely on how much we love the game.

This tension in stories of soccer and development, between the real emotional connection it offers and the structural inequalities it sometimes allows us to ignore, must be addressed if soccer is to contribute to international development. Sociologists such as Douglass Hartmann and Christina Kwauk have proposed distinguishing between SDP programs that operate with a "reproductive vision" designed to "resocialize and recalibrate individual youth and young people" and SDP programs that have a "transformative vision" which "must also involve a concomitant attempt to alter the conditions of inequality" by transforming "the educational space and experience of sport."[14] Hartmann and Kwauk argue that the transformative vision of SDP is much more rare and difficult than the reproductive vision, but essential to consider if sports are going to actually make positive social change.

I have argued in my own scholarly work that sport psychology scholars and practitioners can make practical contributions to SDP with oft-neglected steps such as undertaking genuine needs assessments before implementing programming and using multidisciplinary research to engage in open-minded reflections on impact.[15] The core idea is to approach SDP initiatives with the types of intellectual curiosity and critical consciousness that are essential to both social science and thinking fandom. No soccer-for-development initiative is perfect, but each has something to teach. So let's turn to three examples that can help to illustrate what we might learn from an analysis that goes beyond just the game's obvious emotional appeal.

Grassroot Soccer

While the idea of soccer as a universal language that brings people together is a cliché to be used with caution, the global popularity of the game does create serendipitous opportunities. Take, for example, the origin story of the prominent SDP program Grassroot Soccer—an organization that tries to leverage the appeal of soccer toward HIV education and health promotion.[16] While Grassroot Soccer now spends millions of dollars a year in forty-five participating countries, it started when Scotland's backup goalkeeper in the 1978 World Cup became the coach of Highlanders FC in Bulawayo, Zimbabwe. The coach, Bobby Clark, brought along his then fourteen-year-old son Tommy, who would go on to play for his father at Dartmouth College in New Hampshire, and then return to play for Highlanders and teach English in Zimbabwe. This early exposure helped Tommy recognize the scourge of

HIV in sub-Saharan Africa, go to medical school to become a pediatrician, and put it all together by creating a nonprofit that "leverages the power of soccer to educate, inspire, and mobilize at-risk youth in developing countries to overcome their greatest health challenges."[17] As Tommy Clark explains it on the Grassroot Soccer website,

> Every day as I walked to practice [while playing for Highlanders in Zimbabwe], I was followed by a group of children who would abandon their own pick-up soccer games to join me on my walk. The bolder children would push to the front and walk next to me, practicing their English as I practiced my isiNdebele. Over time the group of children grew as word spread that a Mukiwa (white man) and professional soccer player was in their community. It was on these walks that I further realized the power and draw of soccer.
>
> Zimbabwe, however, had changed since I first arrived as a teenager. City squares that had teemed with artisans selling crafts and vendors selling food and staples were now empty. European tourists who had roamed the graceful streets of Bulawayo were conspicuously absent. Families were missing uncles, mothers, sisters, and grandparents. AIDS had struck.[18]

The basic ingredients of humanitarian soccer initiatives are abundant here: an emotional connection, a shared love of soccer, and a social problem reflecting and accentuating global inequality. Clark eventually flavored those basic ingredients with knowledge from his medical training, working with several cofounders to hatch the idea of using professional soccer players to promote HIV prevention and other health messages in Zimbabwean communities. In 2002, the year of Grassroot Soccer's formal founding, the UNAIDS program estimated the adult HIV/AIDS prevalence in Zimbabwe to be around 33 percent.[19] It is hard to read statistics like that without feeling an emotional tug and wanting to be part of the solution.

Clark went on to draw quite explicitly on social science tools to respond, noting "a chance meeting with Dr. Albert Bandura—a Stanford psychologist famous for articulating 'social learning theory.'" Clark reported this meeting as a prompt to wonder "If Michael Jordan could promote consumer products, why couldn't soccer stars promote health?"[20] That basic question found enough purchase to eventually grow Grassroot Soccer into a global "adolescent health organization."

As of 2018, after focusing initially only on the familiar terrain of Zimbabwe, Grassroot Soccer was working with thirty-five implementing partners and reaching over one hundred thousand youth each year in a wide variety of countries.[21] Grassroot Soccer has plenty of its own promotional material for the curious, and it has broadened its mission considerably over time (now addressing malaria, gender issues, youth development, and other development issues in addition to HIV). But its most basic method historically was to have coaches and mentors implement a "SKILLZ curriculum" that integrates information about HIV risk behaviors and prevention with soccer activities.

As one example of how the SKILLZ curriculum would work, at least one version developed in conjunction with UNAIDS for use in South Africa offers eleven units including activities such as "Make a Choice."[22] In this unit, youth run around a field making choices of who to group with as a coach shouts questions progressing from "Who is your favorite soccer team?" to "What is your favorite subject in school?" The activity would build to groupings that demonstrate that "for every 6 adults in South Africa, 1 had HIV" with an affirmation of the life "choices" we can make "to avoid getting or spreading HIV: Choose to abstain from sex; choose to stick to one partner who sticks only to me; choose to stay away from older partners; choose to always wear a condom if I do have sex."

Has it worked? Does soccer offer a particularly compelling vehicle for these types of public health messages? Here is where the story requires more analysis and less emotional attachment. And here is where the story gets complicated.

Grassroot Soccer, to its great credit, is one of the few SDP organizations that uses a serious research lens to evaluate its programming. It also often makes that evidence public, offering a regular "research report" that as of 2016 provided summaries of "27 research studies since 2005 in over 20 countries, ranging from South Africa to the Dominican Republic. GRS has also conducted the largest school-based randomized controlled trial (RCT) evaluating a sport-based HIV prevention program, called the GOAL Trial."[23] Using an RCT study, considered the gold standard for intervention research, in sport for development is exceedingly rare.

The GOAL Trial drew from large school districts in South Africa to find that Grassroot Soccer programs do indeed increase knowledge related to HIV prevention and rates of HIV testing. But the RCT trial also found that the group of youth exposed to the intervention was actually more likely than a control group to report multiple sexual partners and to perpetrate intimate-partner violence.[24] In some important ways, in other words, soccer made things worse. This finding reinforces a phenomenon that has long been known to social psychologists and that regularly stymies educators—in the realm of youth risk taking, reason is easily hijacked by emotion. More practically, knowledge does not always change behavior. Teens often know, for example, about the risks of driving too fast or of binge drinking. But when it comes to actual behavior, and especially teen behavior in group contexts, teens often prioritize emotional rewards over rational understandings of risk.[25] While the Grassroot Soccer participants seemed to learn lots of useful information about HIV prevention, they also seemed inclined to engage in the kinds of behaviors that might bring some short-term pleasure at the expense of the health and safety of themselves and others.

It is not entirely clear why the GRS GOAL trial participants not only ignored their rational knowledge, but actually increased some problem behaviors. The full details of the randomized control trial's findings have not been shared publicly. It seems, however, that Grassroot Soccer has started to de-emphasize its SKILLZ curriculum and it may be that the randomized control trial results are at least part of the reason. If you have really randomized your intervention group and your control group, and you have the right sample sizes, then there is no other conclusion to draw than that participation in the soccer program contributed to risk behavior. This must have been a hard finding to confront, but Grassroot Soccer should be applauded for being willing to care about the evidence.

Grassroot Soccer should also be applauded for a variety of other ways in which it uses soccer for development. In another program Grassroot Soccer administered and researched in Bulawayo, Zimbabwe, a separate randomized control trial found that a program to encourage voluntary male circumcision as a way of reducing HIV transmission had modest but significant effects.[26] The program revealed that an hour-long informational session using the context of soccer was a cost-effective way to get young men to proceed with the voluntary circumcision. Grassroot Soccer has also been excellent about partnering with other relevant development players to try to scale up its programming. It has teamed with schools, with UNAIDS, with U.S. Peace Corps volunteers, and with the foundations for teams such as Arsenal and Manchester City. It has, in other words, combined an emphasis on the grassroots with significant efforts to think about broader awareness and policy change.

It is also worth noting that recent estimates of the adult HIV prevalence rate in Zimbabwe are approximately half what they were in 2002. The broader global effort towards HIV education and intervention seems to be working.

Although the exact role of soccer in that type of progress is something that would be very difficult to evidence, at least Grassroot Soccer recognizes that the game itself is not enough. But if the game itself is not enough to make development happen, what about the ball?

One World Futbol

Soccer appeals to many in the development world because of its simplicity. You only really need a ball to play. This fact is part of the beauty of the game, and it has also been the font for many international service trips full of warm-hearted travelers with extra luggage packed full of donated soccer balls. In many parts of the developing world, a ball is indeed a magical gift. Of course, the emotional pull of that gesture, like the emotional pull of the game itself, can be misleading. When understood through social science lenses, a ball turns out not to be a simple thing.[27]

In my own work as a Peace Corps volunteer in Malawi, I was actively discouraged from having people send bags of balls and other large quantities of sports equipment because of huge import tariffs that would end up costing more than buying the equipment locally (which was exactly the point of the tariffs, to encourage people to buy local goods). And then, if the equipment did make it to schools or communities, it often would not last very long. Most manufactured soccer balls pop after significant use, particularly on fields of dirt and stone. The clichéd image of barefoot boys playing on dusty streets with an improvised ball is not just a product of poverty. The improvised balls made of collected plastic bags enmeshed in twine or rocks rolled in socks actually can be the most functional way for kids to play the game in communities without access to turf fields and big-box sporting goods stores. But being functional does not necessarily mean being optimal. And that image of the barefoot child with the twine ball feels so powerful emotionally that it practically begs for action.

At least that was the feeling that animates the origin story publicized by the One World Play Project, originally called One World Futbol, which is known in the world of soccer and development for inventing an "indestructible" soccer ball. As the story was explained by Gwen Knapp, writing for *Sports on Earth* in 2013:

> The inventor, Tim Jahnigen of Berkeley, Ca., came up with the idea when he watched a 2006 documentary about Darfur refugees that showed children

in a camp kicking a wad of trash bound by string. In Brazil, where billions have been spent on new stadiums, the game has become an impediment to basic needs. For children in a war zone, Jahnigen recognized that play was essential to their well-being. (The United Nations agrees and lists children's recreation as a human right.)

Jahnigen learned that sending regular soccer balls would be pointless. Aid organizations had done it before, but the balls would quickly deflate or be destroyed on the hard ground. In one African village, he said, the nearest pump required a full day's walk at an adult's pace.[28]

Here again we have an emotional tug, a love of soccer, and a social problem to be solved—but this time a love of soccer was not exactly what drove the initiative. Jahnigen, according to multiple interviews and journalistic reports, was mostly an entrepreneur who did not know much about soccer beyond it being the most popular game in the world. Instead, he saw the issue of soccer balls as a design problem to be solved, and as a business proposition. Drawing on the recent trend in international development work to promote "social entrepreneurship," the One World Play Project officially incorporated as a business—though one certified as a "B-Corp" for its emphasis on social responsibility. The idea behind social entrepreneurship tries to navigate the emotional valence of development by assuming that degrees of a profit motive can help overcome the pitfalls of relying mostly on altruism.

Jahnigen's lack of emotional connection to soccer may ultimately have had significant advantages. On the design side, he needed a material unlike the versions of leather and plastic that are sentimentally familiar to anyone growing up around manufactured balls. He found it in a type of synthetic foam most famous as the ingredient making Croc sandals cheap, durable, reasonably comfortable, and hugely popular. On the business side, he was not limited to connections in the sports world. Instead, needing seed funding to develop and test prototypes, Jahnigen raised $300,000 from an old connection in the music industry (the pop star Sting).[29]

After several iterations of design, and several forms of field testing (apparently including giving the ball to a lion at the Johannesburg Zoo to make sure it was truly indestructible[30]), One World Futbol was ready to play the international development game. The business plan it chose involved a model made famous by TOMS shoes and Warby Parker glasses, often referred to as BOGO: buy one, give one. The basic idea is that every time a (presumably affluent resident of the global north) consumer buys one of these products, another is given away to a (presumably poor resident of the global south) person in need. When I bought my then-three-year-old son a One World Futbol for Christmas a few years back, we got an indestructible soccer ball and we were thanked for donating an unseen other ball to someone somewhere else. We got a ball we could kick around in the backyard without worrying about leaving it out in the rain, and we got to feel good about ourselves for being philanthropic types.

The BOGO model of international development is also rife with critics and complexities. A 2014 exchange in the *Stanford Social Innovation Review,* for example, included arguments both for and against the BOGO model as a way to address global inequality.[31] On the one hand, the model fits well with younger consumers who are concerned with how personal economic choices relate to broader social issues and seems likely to grow in popularity. On the other hand, the BOGO idea is often enacted with more of an emphasis on clever marketing than on transformative social change. Will charitable donations from successful Western companies really address global inequality? One of the founders of One World Futbol, Mal Warwick, chimed in on the issue through the comments section of the *Stanford Social Innovation Review* discussion, arguing that their model was distinctive because: "1. We donate the same soccer ball as the one we sell to paying customers; and 2. The bulk of our donations are made possible through a generous sponsorship by Chevrolet."[32]

In a separate comment on the same article, Warwick pressed the case for social value by using many of the standard arguments about the nearly miraculous power of soccer: "The virtually indestructible One World Futbol—is more than useful to the young people who receive it. Because it enables them to play without fear that the ball will suddenly go flat and become useless, the One World Futbol helps promote health and wellbeing in communities where there may be no other opportunities for organized play. In a great many of these communities, the One World Futbol is employed in 'sport for peace and development' programs undertaken by the UN, the national government, or NGOs—programs that teach conflict resolution, gender equity, HIV/AIDS prevention, and other critical subjects and skills."[33]

The vision of development here is both expansive and reproductive. It is expansive in its ambition, and the idea is that the company is doing more than just giving away soccer balls. This ambition seems to be behind the change of the company's name from "One World Futbol" to the "One World Play Project." But it is also reproductive in that it hopes mostly to "recalibrate individual youth" rather than attempting to "alter the conditions of inequality" (drawing terms from the aforementioned sociologists Hartmann and Kwauk). It is also worth noting that, unlike Grassroot Soccer, the One World Play Project has very little publicly available data to support its claims. There does not seem to be research comparing community levels of physical activity, health, or other measures of well-being before and after the introduction of One World Futbols in marginalized communities.[34] Further, while corporate sponsorship from General Motors may indeed make the business viable, it also means that most One World Futbols are emblazoned with a Chevrolet logo—mixing a strong dose of corporate branding directed at children into what is framed as a social value endeavor.[35]

In short, if the miraculous power of giving away indestructible soccer balls seems too good to be true, then it just may be. When researching One World Futbol, I came across one article on the Sustainable Brands website that claimed the ball was "Saving Soccer in the Developing World."[36] As evidence, the article cited the then-president of Malawi, Joyce Banda, whose foundation received and distributed eleven thousand One World Futbols, explaining on national television that "the balls would go to support the first nationwide youth soccer and netball tournaments, which was previously impossible due to a lack of durable balls."[37] Having worked with school soccer in Malawi for two years between 1997 and 1999, I can definitively say that soccer did not need "saving." Kids and schools were playing constantly. I suspect, however, the honorable President Banda is making a semantic distinction here, because while there may not have been national school tournaments, there was always some type of ball with which to have a game.

Ultimately, while some critical thinking about the One World Futbol initiative raises important qualifications, I generally like the project. The qualifications are mostly questions: how to avoid pandering to stereotypes of deficiency; whether there are advantages to *not* loving soccer; how SDP should factor in the realities of global capitalism; and more. But One World Futbol is ultimately a neat example of how an ultra-rational approach to something as basic as a soccer ball can create innovation and opportunity. And that rational approach gets balance from the emotional resonance of a ball. There is something about a soccer ball, and about the game itself, that represents potential. The potential for joy, for social connections, for achievement, and maybe for development itself if it can be used with a vision to disrupt the underlying structures of inequality. So, what might that look like?

Women Fighters

While Grassroot Soccer and the One World Play Project are variations on the development theme of Westerners perceiving needs in the developing world and exporting ways to address those needs, development experts often emphasize the importance of local solutions to local problems that can then transform policy. What would it look like for local communities to make their own soccer-for-development program? One intriguing possibility is illustrated by a 2007 documentary film titled *Zanzibar Soccer Queens* and its 2016 follow-up *Zanzibar Soccer Dreams* (there is also a 2015 film, *New Generation Queens*, documenting a very similar version of the same story, but the production of that film seems independent of the other two).[38] The film-maker, a Cameroonian academic working at the University of South Wales named Florence Ayisi, explained to the *Mirror* that when she made the film, she was specifically looking for ways to counter negative stereotypes of sub-Saharan Africa: "It was the era of Live Aid and Bob Geldof. I wanted to show the other Africa beyond the headlines."[39] She came upon the story of "Women Fighters FC" on Zanzibar Island off the coast of mainland Tanzania, a team inspired by a Swedish women's team traveling through Zanzibar in 1988, but taken up largely by local women in the decades since.

The name "Women Fighters" is entirely intentional—the women are very conscious of having to fight against not only the argument that soccer is a men's game, but also Zanzibar's broader patriarchy and local interpretations of Muslim strictures against women playing sports. The women are very consciously using soccer to fight for their own development. Though not a glossy big-budget film, the documentary offers a rich analysis from local perspectives on what soccer and sports might mean for development. The Women Fighters talk about how much the game means to them as a chance to express themselves and their strengths, while critics speaking in the films (including a female university student, a male teacher, a female teacher, and some parents) argue that Islam prohibits the display of the body and discourages the female assertiveness inherent to soccer. This tension is central to the film's intent, with an academic reflection on the filmmaking arguing that the local women "metaphorically reveal their inner selves beneath traditional restrictions. This dichotomy of transgression vs. conformity in these women's identities is synecdochal for all women in Ayisi's films."[40]

Soccer for development in this case becomes both a "transgression" and a complicated driver of social transformation. The process involves hard work in both rational and emotional ways. Several of the players become teary when explaining what it is like to see one's name on the back of a real jersey for the first time, or when describing their sadness at being forced to quit the game by a new husband. But watching video of their exuberance during games against men on slippery village fields, or against women in bumpy city parks, it is hard not to feel that soccer can indeed empower and shape transformation. Local critics of the team given voice in the film, on the other hand, articulate an argument that mostly serves to highlight its own limits—their concerns that women in soccer uniforms might throw the whole community into disarray seems more about male fantasies and patriarchal control than it is about respecting local culture.

The challenge of navigating a simplified idea of "local culture" in soccer for development, however, is a real one. One of the classic issues for many development workers interested in gender equity as part of social change is to reconcile conflicting ideas about women's rights with a respect for local (often patriarchal) value systems. This challenge can be particularly pronounced in parts of the world where soccer is gender-typed as masculine in local cultural discourse. In this case, however, there is some good evidence that the idea of "African culture" prohibiting women's soccer is another oversimplification—making the mistake of thinking of culture as static rather than dynamic.

In case studies of "football feminine" in Senegal, Nigeria, and South Africa, for example, the scholar Martha Saavedra finds that the boundaries of who can play and who can't is always more about power than it is about "indigenous culture."[41] In Senegal, women's basketball is among the most popular sports, third only to men's soccer and wrestling in Dakar. And the Senegalese whom Saavedra talked to claim that is partially because basketball is a more graceful, feminine sport than the "brute" game of soccer. Of course, the fact that such an argument is nearly a complete inversion of how the games are perceived in other cultures (including in the United States) demonstrates that it is less about the sport and more about protecting territory.

But even beyond the "traditional culture" argument, there are a constellation of other challenges to the women's soccer in Africa—so much so that when Saavedra went on a research trip to Senegal in 1998–1999 to study women's football, she never actually got to see a women's match. They simply were not playing. In describing the obstacles, Saavedra points out that while men are usually embedded in the power structures and national federations that oversee the game, women in many African communities have less leisure time than men, and there are many other social issues that may necessarily be priorities for African women's activists beyond sports equity (e.g., violence against women, HIV, limited access to education, malnutrition).

The story of women's soccer in Zanzibar is important to understanding soccer and development precisely because it shows locals trying to overcome obstacles and transform power structures. One of the key figures in the films is a local woman named Nassra Mohammed, who founded Women Fighters FC after participating in the 1988 friendly match against the visiting Swedish women's team. In the initial 2007 film Mohammed, who has a career in the local civil service, uses her forceful personality and ingenuity to both train the Women Fighters team and make it sustainable, even organizing the team to open a small provision store to help fund its endeavors.

This bottom-up initiative, with the amplification of Ayisi's storytelling, eventually led to top-down policy change. The initial film about Women Fighters FC "was screened in Zanzibar in 2007 to an audience of more than 1,000, including the country's vice sports minister and secretary general of the Zanzibar Football Association."[42] Not coincidentally, the government has since "changed official policy to encourage schoolgirls to play the sport." This top-down change then, in turn, cycles back to bottom-up participants by influencing grassroots experiences. As Ayisi explained to the *Mirror* newspaper: "Something great has happened to girls. . . . Islam, soccer, and womanhood now seem to converge and coexist in harmony as women experience a significant transformation of their identities—from being 'hooligans' and 'street kids' to being regarded as cultural ambassadors."[43]

As a result, in the 2016 film, we see Mohammed shifting her focus to the new programs in schools. She is now a coaching instructor affiliated with the Confederation of African Football (CAF), training both men and women while helping teachers instantiate soccer for girls in the local school system. There are at least two key lessons here that are surprisingly rare in the use of soccer for development and gender empowerment. First, targeted efforts to spread women's soccer are most likely to lead to social change only when they help transform practices within structural institutions such as schools. Second, soccer for development needs local champions to have any hope of actually making a difference. In combination, this is a small-scale example of David Black's emphasis on the importance of both top-down public policy and bottom-up grassroots community in successful development projects.

The importance of local, bottom-up endeavor to making soccer relevant in development does not, however, mean that international forces are irrelevant. The 2007 film, for example, led to Women Fighter's FC being sponsored for a cultural exchange in Potsdam, Germany, a trip that the women in the 2016 film describe as paradigm shifting. More abstractly, in a short version of the film labeled as an "impact study," coach Nassra Mohammed notes, "This current situation of globalization, with people moving freely has helped us a lot. People from different places have interacted, improving understanding. Society in Zanzibar has now accepted that football can be played by women and men. Even when walking down the street, people stop me and ask: 'How is your team?,' 'How is the game going?'"[44]

Ultimately, as much as we soccer fans in the global north want the game to be something *we* can use as a development tool, the Zanzibar examples makes clear that nothing will do more good than strong women (and men) empowered to work in their own communities with the support of structures such as the education system. This idea was driven home powerfully by the final scene of *Zanzibar Soccer Queens*, a simple shot panning slowly across the faces of Women Fighters FC as they line up in their crisp white uniforms for a game. It is a shot familiar to any soccer fan anywhere, the pregame lineup. But amid the usual mix of emotions these faces also vividly convey something else: people with a sense of purpose—a rationale—toward making soccer a tool for transformation.

Soccer for Development?

In emphasizing the importance of reason in SDP, the intention is not to undervalue emotion. After all, organizations such as Grassroot Soccer, the One World Play Project, and Women Fighters FC are only on the radar of soccer fans when they see an occasional promotional video or blog post that is designed to make us feel good about the game. And that good feeling we get when we learn about soccer and development is important. It taps a deep and often unconscious hope that the game we love is not just a hedonistic entertainment—a hope that it might be a force for good in the world. That hope is closely related to the feelings evoked by the clichéd image of children playing soccer with a rag ball in the streets—the feeling that the game offers human connection. Soccer for development efforts, in other words, tap into our hopes that the love of soccer is meaningful.

The emphasis on reason is, however, a plea to balance the emotional tug of soccer and development with considerations for a basic analytical question: what do people in marginalized communities, kids like Diego, really need? Despite being physically disabled and living in an impoverished refugee community, Diego did not really need mere exposure to the game. He already played more robustly than many children in more privileged circumstances. He also did not really need the soccer to teach him life skills (to "resocialize or recalibrate" his individual self). His personal ability to adapt and persevere was beyond what any curricula could teach. But he did need the types of opportunities and supports that many Western soccer fans take for granted, such as education, health care, living-wage jobs, and decent shelter. He needed transformational change to happen, at least in his small refugee community. And while soccer cannot really make that kind of change by itself, no other single development tool can either.

In that vein, soccer (and thinking soccer fans) can learn from what we know about international development more broadly. Development works best when based on reasonably objective evidence, like that used by Grassroot Soccer to make an impact on global health. Development works best when it embraces innovative problem solving, like that used to create the One World Futbol to extend the ways children around the world can play. Development works best when it empowers people to work for social change and reshape public policy in their own communities, like the Women Fighters working to transform gender relations in Zanzibar.

I have also argued here that development works best when it combines our emotional and our rational selves—and I'd further suggest that this is a key for answering the broader question of how soccer can do good in the world. As I've argued throughout this book, the global resonance of soccer, and its ability to tell engaging stories, makes it a worthy object of study and an important cultural form. And as I've argued in these last two chapters, soccer's importance can extend in small ways to making contributions to the greater good, especially when it is used thoughtfully, modestly, and with a recognition that the social context in which the game takes place is what really matters. Soccer is most likely to do some good in the world if we don't just assume the power of the game but also make critical inquiries into what the game really has to offer. Finally, then, it is worth turning to questions that go beyond what the game can do to think about how we all might use social science to make the game better.

After a goal at the 2015 FIFA Women's World Cup in Canada. Though *but* means goal in French, as an English conjunction it suggests there is more to come ("but that's not all . . ."). Author photo.

CHAPTER 8

Futures

Toward Thinking Fandom

I N FEBRUARY 2020, in my dual identity as soccer fan and social scientist, I had the great privilege of attending the final of the Mbuzi Cup in the shadow of Mount Kilimanjaro. The tournament had riveted the community for weeks, with a group stage and knockout rounds full of spectacular goals, upsets, heartbreaking losses, controversy, and drama on and off the field. On the day of the final fans were packed around the field raising signs and singing songs, separated into sections by their allegiance and by security personnel wielding intimidating bats. When the players stepped onto the field, they represented many of the greatest clubs in world soccer—Manchester United, Real Madrid, Roma, Barcelona, Juventus, to name just a few—and they were bubbling with the kinetic energy that comes from playing in a final. The cup itself sat alone on a small platform just off the field at the extension of the midfield line, its golden glow sharp in the warm equatorial sunshine. So much of the scene would have been intimately familiar to any devotee of the global game. Except that this particular tournament was merely the intramural championship for a secondary school in Moshi, Tanzania, the titular prize of an *mbuzi* referring to the right to slaughter a goat (*mbuzi* in Kiswahili) for a team feast, and the most interesting things to see had little to do with the quality of the soccer and everything to do with watching the game as a thinking fan.

I'll return below to explain what exactly made the Mbuzi Cup so interesting to watch, but I first need to return to the concept of thinking fandom—a way of watching soccer that underlies the entirety of this book. As introduced briefly in chapter 1, I define thinking fandom as an approach that depends on a broad intellectual curiosity and an engaged critical consciousness. Thinking fandom is a natural outgrowth of the very social science of soccer. It is a way of thinking about the game with a scientific mindset while centering the messiness of human experience. It is something I've tried to demonstrate through all the preceding chapters, and here I hope to further promote as something anyone can use to enrich their own experience of soccer—and, just maybe, also as a way to make soccer a bit better for others. After considering how soccer might do some good in the world, in other words, it's important to consider how those of us who care about the game might do some good ourselves.

Note first that when I refer to a "thinking fan" I'm referring loosely to anyone who cares about the game—whether players, coaches, administrators, or supporters. And care in this formulation means having concerns beyond profit. Global soccer in the twenty-first century is a heavily commercialized endeavor; many see soccer primarily as a business concern. The commodification of soccer is also sometimes enabled by others who think of soccer as nothing more than a trivial pastime. Thinking fandom starts with a willingness to position one's self in between soccer as a business and soccer as a triviality and to actively engage soccer as one of the world's most broadly shared cultural forms with very social meanings.

The active engagement of thinking fandom is then primarily tautological: it is founded on thinking. This is not to question the aesthetic pleasure of watching players with special skills perform at their best. Nor is it to question the happiness that comes from seeing a team with which one feels a deep connection win, nor the elemental joy that comes from playing the game itself. In fact, I will argue at the end of this chapter that thinking fandom dovetails well with play and can be complementary and deeply satisfying in its emphasis on learning and playing with ideas. Soccer can simultaneously trigger our most ancient *as well as* our most evolved instincts, providing us both reflexive joy and deliberate opportunities to better understand ourselves and our world.

We'll start by integrating some of the understandings offered throughout this book through a thinking fans' take on that Mbuzi Cup final, and then offer further ideas of how thinking fandom can be enacted and embodied. Those ideas, including celebrating diversity, supporting locally, thinking culturally, and promoting accessibility, are discussed in relation to possible futures for soccer at both elite and grassroots levels. The point is not to predict the future, nor is it to necessarily suggest soccer's future is bright; if anything, there seems to me a significant risk that soccer will continue to become more commercial, more unequal, more artificial, less fun, and less human. The point instead is to explore how the very social science of soccer can offer counterpoints to those risks with reasons for optimism and visible pathways to a better game. Thinking fandom can make the game more enjoyable, and it might just possibly make the game better.

A Thinking Fan's Guide to the Mbuzi Cup

I was at the Mbuzi Cup final that day in Tanzania because I'd spent most of the 2019–2020 academic year in Moshi as a Fulbright Scholar doing research on youth development in extracurricular activities at Kilimanjaro-region schools. It turned out that slightly different versions of the Mbuzi Cup were a regular feature of many school extracurricular calendars—and were a common way to engage youth throughout northern Tanzania in both villages and schools. For a thinking fan, the Mbuzi Cup was a perfect opportunity to apply the very social science of soccer.

Thinking like a sociologist, I was consistently impressed with the many local adaptations Tanzanian schools used to ensure soccer tournaments fit their particular community context, modifying the rules, the brackets, the prizes, and the social organization of the whole event. One school, for example, had changed its tournament into a *N'Gombe* [Cow] Cup so that there was more meat for the post-tournament feast and so that all students—rather than just the winning team—could share.[1] Other schools combined the soccer tournament with sports such as volleyball and basketball to encourage broader participation. Changing gender norms meant integrating girls' teams at many schools.

Thinking like a psychologist, I was struck by the different leadership styles and interpersonal dynamics evident in the tournament structure. At some schools, teachers took on much of the organizing, but most schools let students take the lead and made the organizing itself an educational experience. Games often became emotionally charged—and the ways students navigated moments of anger, joy, and anxiety on the field offered insight into deeper dynamics of human development. Watching it all through the social science lenses introduced at the beginning of the book didn't allow for a conclusive psychoanalysis of any individual student, but it did offer a vision of the human psyche—shaped and constrained by community and culture—in furious action.

At that particular cup final in Moshi, the fans ringing the field demonstrated a rich and unconscious hybridizing of global soccer, local meanings, and human psychological tendencies. They had created signs for their favorite players, hand-painting "RAMOS" as a simple tribute to the captain of one of the school teams whose play reminded them of the man they told me was "the best defender in the world," the Spaniard Sergio Ramos (the attraction of global soccer icons was robust even in small-town Tanzania). The fans also formed social groups in the spaces around the field—mostly delineating themselves by year in school, subjects studied, and team affiliation, with group membership further cemented by songs and celebrations. At multiple points in the game, the winning fans succumbed to the neurophysiological rush that universally associates with a well-taken goal, rushing the field en masse and singing a collective rendition of "Olé, Olé, Olé." Toward the end of the game the fans concocted a cruder song to sing to the losers, cementing in-group and out-group status with the types of symbols and rituals that soccer fans around the world use to feel like they belong. It was, in other words, a distillation of what I earlier described as the particular power of soccer fandom to tap primal emotions, create imagined communities, and cement social bonds.

The teams on the field joined the fans in hybridizing the global and the local, having improvised their uniforms for the final by combining vaguely similar colorways from the replica soccer jerseys available at virtually every Tanzanian used clothing market. So, most all of the great European clubs really were represented, but only insofar as the reds of old Manchester United kits were deemed similar enough to the red of old Roma shirts, Arsenal shirts, and so forth to demarcate one team, while the white base for old Real Madrid shirts, Juventus stripes, and many other home whites identified the other. The students themselves had determinedly collected enough shirts from friends and schoolmates to create two pastiches of color that simultaneously paid tribute to the global commercial reach of elite soccer and allowed local allegiances to make identity claims through the simple act of choosing a color. This "glocal" manifestation of soccer, making a school soccer tournament simultaneously familiar and strange, was just one example of how the cultures of soccer described earlier make for both themes and variations in the game.

The play itself also reflected themes and variations, combining the universal vim and vigor of adolescent boys with occasional dashes of skill honed through something like the "romantic" model of talent development. Youth players in Tanzania mostly learned the game through years of pickup village soccer with friends and peers, rarely benefiting (or suffering) from the type of organized coaching that predominates in the professionalized youth soccer environments of North America and Europe. That made it all the more interesting to watch the ways the psychology manifested within the game—the visible physical withering of one team after conceding several early goals, the confident and composed penalty kick taken by a senior player on the winning team, the moist eyes of the losers after investing so much of their selves into a tournament that only really mattered to them. It reinforced the universality of much of what was described as the psychology of soccer: the need to manage anxiety and arousal, different responses to pressure in critical moments, and the ways people can invest too much of a self-concept in something as capricious as soccer.

The deep emotional investment of the players and fans at that Mbuzi Cup final also made me curious about the impact of the tournament on the school. The headmaster of the school told me he saw the tournament as a chance for the students to get some healthy recreation, to build a sense of community, and to learn life lessons. He had, for example, felt the need to intervene in the early stages of the tournament when one of the teams became excessive in accusing the student referees and organizers of corruption—making the members of the team apologize in front of a whole-school assembly. The headmaster was also determined to ensure the tournament didn't distract students from the actual school year. One reason intramural tournaments are so popular in Tanzanian secondary schools is because, unlike interscholastic competitions, they don't take students away from their home campuses and thus away from valuable class time. The game can indeed do some good in the world but its social impact is not guaranteed. Soccer is distinct as a tool for development in its universal appeal and its ability to tell compelling stories, but its actual impact depends almost entirely on context and requires a type of rational analysis that is sometimes hard to come by with such an emotionally engaging game.

The game itself that February day in Moshi was ultimately unexceptional, ending as a 4–0 blowout that might not really have been worth watching—except for the simple fact that the whole scene was so damn interesting. It was just one of millions of soccer games that provide fun real-world laboratories for exploring ideas about how things do and should work in distinct social contexts. Using those laboratories, watching the game as a thinking fan, often starts with just noticing patterns, trends, symbols, behaviors, and other things with a sense of intellectual curiosity—and then, drawing on a critical consciousness, asking questions about those things. What, for example, was the actual impact of that Mbuzi Cup tournament on the school and the experience it offers students? Is sports really worth time and resources for a school struggling to meet basic educational needs? Does the emotional engagement of the fans bring the school community together or create divisions? Do the fundamental experiences of those emotions depend upon the cultural context of the games? How should players balance the possibilities of using their soccer talents while also fulfilling other aspects of their human potential? Are there ways such tournaments could be organized to maximize not just the soccer performance but also the development possibilities? Is there anything special about the sport being soccer?

The last question may be the easiest for me to answer. Yes, there is something special about soccer. We could have fun debating what exactly that something is, but the fact that soccer is the world's most popular game is meaningful in itself. Soccer, whether on a dirt pitch in the shadow of Mount Kilimanjaro or on the verdant green carpet of a World Cup stadium, distinctively combines play, competition, business, and science with identity, culture, reason, and emotion. Soccer integrates the science of human potential with humanistic concerns such as storytelling and the common good. The fact that soccer is also a relatively low-stakes endeavor—it is, ultimately, still a game—taken up virtually everywhere in the world makes it all the more useful as a space for exploring big questions. Thinking fandom in these contexts becomes a fun way to imagine new possibilities.

An Alternative Soccer?

Patterns, questions, and possibilities are as evident at the highest-profile version of the game as at the grassroots. We can take, for example, the men's World Cup. Starting with South Africa 2010, moving through Brazil 2014 and Russia 2018, and now building to Qatar 2022, the discourse around each tournament has a clear pattern of stages. These stages seem sadly predictable, but they also raise critical questions about what soccer might be.

The first stage around recent World Cups is unbridled and unrealistic promises for the power of soccer to change the world. A World Cup in South Africa was going to accelerate development across an entire continent; the 2014 World Cup was to be a crowning achievement for Brazil as an emerging world power; 2018 was to show Russia's openness to the global community; Qatar 2022 will, supposedly, showcase a new modernity in the Arab world.

The second stage, closely following the first, is skepticism and doubt. South Africa, the doubters thought, was too crime-ridden and poor. Brazil was too politically divided and corrupt. Russia was too autocratic and inept. Qatar, the critics say, is too small and immoral.

The third stage is nervous anticipation. There are regular stories about delayed stadium construction; intense coverage of political accommodations to buffer national image; and a sharp uptick in attention to the players and teams that just might actually be playing soccer sometime soon.

The fourth stage, at least in South Africa, Brazil, and Russia, is an amazingly fun and anodyne month of soccer—largely devoid both of global change (as promised in the first stage) and of major problems (as anticipated in the second stage). Despite irrational optimism, legitimate skepticism, genuine political and logistical problems, and a raft of real corruption, the soccer just keeps going.

The pattern here is simultaneously comforting and worrisome. It is comforting that the naysayers are often wrong about what happens when countries and communities away from the global north are given opportunities to join the party. The success of places such as South Africa and Brazil hosting the World Cup reinforces to a global audience the resourcefulness and talent distributed relatively evenly across the globe even when opportunities are not. It also reinforces the simple fact that soccer itself is indeed powerful. Remember, however that the power of soccer has a Janus-face. In the wrong hands, sportwashing—the use of soccer to deflect and distract from real social problems—can work. There is an obvious bread-and-circus component to elite soccer, providing moments of entertainment that produce misapprehensions of community harmony and illusions of equal opportunity. The power of soccer sometimes plays havoc with our critical faculties.

So, what is a thinking fan to do? One tempting option is to largely boycott mega-events such as the men's World Cup. This was the tactic, for example, of the thoughtful soccer writer and columnist Ian Plenderleith: "In 2018 I personally boycotted the Russia World Cup and used my writing to try and persuade others to do likewise." It didn't work. "The morning after England's quarterfinal game against Sweden I read that 22 million people watched the game on TV in Britain, and at that point I threw in the towel and ended up watching the last four matches."[2]

Plenderleith described his aborted boycott in an interview with German author Ronny Blaschke during a discussion of soccer and political exploitation. Blaschke's work highlights the various ways soccer has been used to garner political power for grassroots social movements, despite opposition from the powers that be, in places ranging from Turkey to Egypt to Argentina. Blaschke sees evidence in these examples that soccer can "politicize" people in positive ways, arguing that "an alternative soccer is a real possibility."[3]

While the politics of soccer is a topic for another book, imagining the possibility of "an alternative soccer" is at the heart of thinking fandom. I suspect Qatar 2022, the 2026 World Cup in North America, and many future elite competitions will perpetuate at least the broad outlines of the historical pattern. There will be debates and protests about broken promises, corruption, commercialization, inequality, misplaced priorities, and all the social problems embedded in global soccer, until the soccer becomes so fun that we all just end up watching. But if we watch with intellectual curiosity and critical consciousness, if we ask questions about alternative ways of hosting mega-sporting events and alternative ways of supporting the game, the important details of future World Cups might be different. There are ways to imagine an alternative soccer for the future, mostly aside from anything to do with the men's World Cup, that start with possibilities already available to thinking fans. What follows are examples of some such possibilities—modest ideas, suggested by the very social science of soccer, for using thinking fandom toward the greater good.

Celebrating Global Diversity

Though it risks sounding like a bland FIFA marketing slogan, the diversity embedded in soccer as a global game accessible across community types offers rich possibilities for a thinking fan. As just one prominent example, the standard trajectory described above for the men's World Cup does not yet hold on the women's side. Though women's soccer in much of the world is underfunded and undervalued, the game has grown rapidly and demonstrated an ability to destabilize gender norms, envision a more inclusive game, and empower players rather than administrators. More generally, women's soccer offers rich opportunities for using social science lenses by creating points of contrast and comparison—and for providing evidence that soccer can change. Diverse forms of the game, from this perspective, are critical for thinking about why soccer works the way it works, and for thinking about alternatives.

The ability of the women's game to help imagine an alternative soccer relates to its potential for countering hegemonic norms. In the classic social theory of Antonio Gramsci, hegemony is the process whereby the powers that be implicitly and explicitly set social norms in ways that earn tacit consent from those who are marginalized. These powers that be set the terms for social change so that any progress fails to challenge underlying power structures or ideologies.[4] Men's soccer, and men's sports more generally, often exerts hegemonic power by implicitly setting the standards for how the game should be organized and played. The growing interest in women's soccer is an important part of the hegemonic process in which men's norms are set as the standards for progress, which implicitly reinforces that those norms are right and true. The trick is that the norms of modern men's soccer, particularly at the elite level, are often deeply problematic in the ways they commodify players, prioritize private gains over public goods, emphasize winner-take-all competitions, glorify pain and aggression, promote illusions of meritocracy in the face of growing inequality, and reinforce other ugly (and potentially unnecessary) by-products of sport as an unfettered business.[5]

As women's soccer has battled for opportunities, the fight has often revolved around making women's soccer more like men's soccer, sometimes without due consideration of whether men's soccer offers a model worth emulating. Given the corruption, commercialism, and cynicism of men's elite soccer, why not pay as much attention to making men's soccer more like women's soccer? Women's soccer can help us envision a game that is more empowering to people than to business interests, a game where much of the initiative comes from the bottom up rather than from the top down, a game where a love of the sport still has a chance to thrive at the highest levels, and a game with the potential to transform social relations. Even on the field, research finds that women are less likely to dive and fake injuries to bait referees and opponents[6]—though that may be changing as the game adopts more of the men's model.[7]

If women's soccer might be used to reimagine hegemonic norms *in* the game, women's soccer supporters may also be able to help reimagine norms *around* the game. In my research on Portland Thorns fandom, I was interested to learn what made the Thorns an outlier as the highest-drawing women's professional sports team in the world. While some of the answer was similar to what makes for success in any spectator sports context, such as an appreciation for world-class soccer played in a quality venue with an energizing atmosphere, some of the answer was different from the hegemonic norm. Thorns fans felt that supporting local women's soccer fit with personal values around empowering women, diversity, and inclusion. Unlike many professional sports contexts, women's soccer has the possibility of bringing together diverse fans ranging from suburban soccer families to working-class fans who appreciate seeing world-class athletes at affordable prices to urban hipsters across gender and sexuality spectrums.

Women's soccer in the United States, and American soccer more broadly, has unfortunately not been as good at integrating diversity across racial, ethnic, and class groups. This has been particularly evident in the limited integration of official U.S. Soccer programs with widespread leagues and youth programs serving Latinx players and families,[8] but it is also evident in the coding of soccer in the United States as a "suburban" sport[9]—implying that soccer insulates itself from having to confront dramatic racial and economic inequities. Yet even here the truly global reach of soccer—the fact that it is the most popular sport across racial and class lines in most countries of the world—offers opportunities for thinking fandom. American soccer, like all of American society, needs to more intentionally work toward racial and economic justice. Empowering diverse voices and enabling thinking fandom can help with that work.

From a pure popularity perspective, an embrace of diversity and inclusion brings more people to the game. Soccer becomes accessible to those who might never otherwise engage with sports. From a more human perspective, embracing diversity and inclusion is a simple matter of justice, promoting genuinely equal opportunities and human rights. And for a thinking fan, embracing diversity in the game brings opportunities to learn more about how people work, how the world works, and what might be possible alternatives we can both imagine and, potentially, enact.

Acting Locally

The argument for diversity from social science also extends to the types of teams and leagues we follow. Homogeneity in playing styles, fan cultures, stadium designs, team aesthetics, coaching tactics, player development systems, and any other variable in the modern soccer equation is deadening. Heterogeneity can also go too far. Early incarnations of professional soccer in the United States, which included innovations such as one-on-one penalty shootouts starting thirty-five yards from goal, were at first weird and off-putting. But many fans also find it weird and off-putting when U.S. teams identify themselves as derivatives of famous European teams with no authentic connection to local communities. The fact that the men's professional team representing Utah is named Real Salt Lake, borrowing a name from Spanish tributes to their monarchy, is just bizarre. If I lived in Salt Lake City, however, I'd certainly be a full-blooded Real Salt Lake fan. Promoting diversity in the game, and fully engaging thinking fandom, compels us to support our local teams.

The idea of football localism is similar in concept to other forms of localism that have gained popularity in the midst of accelerating globalization. The local food movement has raised awareness that the ease of shipping and stocking food from far away is a problem for the environment, for local farms, and for meaningful food cultures. Local political movements build off the old cliché to "think globally, act locally" in recognition of the ways that democracy works best when people engage with the issues immediately outside their front door. And, likewise, the "support your local team" movement recognizes that global soccer will continue to thrive only if people have opportunities to engage with the game in their own communities.

Prioritizing localism in soccer is not always easy in our mass media age, where slickly produced games from England or Germany are available for streaming with just a few clicks. And this has been a real problem for soccer outside the big-money leagues. Whether in relatively wealthy countries, such as those of Scandinavia,[10] or in relatively poor countries, as in much of sub-Saharan Africa,[11] the media and marketing of leagues such as the English Premier League has drawn attention away from local teams and local football cultures. And this, in turn, is a problem for the global game, producing less diversity and more homogeneity. This then leads to fewer opportunities for innovation and fewer ways to foment grassroots engagement.

This is not, however, a call for thinking fans to abandon the wonders of the polished entertainment machines that are the top professional leagues. It can be great fun to pick an affiliation in the Premier League and look forward to that team's weekend fixture, even if it only provides a sense of imagined community and an opportunity to bask in reflected (or branded) glory.[12] The idea here, instead, is to return to the hybrid realities of globalization: fandom can also be "glocal." The game as a whole is more vibrant when fans can follow both Manchester United and Malmö, Bayern Munich and Mamelodi Sundowns, Real Madrid and Real Salt Lake. During my Fulbright year in Moshi, Tanzania, I took it as a fortuitous sign that the local Tanzanian *Ligi Kuu* team, Polisi Tanzania FC, had the same PTFC initials as my hometown Portland Thorns FC and Portland Timbers FC. None of those teams could actually expect to compete in head-to-head competition with teams I enjoy watching on TV, ranging from Barcelona to Brighton & Hove Albion, but each is immensely fun to follow when local. Each taps the ability of soccer to engage us emotionally and to tell stories about our communities and ourselves.

Some fans claim they don't like to watch their local teams, whether in Major League Soccer or the National Women's Soccer League or the minor leagues, because in terms of direct competition, the individual teams could not hold their own with teams from the Premier League or the Bundesliga. But sports entertainment is always personal. Americans enjoy college sports as much as professional sports not because the college athletes would beat the pros head-to-head, but because college teams make meaningful connections with communities while entertaining fans. Fans of combat sports enjoy watching lightweights as much as heavyweights because each offers an intriguing spin on the many different ways to excel. Supporting local soccer, in other words, offers thinking fans raw entertainment, a chance to build community, and further ideas for how an alternative soccer might be possible.

Thinking Culturally

One further benefit of supporting local soccer is the opportunity to appreciate different soccer cultures. These cultures are sometimes on display superficially at the elite level, but more often they are instantiated through the grassroots of the game. In fact, cultural variations in the elite game are only the tip of the proverbial iceberg—or, in parlance more often used by sports administrators, the tip of the pyramid. National soccer associations often talk about soccer using a pyramid metaphor, recognizing that World Cup teams and top professional leagues are only the narrow point at the top of a much wider base. If the base of the pyramid, the youth game and the recreational game, is not solid then nothing good can go on top. To have a solid base, to have a robust and vibrant grassroots game that engages local communities, requires thinking culturally.

American grassroots soccer offers a useful example of how culture infuses the base of the soccer pyramid. U.S. soccer is somewhat distinct in the world for its heavy emphasis on a "pay-for-play" system of largely privatized youth soccer. Though there are still many recreational soccer leagues for younger players and organizations such as AYSO that offer reasonable-cost leagues, beyond a certain level the U.S. youth soccer scene is dominated by private clubs with coaches paid primarily from team fees. One survey of youth sports costs undertaken by the Aspen Institute and Utah State University, for example, found that soccer parents can spend up to $9,500 per year for one child (though average spending was much lower due to younger recreational participation).[13] Further, children in the United States quit playing soccer at only nine years of age on average, the second-earliest age of quitting among the twenty-one sports included in the Aspen Institute survey (behind only gymnastics). Only 7 percent of American parents reported that their kids play soccer for free.

These costs are partially about the cultural history of soccer in the United States. Unlike other parts of the world, the United States has few community sports clubs that encourage mass participation across a variety of sports. The most famous Spanish and German clubs, such as Barcelona and Bayern Munich, sponsor a range of teams and have huge membership rolls in their communities. Further, nearly all major European professional teams have long had extensive youth programs that offer elite training for players of all ages—funded largely by the promise of at least a few of those players eventually joining the first team, rather than being funded by a family budget. As we learned in the discussion on talent development, some of these models have also become infused with a business ethos that commodifies youth players. But that business mindset is filtered to some extent by the deep cultural roots and broader accessibility of many global soccer clubs.

In the United States, the idea that soccer, and sports more generally, should be broadly accessible has largely been the domain of schools, along with some civic parks and recreation departments. High school and college sports are culturally distinct in their prominence; virtually no other national sports systems rely on the broader educational system to provide

opportunities for talented athletes. But schools have often filled the gap created by the absence of community sports clubs in other parts of the world
and have, at least in concept, added an educational mission to youth sports.

In a vain and countercultural effort to adopt a more European model of
youth soccer, however, U.S. soccer has consistently tried to marginalize
school soccer and recreational soccer in favor of a professional academy system. This was most dramatic when the U.S. Soccer Federation started its
elite "U.S. Soccer Development Academy" program in 2007. The intention
was to separate out a group of elite youth clubs and youth teams from American professional clubs into a year-round academy system that would try to
mimic the European professional model. Part of that was explicitly forbid-
ding academy players from playing high school soccer, which was a massive
change for American players that generated much controversy and discussion. When explaining this thinking, the U.S. Soccer Federation made an
explicit argument for homogenizing global systems and for treating players as
commodities, appealing to the need to compete in a "global marketplace."[14]

Apparently, the U.S. Development Academy lost in this market competition because in March 2020, under the cover of the COVID-19 lockdown,
U.S. Soccer folded the Development Academy program entirely. Though
some good players came through the Development Academy system, there
was no compelling evidence that U.S. talent development had improved its
productivity through the global market-driven academy model. Instead, the
demise of the Development Academy may offer some grudging recognition
that what works in Europe may not work in the United States. In the wake of
the Development Academy's collapse there have been moves to ensure more
collaboration between U.S. professional franchises and U.S. youth soccer
clubs, including broadening opportunities outside the professional pipeline.
What evolves will likely work best if it recognizes that the global oddity of
American soccer, including school soccer, is simply an example of how soccer cultures can vary according to history and social context.

Though this is just one example of how thinking culturally can shape the
game, culture is as ubiquitous in soccer as it is in our lives and communities.
As discussed throughout this book, culture is not all-powerful. There are
some universal themes to how the human mind works, how societies work,
and maybe even how to produce talented soccer players. But there are also
always important cultural variations. Recognizing the way cultural mean-

ings weave into both the tip and the base of any given soccer pyramid offers thinking fans deeper insights into both the past and future of soccer.

Promoting Accessibility

As should by now be obvious, I am a big fan of school soccer in most any cultural context. This is not because school soccer by itself is particularly entertaining or pure—school soccer is often a scrappy game with uneven levels of competition, and sports can quickly muddle educational priorities. Instead, my fandom of school soccer derives from the fact that schools in most societies are relatively equal-access social institutions with deep community roots that offer the best chance to distribute sports widely and equitably. The principle is to support any community-based effort to make soccer more accessible, and to strengthen the base of the soccer pyramid. Thinking fans interested in accessibility need to pay attention to school soccer, but also to youth soccer, recreational soccer, and spaces for soccer that make the game available more broadly from the bottom up.

Promoting accessibility sometimes requires thinking conceptually about the structural organization of soccer. When, for example, international organizations try to use soccer for development purposes, they often undertake targeted programs in a few marginalized communities. While those programs can be great on their own, they do not have much chance of creating broader social change unless explicitly attached to policy agendas. Likewise, as a related example, when elite youth soccer clubs try to promote access, they often focus on enrolling a few marginalized—but very talented—youth players. While scholarships for talented players do result in compelling individual stories, they do little to genuinely broaden the talent pool or the opportunity structure. Schools, on the other hand, serve most children in most places and offer a chance to find hidden talent, broaden participation opportunities, and potentially infuse some educational values into the game. Whether in rural Tanzania or suburban Portland, a future with more school soccer seems to me the best chance for the game to be more genuinely accessible.

Even in schools, though, not everyone who might benefit from the game gets to play. School teams still tend to select only the most talented players, and filter others who might enjoy playing. This is where investments in community spaces and places should also be important to the thinking fan. Park spaces, public fields, and community recreation programs that promote "sport for all" are an essential component of a healthy grassroots soccer culture, as we saw in examples like the development of soccer in Iceland. American soccer fans often bemoan the lack of opportunities for kids to play the types of "street soccer" famously associated with the skills of Brazilians or Ghanaians or others who grew up playing freely with friends. But street soccer isn't possible without shared public spaces where kids can gather and play.

As one example of an effort that encapsulates thinking fandom and accessibility, the Timbers Army 107 Independent Supporters Trust (in my hometown of Portland, Oregon) has operated "Operation Pitch Invasion" since right around the time their Timbers joined Major League Soccer in 2011. Their mission is to use the volunteer power of Timbers fans, along with charitable donations, to "Build. Revitalize. Maintain . . . soccer fields and futsal courts in parks and schools so that kids of all ages have high-quality and safe playing surfaces to enjoy the beautiful game."[15] In practice they have engaged in several significant projects, in collaboration with the Portland Timbers' "Stand Together" corporate social responsibility initiative, to create "Fields for All" at several Portland-area schools and parks, often successfully repurposing underused and ill-maintained spaces, such as old tennis courts, into futsal courts.[16]

While we've seen that these types of projects are never as simple as they first seem, the concept of using fan initiative and local team resources to make soccer more accessible through the simple act of creating spaces to play is something any thinking fan should get behind. The tagline on the Operation Pitch Invasion website is "soccer from the grassroots up," and the principles that guide the group's work include health, access, talent, and community—a worthy articulation of what soccer at its best can provide. The chances of soccer actually being at its best, along with opportunities for employing very social science of soccer, depend on the types of grassroots accessibility that schools, youth programs, recreational leagues, parks, and, just perhaps, thinking fans can provide.

The Future of the Very Social Science of Soccer

One final example of ways to enact thinking fandom may be the noblest of all: play. I mean that literally for those of us privileged enough have opportunities to get out on the field, but I also mean that metaphorically as a reminder of what soccer should ultimately be about. In his book *The Age of Football*, writer, journalist, and sociologist David Goldblatt contrasts the logics of money and power surrounding modern soccer with "the logics of play" at the game's core.[17] He suggests that, in the face of the blinding spectacle that is much of elite soccer, "if we wish to retain some of the life and spontaneity of our game, if we want to preserve the real solidarities and collective identities we derive from it, if we think football should not be dominated by money and power alone," then we have to engage the game by centering play.

In my own journey as a thinking fan, play has provided an essential balance to my more cerebral work as a teacher and scholar. I had, for example, one of my favorite soccer experiences while undertaking the research on school extracurriculars in Tanzania described briefly at the start of this chapter. It turned out that a teammate of mine from my college soccer days twenty-five years prior had settled in a small village sixty kilometers down the road and was organizing a regular pickup game. Every Tuesday and Friday, an eclectic group of Tanzanians and expats ranging in age from twenty-ish to fifty-ish gathered at the local international school in the shadow of Mount Meru, ending the game only when it was too dark to see the ball. The field was mostly pristine green, bar the occasional invasion of termites building mounds that could twist an ankle with their sturdiness. The game was often intense but almost never angry. We refereed ourselves, and one of the senior Tanzanians always distributed the colored training bibs in a way that ensured a competitive game and a healthy mix of personalities. The primary language was Kiswahili, but there was also a regular smattering of English, German, Dutch, Hindi, French, and other local dialects. I only occasionally understood the verbal banter and playful jousting that seems to be a universal feature of pickup soccer, but I quite regularly recognized the emotional engagement that had been there all my life in moments of joy, frustration, comradery, focus, and curiosity that make me feel alive.

After the sun had set, some of us would retreat to a roadside bar with plastic chairs, friendly service, and a "chef" with a reputation for grilling particularly prime cuts of goat from the carcass hanging in the window. Though I personally preferred the *mkuku* (chicken), having the goat available made me feel like I had won the Mbuzi Cup every time. Then, over a few beverages, we'd trade stories. Some were about events of the week, local politics, family, or work. But most were about soccer. What was the latest update on Arsenal in the EPL? Eintracht Frankfurt in the Bundesliga? The U.S. Women's National Team? The Taifa Stars representing Tanzania in World Cup qualifiers? The Asian Cup? The Portland Timbers in MLS or the Thorns in the NWSL? Angers SCO in France's Ligue 1? Polisi Tanzania FC or Simba or Yanga in Ligi Kuu? FC Utrecht in the Erdivisie? The conversations, and the possibilities offered by the global game, were endless.

The very social science of soccer was, in other words, all there. There were the identity claims that came with our fandom, the cultural pluralism evident in different languages and experiences engaging one shared interest, the delicate balance between our rational and emotional selves—on show in moments of overzealousness on the field or in arguments about the World Cup or the Champions League. There was the universality of soccer, its ability to serve as a vessel for deep human needs including emotional engagement and storytelling. There were opportunities to play, and to play with ideas, in ways that only soccer can provide.

I've only had space in this book to play with some of the many ideas prompted by the very social science of soccer. The intention was not to be comprehensive, but to offer a way of engaging with the game that can be enriching, educational, and impactful. In this final chapter, in exploring what the future of the game could look like, I've suggested there are some specific ways to use social science perspectives to be a thinking fan: celebrating diversity, supporting locally, thinking culturally, and promoting accessibility. But that too is not a comprehensive list. Ultimately, thinking fandom is a habit of mind that should be supple enough to adapt over time and across the places both soccer, and our lives more generally, may take us.

There is, in other words, no one right way to do thinking fandom just as there is no one right way to do soccer itself. No one grand scientific theory will ever explain soccer. Using data and systematic research is important as long as it is done with a recognition that soccer is a social phenomenon engaged by people, not a controlled experiment designed for robots. Using accumulated knowledge, concepts, and theories also offers rich possibilities for understanding—as long as they are used with a recognition that soccer is a deeply cultural game with meanings that are pluralistic and dynamic.

For those involved in the soccer industry, soccer has increasingly become a business, a chance to make money or market products. For many others the game is just an escape from the rest of the world, a televised distraction, a way to run off excess energy, or a chance to go to a stadium and emote. For a thinking fan it can be those things. But with intellectual curiosity, critical consciousness, and social science lenses, it can also be more. Soccer, with a particular way of thinking, is a rare chance to be actively engaged in stories that say something about people, society, and a global community transfixed by playing a game.

NOTES

Chapter 1: Lenses

1. "ŠIMUNIĆ-za dom spremni; Nazi Chanting Croatian Soccer Player?" YouTube, November 20, 2013, https://www.youtube.com/watch?v=Scz QKPkuA_4.

2. Associated Press, "Croatia's Josip Simunic Defends 'Pro-Nazi' World Cup Celebration Chant," *The Guardian*, November 20, 2013, https://www .theguardian.com/football/2013/nov/20/croatia-josip-simunic-defends-apparent -pro-nazi-chant.

3. News Corp Australia, "Aussie-Born Croatia Player Josip Simunic Banned from World Cup over Nazi Chants," *The Advertiser*, May 12, 2014, https://www .adelaidenow.com.au/sport/football/aussieborn-croatia-player-josip-simunic -banned-from-world-cup-over-nazi-chants/. For an academic analysis of how the Balkan conflict plays out in Australian soccer, see Binoy Kampmark, "Australian Soccer Rivalries: Diasporas, Violence and the Balkan Connection," *Soccer & Society* 19, no. 5–6 (July 2018): 875–887. doi:10.1080/14660970.2017.1399603.

4. Mister Football, "The Man Who Earnt Three Yellow Cards," *Roar*, February 7, 2016, https://www.theroar.com.au/2016/02/08/the-man-who-earnt-three -yellow-cards/.

5. Franklin Foer, *How Soccer Explains the World: An Unlikely Theory of Globalization* (New York: Harper Perennial, 2010).

6. David Goldblatt, *The Ball Is Round* (New York: Riverhead Books, 2006); Simon Kuper and Stefan Szymanski, *Soccernomics: Why England Loses; Why Germany, Spain, and France Win; and Why One Day Japan, Iraq, and the United States Will Become Kings of the World's Most Popular Sport* (New York: Nation Books, 2018).

7. See: http://footballscholars.org/ and https://footballcollective.org.uk/.

8. National Federation of State High School Associations, "Participation Statistics," accessed April 27, 2021, https://members.nfhs.org/participation _statistics.

9. Erik H. Erikson, *Childhood and Society* (New York: W. W. Norton, 1950).

10. Eric J. Hobsbawm, *Nations and Nationalism since 1780: Programme, Myth, Reality* (Cambridge: Cambridge University Press, 1990), 143.

11. Benedict R. Anderson, *Imagined Communities: Reflections on the Origin and Spread of Nationalism* (London: Verso, 1991).

12. "Theory: Floating Signifier," Beautiful Trouble, https://beautifultrouble .org/theory/floating-signifier/.

13. See Alexander Abnos, "Start of Something Big," *Sports Illustrated*, accessed April 27, 2021, https://www.si.com/longform/soccer-goals/goal4.html. There were prior efforts at holding women's soccer world championships, such as the 1971 Copa Mundial de Futbol Femenina in Mexico City; though the 1995 event was the first FIFA sanctioned, it is important to emphasize that the history of women's soccer does not start with FIFA. For some of the more nuanced history, see Jeré Longman, "In Women's World Cup Origin Story, Fact and Fiction Blur," *New York Times*, June 25, 2019, https://www.nytimes.com/2019/06/25/sports /womens-world-cup-france.html.

14. See, for example, Tim Rees, S. Alexander Haslam, Pete Coffee, and David Lavallee, "A Social Identity Approach to Sport Psychology: Principles, Practice, and Prospects," *Sports Medicine* 45, no. 8 (2015): 1083–1096.

15. Mark Dyreson, *Crafting Patriotism for Global Dominance: America at the Olympics* (New York: Routledge, 2009).

16. Andrei S. Markovits and Steven L. Hellerman, *Offside: Soccer and American Exceptionalism* (Princeton, NJ: Princeton University Press, 2001). See also Stefan Szymanski and Andrew S. Zimbalist, *National Pastime: How Americans Play Baseball and the Rest of the World Plays Soccer* (Washington, D.C.: Brookings Institution Press, 2006).

17. Andrei S. Markovits and Steven L. Hellerman, "Women's Soccer in the United States: Yet Another American 'Exceptionalism,'" *Soccer & Society* 4, no. 2–3 (2003): 14–29.

18. FIFA Women's Football Survey 2014, accessed April 27, 2021, https:// resources.fifa.com/image/upload/fifa-women-s-football-survey-2522649.pdf ?cloudid=emtgxvpoibnebltlvi3b.

19. C. Wright Mills, *The Sociological Imagination* (New York: Oxford University Press, 2000).

20. Stefan Szymanski and Silke-Maria Weineck, *It's Football, Not Soccer (and Vice Versa): On the History, Emotion, and Ideology Behind One of the Internet's Most Ferocious Debates* (n.p., 2018).

21. Steve Hendricks, "Letter from America: Happy 130th Birthday to English 'Soccer,'" *Sporting Intelligence*, December 6, 2015, http://www.sportingintelligence .com/2015/12/06/letter-from-america-happy-130th-birthday-to-english-soccer -071201/.

22. Stefan Szymanski, "It's Football Not Soccer," May 2014, http://ns.umich .edu/Releases/2014/June14/Its-football-not-soccer.pdf.

23. Szymanski, 4.

24. Hendricks, "Letter from America."

25. David Polkinghorne, "Documentary Helps Josip Simunic Continue His Fight to Clear His Name after FIFA Ban," *Sydney Morning Herald*, February 5, 2016, https://www.smh.com.au/sport/soccer/documentary-helps-josip-simunic -continue-his-fight-to-clear-his-name-after-fifa-ban-20160204-gmleu8.html.

Chapter 2: Fans

1. I have written about this experience previously, and some of this introductory section borrows from Andrew Guest, "Screaming U-S-A! (and Other Imagined Things): Us versus Them at South Africa 2010," in *Africa's World Cup: Critical Reflections on Play, Patriotism, Spectatorship, and Space,* eds. Peter Alegi and Chris Bolsmann (Ann Arbor: University of Michigan Press, 2013).

2. See, for example, Daniel L. Wann and Jeffrey D. James, *Sport Fans: The Psychology and Social Impact of Fandom* (New York: Routledge, 2018); Erin C. Tarver, *The I in Team: Sports Fandom and the Reproduction of Identity* (Chicago: University of Chicago Press, 2017); Justine Gubar, *Fanaticus: Mischief and Madness in the Modern Sports Fan* (Lanham, MD: Rowman & Littlefield, 2015); and George Dohrmann, *Superfans: Into the Heart of Obsessive Sports Fandom* (New York: Ballantine Books, 2018).

3. Emile Durkheim, *The Elementary Forms of Religious Life*, trans. Joseph Ward Swain (London: George Allen & Unwin, 1915). https://www.gutenberg.org /files/41360/41360-h/41360-h.htm.

4. Durkheim, 218.

5. Sven Ismer, "Embodying the Nation: Football, Emotions and the Construction of Collective Identity," *Nationalities Papers* 39, no. 4 (2011): 547–565.

6. See A. J. McCarthy, "This World Cup Commercial Featuring the Chilean Miners Will Give You Chills," *Slate*, June 13, 2014, https://slate.com/culture /2014/06/chilean-miners-world-cup-commercial-this-amazing-banco-de-chile -ad-will-give-you-chills-video.html.

7. William James, *The Varieties of Religious Experience* (1902; repr., Cambridge, MA: Harvard University Press, 1985).

8. Eric Simons, *The Secret Lives of Sports Fans: The Science of Sports Obsession* (New York: Overlook Duckworth, 2013).

9. See Paul C. Bernhardt, James M. Dabbs Jr., Julie A. Fielden, and Candice D. Lutter, "Testosterone Changes during Vicarious Experiences of Winning and Losing among Fans at Sporting Events," *Physiology & Behavior* 65, no. 1 (1998): 59–62.

10. Simons, *Secret Lives of Sports Fans*, 35.

11. Simons, 49.

12. Exact figures for women's sports leagues around the world are difficult to find, but in 2020 FIFPRO, the global organization representing professional football players, published a report on global women's football listing the average attendance for the U.S.-based NWSL in the most recent 2018–2019 season as 7,337 (skewed by the Thorns as an outlier); for the Australian W-League as 1,796; for the English WSL as 1,010; for the Swedish Damallsvenskan as 870; for the German Frauen-Bundesliga as 833; for France's Division 1 Féminine as 920; and for Norway's Toppserien as 269. See FIFPRO, "Raising Our Game: 2020 Women's Football Report," accessed June 24, 2020, https://www.fifpro.org/media/vd1pbtbj/fifpro-womens-report_eng-lowres.pdf, 33.

13. For the original research paper, some of which is included in this chapter, see Andrew M. Guest and Anne Luijten, "Fan Culture and Motivation in the Context of Successful Women's Professional Team Sports: A Mixed-Methods Case Study of Portland Thorns fandom," *Sport in Society* 21, no. 7 (2018): 1013–1030.

14. For the original BIRGing research, see Robert B. Cialdini, Richard J. Borden, Avril Thorne, Marcus Randall Walker, Stephen Freeman, and Lloyd Reynolds Sloan, "Basking in Reflected Glory: Three (Football) Field Studies," *Journal of Personality and Social Psychology* 34, no. 3 (1976): 366. For a more recent review, see Jonathan A. Jensen, Brian A. Turner, Jeffrey James, Chad McEvoy, Chad Seifried, Elizabeth Delia, T. Christopher Greenwell, Stephen Ross, and Patrick Walsh, "Forty Years of BIRGing: New Perspectives on Cialdini's Seminal Studies," *Journal of Sport Management* 30, no. 2 (2016): 149–161.

15. Daniel L. Wann, Merrill J. Melnick, Gordon W. Russell, and Dale G. Pease, *Sport Fans: The Psychology and Social Impact of Spectators* (New York: Routledge, 2001).

16. Cialdini et al., *Basking in Reflected Glory*.

17. D. L. Wann, P. J. Waddill, J. Polk, and S. Weaver, "The Team Identification–Social Psychological Health Model: Sport Fans Gaining Connections to Others via Sport Team Identification," *Group Dynamics: Theory, Research, and Practice* 15, no. 1 (2011): 75.

18. For these and other findings, see Guest and Luijten, "Fan Culture and Motivation."

19. Amir Ben Porat, "Football Fandom: A Bounded Identification," *Soccer & Society* 11, no. 3 (2010): 277–290. doi:10.1080/14660971003619594.

20. Richard Giulianotti, "Supporters, Followers, Fans, and Flaneurs: A Taxonomy of Spectator Identities in Football," *Journal of Sport and Social Issues* 26, no. 1 (2002): 25–46.

21. Desmond Morris, *The Soccer Tribe* (London: Jonathan Cape, 1981).

22. Morris, 8.

23. Roy F. Baumeister, *The Cultural Animal: Human Nature, Meaning, and Social Life* (New York: Oxford University Press, 2005).

24. For an academic overview, see Dominic Ed Abrams and Michael A. Hogg, *Social Identity Theory: Constructive and Critical Advances* (London: Pearson Education, 1990).

25. Muzafer Sherif, O. J. Harvey, B. Jack White, William R. Hood, Carolyn W. Sherif, *Intergroup Conflict and Cooperation: The Robbers Cave Experiment*, originally published 1954/1961, accessed May 1, 2021, https://psychclassics.yorku .ca/Sherif/index.htm.

26. There is some recent debate about the extent to which Sherif and his research team actively facilitated the group enmity in the original Robbers Cave study; see Gina Perry, *The Lost Boys: Inside Muzafer Sherif's Robbers Cave Experiment* (Victoria, Australia: Scribe Publications, 2018). In my reading it seems true that Sherif did not fully disclose the active efforts of his research team, but it is also true that under the right conditions the boys were primed to form into competitive groupings.

27. Though not a scholarly work, the video of Jane Elliot's experiment is available through PBS at "A Class Divided," PBS Frontline, March 26, 1985, accessed May 1, 2021, https://www.pbs.org/wgbh/frontline/film/class-divided/.

28. Judith Rich Harris, "Where Is the Child's Environment? A Group Socialization Theory of Development," *Psychological Review* 102, no. 3 (1995): 458–489.

29. Judith Rich Harris, *The Nurture Assumption: Why Children Turn Out the Way They Do* (New York: Free Press, 2009).

30. Jeffrey W. Kassing and Lindsey J. Meân, eds., *Perspectives on the U.S.– Mexico Soccer Rivalry: Passion and Politics in Red, White, Blue, and Green* (Palgrave Macmillan, 2017).

31. Kassing and Meân, viii.

32. See Dave Zirin, "After Donovan's Goal: Joy or Jingoism?," *The Nation*, June 23, 2010, https://www.thenation.com/article/after-donovans-goal-joy-or-jingoism/.

33. Roxane Coche and Oscar Guerra, "Food-Ball: Tailgates That Enculturate before US–Mexico Fútbol Matches," in *Perspectives on the U.S.–Mexico Soccer Rivalry* (Cham, Switzerland: Palgrave Macmillan, 2017), 223–241.

34. For an academic overview of the meaning of the term in soccer contexts, see Nathian Shae Rodriguez, "# FIFAputos: A Twitter Textual Analysis Over 'Puto' at the 2014 World Cup," *Communication & Sport* 5, no. 6 (2017): 712–731.

35. See Victor Balta, "'Homophoic and Not Very Clever': Why Puto Chants Haunt Mexican Football," June 18, 2018, https://www.theguardian.com/football /2018/jun/18/puto-chants-mexico-football-world-cup.

36. Coche and Guerra, "Food-Ball," 228.

37. Coche and Guerra, 233–234.

38. Roxane Coche, Lindsey J. Meân, and Oscar Guerra, "Bicultural Stress, Soccer, and Rivalry: How Mexican-Americans Experience the Soccer Competition between Their Two Countries," in *Perspectives on the US-Mexico Soccer Rivalry* (Cham, Switzerland: Palgrave Macmillan, 2017), 265–287.

39. Coche, Meân, and Guerra, 273–274.

Chapter 3: Cultures

1. The league was technically amateur, though it was the top national league and the best teams had generous sponsors that also provided jobs for the best players. It was well covered in the local news and an object of much local interest, though the fact that Malawi was then one of few remaining countries in the world without any local television stations contributed to decidedly low-budget operations.

2. For classic critiques from cultural anthropology see, for example, Lila Abu-Lughod, "Writing against Culture," in *Recapturing Anthropology: Working in the Present*, ed. Richard Fox (Santa Fe, NM: School of American Research Press, 1991), 137–162, and James Clifford, *The Predicament of Culture: Twentieth-century Ethnography, Literature, and Art* (Cambridge, MA: Harvard University Press, 1988).

3. See chapter 4 on "bio-banding" and the idea of grouping players by size and ability rather than by strict chronological age.

4. See, for example, Joseph Maguire, "Sport and Globalization," *Handbook of Sports Studies* (2000): 356–369, or Mauro F. Guillén, "Is Globalization Civilizing, Destructive or Feeble? A Critique of Five Key Debates in the Social Science Literature," *Annual Review of Sociology* 27, no. 1 (2001): 235–260.

5. George Ritzer, *The McDonaldization of Society* (Thousand Oaks, CA: Pine Forge Press, 1993).

6. David L. Andrews and George Ritzer, "The Grobal in the Sporting Glocal," *Global Networks* 7, no. 2 (2007): 135–153.

7. Richard A. Shweder, Jacqueline J. Goodnow, Giyoo Hatano, Robert A. LeVine, Hazel R. Markus, and Peggy J. Miller, "The Cultural Psychology of Development: One Mind, Many Mentalities," *Handbook of Child Psychology* 1 (2007).

8. Gary Chick, "Games and Sports," in *Explaining Human Culture*, ed. C. R. Ember (2015). Human Relations Area Files, accessed January 10, 2020, http:// hraf.yale.edu/ehc/summaries/games-and-sports.

9. "Why Does Every Soccer Player Do This?," *New York Times*, July 10, 2018, https://www.nytimes.com/2018/07/10/sports/world-cup/england-croatia-france-belgium.html.

10. Jessica L. Tracy and David Matsumoto, "The Spontaneous Expression of Pride and Shame: Evidence for Biologically Innate Nonverbal Displays," *Proceedings of the National Academy of Sciences* 105, no. 33 (2008): 11655–11660.

11. See also David Goldblatt, "How Soccer Enables the English to Feel . . . Well, English," Al Jazeera America, June 13, 2014, accessed June 9, 2020, http://america.aljazeera.com/articles/2014/6/13/england-soccer-identity.html.

12. Tom Gibbons, "Contrasting Representations of Englishness during FIFA World Cup Finals," *Sport in History* 30, no. 3 (2010): 422–446.

13. Gibbons also argues that the use of different flags may not mean as much to fans as it does to academics, and sees the shift to the St. George's Cross flag as a largely practical one. See Tom Gibbons, *English National Identity and Football Fan Culture: Who Are Ya?* (Surrey, England: Ashgate Publishing, 2014).

14. Though there is some dispute about where and how soccer was invented, there is little dispute that the British were the first to codify the rules in 1863 when the Football Association (FA) was formed and a formal distinction was made between "Rugby football" (favored at the English prep school of Rugby) and "association football"—from which the term "soccer" likely derives.

15. John Hughson, *England and the 1966 World Cup: A Cultural History* (Manchester, England: Manchester University Press, 2016).

16. For an academic analysis, see Neil Ewen, "Team GB, or No Team GB, That Is the Question: Olympic Football and the Post-war Crisis of Britishness," *Sport in History* 32, no. 2 (2012): 302–324.

17. The women's situation is potentially more complicated because the Olympics are considered an international tournament on par with the FIFA World Cup, and thus there is more determination for a full team from Great Britain to participate. See, for example, "Home Nations Far from United Over GB Women's Olympic Football Team," *The Guardian*, November 5, 2019, https://www.theguardian.com/football/blog/2019/nov/05/home-nations-gb-womens-olympic-football-team-tokyo-2020.

18. See Kris Voakes, "Forty Years On—How Viv Anderson Became England's First Black Player," *Goal*, November 29, 2018, https://www.goal.com/en-tza/news/forty-years-on-how-viv-anderson-became-englands-first-black/1dbgnwzdcilw51rn26wdxrizkv.

19. Kuper and Syzmanski argue this is a significant problem for England—limiting the country's talent pool and perpetuating a single-minded approach to the game. See Simon Kuper and Stefan Szymanski, *Soccernomics: Why England Loses, Why Spain, Germany, and Brazil Win, and Why the US, Japan, Australia—and*

Even Iraq—Are Destined to Become the Kings of the World's Most Popular Sport (New York: Nation Books, 2014).

20. Jean Williams, *A Game for Rough Girls?: A History of Women's Football in Britain* (London: Routledge, 2003), 6.

21. Alex Dibble, "Proportion of British BAME Players Has Doubled Since the Premier League Began—talkSPORT Special Report," talkSPORT, August 15, 2017, https://talksport.com/football/269320/proportion-british-bame-players -has-doubled-premier-league-began-talksport-special-report/.

22. See Williams, *A Game for Rough Girls?*

23. "In Game Anti-Racism Warnings As Rüdiger Faces Abuse at Spurs," AP News, December 22, 2019, https://apnews.com/a30f2df110705d066d706a2d7c0096ff.

24. "Tottenham Promise to Take 'Strongest Action' Over Racial Abuse," *The Guardian*, December 22, 2019, https://www.theguardian.com/football/2019/dec /22/chelsea-tottenham-premier-league-racist-abuse-stadium-announcement.

25. David Goldblatt, *The Game of Our Lives: The Meaning and Making of English Football* (New York: Nation Books, 2014).

26. See David Hirshey and Roger Bennett, "Soccer Isn't For Ballerinas," ESPN .com, April 29, 2010, https://www.espn.com/world-cup/columns/story/_/id /5146962/ce/us/thugs-hard-men.

27. Eduardo Galeano, *Soccer in Sun and Shadow* (London: Verso, 1998), 209.

28. Scott Waalkes, "Does Soccer Explain the World or Does the World Explain Soccer? Soccer and Globalization," *Soccer & Society* 18, no. 2–3 (2017): 166–180.

29. Pelé with Brian Winter "Why Soccer Matters," (New York: Celebra, 2014), 92.

30. Galeano, *Soccer in Sun and Shadow*, 209.

31. Alex Bellos, *Futebol: The Brazilian Way of Life-Updated Edition* (New York: Bloomsbury Publishing, 2014), 361.

32. For an academic analysis of the protests, see James Holston, "'Come to the Street!'": Urban Protest, Brazil 2013," *Anthropological Quarterly* 87, no. 3 (2014): 887–900.

33. "Brazil's Leaders Caught Out by Mass Protests," BBC News, June 18, 2013, https://www.bbc.com/news/world-latin-america-22947466.

34. "Police Clashes at Start of Brazil Confederations Cup Final," BBC News, July 1, 2013, https://www.bbc.com/news/world-latin-america-23121532.

35. Janet Lever, "Soccer: Opium of the Brazilian people," *Trans-action* 7, no. 2 (1969): 36–43.

36. Roberto DaMatta, "Soccer: Opium for the People or Drama of Social Justice?" *Social Change in Contemporary Brazil* (1988): 125–133.

37. Roberto DaMatta, "Sport in Society: An Essay on Brazilian Football," *VIBRANT-Vibrant Virtual Brazilian Anthropology* 6, no. 2 (2009): 98–120. https://www.redalyc.org/pdf/4069/406941908006.pdf.

38. DaMatta, "Sport in Society," 107.

39. "Neymar Draws Inspiration from Protests," *The Irish Times*, June 20, 2013, https://www.irishtimes.com/sport/soccer/neymar-draws-inspiration-from -protests-1.1436528.

40. "Football in South Africa," South Africa History On-Line, accessed June 6, 2020, https://www.sahistory.org.za/article/football-south-africa.

41. "60th FIFA Congress, Johannesburg 2010," FIFA.com, June 9, 2010, https://www.fifa.com/who-we-are/news/congress-opens-with-message-from -mandela-1232711.

42. Lloyd Hill, "Football as Code: The Social Diffusion of 'Soccer' in South Africa," *Soccer & Society* 11, no. 1–2 (2010): 12–28.

43. Hill, 23–24.

44. Chris Bolsmann, "White Football in South Africa: Empire, Apartheid and Change, 1892–1977," *Soccer & Society* 11, no. 1–2 (2010): 29–45.

45. Cynthia Fabrizio Pelak, "Women and Gender in South African Soccer: A Brief History," *Soccer & Society* 11, no. 1–2 (2010): 63–78.

46. "Eudy Simelane," South Africa History On-Line, accessed June 4, 2020, https://www.sahistory.org.za/people/eudy-simelane.

47. Sifiso Mxolisi Ndlovu, "Sports as Cultural Diplomacy: The 2010 FIFA World Cup in South Africa's Foreign Policy," *Soccer & Society* 11, no. 1–2 (2010): 144–153.

48. Ashwin Desai and Goolam Vahed, "World Cup 2010: Africa's Turn or the Turn on Africa?" *Soccer & Society* 11, no. 1–2 (2010): 154–167.

49. Peter Alegi and Chris Bolsmann, eds., *Africa's World Cup: Critical Reflections on Play, Patriotism, Spectatorship, and Space* (Ann Arbor: University of Michigan Press, 2013), vii.

50. Loenard Solms, "Football and Feminism: South African Football Still Grappling with Toxic Masculinity," Extratime Media, January 24, 2020, https:// extratime.media/2020/01/24/football-and-feminism-south-african-football-still -grappling-with-toxic-masculinity/.

51. "Premier League Fans Summary," Global Web Index, accessed June 9 2020, https://insight.globalwebindex.net/hs-fs/hub/304927/file-2593818997-.

Chapter 4: Players

1. "Qatari Soccer Empire Buys a Foothold in Europe," *New York Times*, July 15, 2014, https://www.nytimes.com/2014/07/16/sports/worldcup/a-qatari -soccer-program-looking-to-rise-buys-a-foothold-in-europe.html; and "Seeking Soccer Respect, Qatar Looked Abroad," *New York Times*, July 14, 2014, https:// www.nytimes.com/2014/07/15/sports/worldcup/in-qatars-bid-for-soccer

-respect-big-bankroll-and-imported-talent.html; Sebastian Abbot, *The Away Game: The Epic Search for Soccer's Next Superstars* (New York: W. W. Norton, 2018).

2. No Portland-bred player has yet even contributed significantly to the Portland Timbers professional team.

3. "Seeking Soccer Respect, Qatar Looked Abroad," *New York Times*.

4. "Football Dreams," Aspire Academy, accessed June 8, 2020, https://www .aspire.qa/football/football-dreams.

5. Abbot, *The Away Game*, xviii.

6. Qatar has generated some controversy for "naturalizing" a few star players for its national team who weren't born in Qatar, but that is not uncommon practice even for teams like the United States and Italy. Further, none of the naturalized Qatar players came through the Football Dreams project.

7. Of the players Abbot followed for years in *The Away Game*, the most successful was Diawandou Diagne from Senegal, who made twenty-seven appearances for the Barcelona B team. The book ends with the hint that Diagne might just break through, but at last report he had long since left *La Liga* for a stint in Belgium and then a swan song with less-than-famous Odisha FC in the Indian Super League. There were two Aspire players at the 2018 World Cup (Senegalese defender Moussa Wagué and Nigerian goalkeeper Francis Uzoho) but neither is yet considered truly world class.

8. Abbot, *The Away Game*, 45.

9. Abbot, 212.

10. These quotes are all widely available on the Internet, but are nearly impossible to trace to a specific source. It is thus possible they are not perfectly accurate to the speaker, but they are included here because the sentiment is plausible enough to exemplify a common popular discourse in sports.

11. See, for example, Martin E. P. Seligman and Raymond D. Fowler, "Comprehensive Soldier Fitness and the Future of Psychology," *American Psychologist* 66, no. 1 (2011): 82–86, and Angela Duckworth, *Grit: The Power of Passion and Perseverance* (New York: Scribner, 2016).

12. Robert Hughes and Jay Coakley, "Positive Deviance among Athletes: The Implications of Overconformity to the Sport Ethic," *Sociology of Sport Journal* 8, no. 4 (1991): 307–325.

13. Jay Coakley, "Burnout among Adolescent Athletes: A Personal Failure or Social Problem?," *Sociology of Sport Journal* 9, no. 3 (1992): 271–285.

14. Abbot, *The Away Game*, 18.

15. "The 20 Greatest Ray Hudson Quotes That Sum Up Lionel Messi," Sport Bible, accessed June 8, 2020, https://www.sportbible.com/football/reactions -take-a-bow-news-the-20-greatest-ray-hudson-quotes-that-sum-up-lionel-messi -20190328.

16. Marleen H. M. De Moor, Tim D. Spector, Lynn F. Cherkas, Mario Falchi, Jouke Jan Hottenga, Dorret I. Boomsma, and Eco J. C. De Geus, "Genome-Wide Linkage Scan for Athlete Status in 700 British Female DZ Twin Pairs," *Twin Research and Human Genetics* 10, no. 6 (2007): 812–820.

17. Tena Vukasović and Denis Bratko, "Heritability of Personality: A Meta-Analysis of Behavior Genetic Studies," *Psychological Bulletin* 141, no. 4 (2015): 769–785.

18. Ana Maria Fernandez-Pujals, Mark James Adams, Pippa Thomson, Andrew G. McKechanie, Douglas H. R. Blackwood, Blair H. Smith, Anna F. Dominiczak, et al., "Epidemiology and Heritability of Major Depressive Disorder, Stratified by Age of Onset, Sex, and Illness Course in Generation Scotland: Scottish Family Health Study (GS: SFHS)," *PLOS One* 10, no. 11 (2015).

19. Collin Moran, "Born to Win: Top Athletes Don't Share a Single Talent Gene, but Hundreds of Them," *The Conversation*, June 25, 2015, https://theconversation.com/born-to-win-top-athletes-dont-share-a-single-talent-gene-but-hundreds-of-them-43816.

20. Tim Rees, Lew Hardy, Arne Güllich, Bruce Abernethy, Jean Côté, Tim Woodman, Hugh Montgomery, Stewart Laing, and Chelsea Warr, "The Great British Medalists Project: A Review of Current Knowledge on the Development of the World's Best Sporting Talent," *Sports Medicine* 46, no. 8 (2016): 1041–1058.

21. Likewise, one soccer-specific meta-analysis found 2,944 academic articles related to talent development, drawing on only the highest-quality evidence to conclude "the most successful players present technical, tactical, anthropometric, physiological and psychological advantages that change non-linearly with age, maturational status and playing position." See Hugo Sarmento, M. Teresa Anguera, Antonino Pereira, and Duarte Araújo, "Talent Identification and Development in Male Football: A Systematic Review," *Sports Medicine* 48, no. 4 (2018): 907–931.

22. Malcolm Gladwell, *Outliers: The Story of Success* (New York: Little, Brown, 2008).

23. K. Anders Ericsson, Ralf T. Krampe, and Clemens Tesch-Römer, "The Role of Deliberate Practice in the Acquisition of Expert Performance," *Psychological Review* 100, no. 3 (1993): 363–406.

24. K. Anders Ericsson, "Towards a Science of the Acquisition of Expert Performance in Sports: Clarifying the Differences between Deliberate Practice and Other Types of Practice," *Journal of Sports Sciences* 38, no. 2 (2020): 159–176.

25. See, for a review, Joseph Baker and Bradley Young, "20 Years Later: Deliberate Practice and the Development of Expertise in Sport," *International Review of Sport and Exercise Psychology* 7, no. 1 (2014): 135–157.

26. See, for example, John O'Sullivan, "The 10,000 Hour Myth," *Changing the Game Project* (blog), February 12, 2014, https://changingthegameproject.com/the-10000-hour-myth/.

27. Arne Güllich, "'Macro-structure' of Developmental Participation Histories and 'Micro-structure' of Practice of German Female World-Class and National-Class Football Players," *Journal of Sports Sciences* 37, no. 12 (2019): 1347–1355; Manuel Hornig, Friedhelm Aust, and Arne Güllich, "Practice and Play in the Development of German Top-Level Professional Football Players," *European Journal of Sport Science* 16, no. 1 (2016): 96–105.

28. Hornig, Aust, and Güllich, "Practice and Play," 103.

29. "Barcelona Superstar Lionel Messi Opens Up about Details of Childhood Hormone Injections," *Daily Mail*, March 20, 2018, https://www.dailymail.co.uk/sport/football/article-5523775/Barcelonas-Lionel-Messi-opens-childhood-hormone-injections.html.

30. Brenda Elsey and Joshua Nadel, *Futbolera: A History of Women and Sports in Latin America* (Austin, TX: University of Texas Press, 2019).

31. Jean Williams, *A Game for Rough Girls?: A History of Women's Football in Britain* (London: Routledge, 2003).

32. "When the German FA Banned Women's Football," World Soccer Talk, March 18, 2019, https://worldsoccertalk.com/2019/03/18/when-the-german-fa-banned-womens-football/.

33. "More than 76 Million Students Enrolled in U.S. Schools, Census Bureau Reports," United States Census Bureau, December 11, 2018, https://www.census.gov/newsroom/press-releases/2018/school-enrollment.html.

34. This is an improvement from 2008, when 86 percent of NCAA women's players were White—during that same time period, head coaches for women's teams went from 89 percent White to 87 percent White. See "NCAA Demographics Database," NCAA, http://www.ncaa.org/about/resources/research/ncaa-demographics-database.

35. Jennifer McGovern and Esther Wellman, "Women's Soccer in the United States: A 'Wealth' of Talent," *Engaging Sports*, June 24, 2019, https://thesocietypages.org/engagingsports/2019/06/24/womens-soccer-in-the-united-states-a-wealth-of-talent/.

36. Michael Sagas and George Cunningham, "Sport Participation Rates among Underserved American Youth," *Aspen Institute* (2014), https://assets.aspeninstitute.org/content/uploads/files/content/docs/pubs/Project_Play_Underserved_Populations_Roundtable_Research_Brief.pdf.

37. I return to this issue in chapter 8.

38. Michael Sokolove, "How a Soccer Star is Made," *New York Times Magazine*, June 6, 2010, https://www.nytimes.com/2010/06/06/magazine/06Soccer-t.html.

39. "The Coerver Coaching Method," Soccer Training Info, June 26, 2019, https://soccer-training-info.com/the_coerver_coaching_method/.

40. See particularly the interview with Paul van Veen, "editor in chief of the internationally renowned Dutch coaching technical magazine *Trainers Magazine*," in Peter Hyballa and Hans-Dieter Te Poel, *Dutch Soccer Secrets* (Maidenhead, UK: Meyer & Meyer Sport, 2012).

41. "Youth Academy," Ajax Amsterdam, accessed June 8, 2020, https://english.ajax.nl/youth-academy/youth-academy.htm.

42. Hyballa and Te Poel, *Dutch Soccer Secrets*, 43, 123–130.

43. Hyballa and Te Poel, 32.

44. Les Murray, "Double Dutch on Talent Development," The World Game, February 2, 2016, https://theworldgame.sbs.com.au/les-murray-double-dutch-on-talent-development.

45. I had personal experience with the export of Dutch methods when coaching with the Illinois Youth Soccer Association, which brought in a Dutch federation coach to lead a workshop on coaching methods. The workshop consisted of lots of time dribbling balls through cones and little inspiration for how to engage more American kids with the game.

46. David Winner, *Brilliant Orange: The Neurotic Genius of Dutch Football* (London: Bloomsbury, 2001).

47. A lack of fun that seemed to reach an apotheosis with a brutal display of cynical soccer by the Dutch men's national team in that 2010 World Cup final.

48. "MLS Players by Birthplace," Major League Soccer, March 7, 2019, https://www.mlssoccer.com/media-resources/players-by-birthplace.

49. "Player Export," CIES Football Observatory, November 11, 2019, https://football-observatory.com/IMG/sites/b5wp/2019/wp275/en/.

50. Peter Alegi, *African Soccerscapes: How a Continent Changed the World's Game* (Athens, OH: Ohio University Press, 2010), 68.

51. Paul R. Ford, Christopher Carling, Marco Garces, Mauricio Marques, Carlos Miguel, Andrew Farrant, Andreas Stenling, et al., "The Developmental Activities of Elite Soccer Players Aged Under-16 Years from Brazil, England, France, Ghana, Mexico, Portugal and Sweden," *Journal of Sports Sciences* 30, no. 15 (2012): 1653–1663.

52. See, for example, Robert F. LaPrade, Julie Agel, Joseph Baker, Joel S. Brenner, Frank A. Cordasco, Jean Côté, Lars Engebretsen, et al., "AOSSM Early Sport Specialization Consensus Statement," *Orthopaedic Journal of Sports Medicine* 4, no. 4 (2016): doi:10.1177/2325967116644241 and Michael F. Bergeron, Margo Mountjoy, Neil Armstrong, Michael Chia, Jean Côté, Carolyn A. Emery, Avery Faigenbaum, et al., "International Olympic Committee Consensus

Statement on Youth Athletic Development," *British Journal of Sports Medicine* 49, no. 13 (2015): 843–851.

53. See, for example, J. R. Eskilson, "From Ghana to Hollywood," Top Drawer Soccer, July 12, 2012, https://www.topdrawersoccer.com/club-soccer-articles/from-ghana-to-hollywood:-boatengs-rise_aid24588.

54. Paul Darby, James Esson, and Christian Ungruhe, "Africa: SDP and Sports Academies," in *Routledge Handbook of Sport for Development and Peace*, ed. Holly Collison, Simon C. Darnell, Richard Giulianotti, and P. David Howe (New York: Routledge, 2018), 419–429.

55. See, for example, James Esson, "Better Off at Home? Rethinking Responses to Trafficked West African Footballers in Europe," *Journal of Ethnic and Migration Studies* 41, no. 3 (2015): 512–530.

56. See, for example, Sean P. Cumming, Chris Searle, Janie K. Hemsley, Finlay Haswell, Hannah Edwards, Sam Scott, Aleks Gross, et al., "Biological Maturation, Relative Age and Self-Regulation in Male Professional Academy Soccer Players: A Test of the Underdog Hypothesis," *Psychology of Sport and Exercise* 39 (2018): 147–153.

57. This does not necessarily mean the many unsuccessful Ghanaian players are passive victims; a group of sociologists studied players who had failed to leverage Ghanaian academy play into overseas contracts quoted in the title of their scholarly analysis: "The downfall of a man is not the end of his life." See Nienke Van der Meij, Paul Darby, and Katie Liston, "'The Downfall of a Man Is Not the End of His Life': Navigating Involuntary Immobility in Ghanaian Football," *Sociology of Sport Journal* 34, no. 2 (2017): 183–194.

58. Emma Young, "Iceland Knows How to Stop Teen Substance Abuse but the Rest of the World Isn't Listening," Mosaic Science, January 17, 2017, https://mosaicscience.com/story/iceland-prevent-teen-substance-abuse/.

59. Frode Telseth and Vidar Halldorsson, "The Success Culture of Nordic Football: The Cases of the National Men's Teams of Norway in the 1990s and Iceland in the 2010s," *Sport in Society* 22, no. 4 (2019): 689–703.

60. Telseth and Halldorsson, 690.

61. Telseth and Halldorsson, 694

62. Telseth and Halldorsson, 699.

63. Vidar Halldorsson, *Sport in Iceland: How Small Nations Achieve International Success* (New York: Routledge, 2017).

64. Halldorsson, 29.

65. Telseth and Halldorsson, "The Success Culture," 701.

66. John M. Hoberman, *Mortal Engines: The Science of Performance and the Dehumanization of Sport* (New York: Free Press, 1992).

Chapter 5: Performances

1. Matt Bonesteel, "Brazil's Weepy World Cup Players Need a Tissue and a Psychologist," *Washington Post*, July 3, 2014, https://www.washingtonpost.com /news/soccer-insider/wp/2014/07/03/brazils-weepy-world-cup-players-need-a -tissue-and-a-psychologist/.

2. Translation from "Psicólogo Teme Choradeira da Seleção e Erro de Capitão," Terra.co.br, June 30, 2020, https://www.terra.com.br/esportes/brasil /psicologo-teme-choradeira-da-selecao-e-erro-de-capitao,2dd3b448c8ce6410Vg nVCM10000098cceboaRCRD.html.

3. Jonathan Watts, "Brazil World Cup Team Calls in Psychologist after Chile Match Tears," *The Guardian*, July 3, 2014, https://www.theguardian.com /football/2014/jul/03/brazil-world-cup-2014-psychologist-tears.

4. Jim Powell, "World Cup Massacre . . . 'Historic Humiliation': Front-Page Reaction around the World to Brazil v Germany—In Pictures," *The Guardian*, July 9 2014, https://www.theguardian.com/football/gallery/2014/jul/09/world -cup-brazil-germany-front-pages.

5. Local academics noted that the events of 2014 were not good for the broader field of sport psychology in Brazil. In one 2016 academic overview of sport psychology in Brazil, the authors suggested that high-profile events such as the Olympics and the World Cup bring both opportunities and threats for the broader field:

> The last major sporting event in Brazil, the 2014 World Cup, did not positively influence the image of sport psychology. Unfortunately, the sport psychologist working with the national team was heavily criticised for her approach. The Brazilian players were deemed to be "too emotional" and there were many commentaries about the psychological preparation by the national media. In this discussion, many sport psychologists gave their opinions about the situation. Regrettably, not all comments were positive to the image of sport psychology in Brazil. The comments were more personal views rather than a position held by a national organisation. The sport psychologist working with the national soccer team for the 2014 World Cup is a highly respected professional in Brazil and internationally. Polemic situations like the World Cup elimination require an official statement from an organisation representing the view of all sport psychologists in Brazil. Another possible threat with the proximity of the Rio Olympic Games and the increase in pressure because Brazil is the hosting country is sport psychologists being hired at the last minute to work with teams. According to the information published in the media for the World Cup, the team sport psychologist started to work with the athletes during the competition.

See Fernanda Serra de Queiroz, Janaina Lima Fogaça, Stephanie J. Hanrahan, and Samuel Zizzi, "Sport Psychology in Brazil: Reflections on the Past, Present, and Future of the Field," *International Journal of Sport and Exercise Psychology* 14, no. 2 (2016): 180–181.

6. Andrew Lane, "The Psychology behind Brazil's Semi-final Downward Spiral," *The Conversation*, July 9, 2014, https://theconversation.com/the -psychology-behind-brazils-semi-final-downward-spiral-29003.

7. Angela Patmore, "Why Sports Psychologists Couldn't Save Brazil's World Cup Hopes," *The Guardian*, July 9, 2014, https://www.theguardian.com/football /2014/jul/09/why-sports-psychologists-couldnt-save-brazil-world-cup.

8. Gavin Brent Sullivan, "Collective Emotions and the World Cup 2014: The Relevance of Theories and Research on Collective Pride and Shame," *Psicologia e Saber Social* 3, no. 1 (2014): 112–117.

9. The 50 percent figure is based on estimated lifetime prevalence of any mental disorder; see, for example, "CDC Statistics: Mental Illness in the US," PsychCentral, accessed May 2 2021, https://psychcentral.com/blog/cdc -statistics-mental-illness-in-the-us/.

10. Jay Coakley, "Burnout among Adolescent Athletes: A Personal Failure or Social Problem?," *Sociology of Sport Journal* 9, no. 3 (1992): 271–285.

11. Raúl Vilchis, "Mexico Wages a Psychological Battle against Its World Cup Demons," *New York Times*, June 6, 2018, https://www.nytimes.com/2018/06/06 /sports/soccer/mexico-world-cup-psychologist.html. The article explains that "Ibarrondo is not a licensed psychologist," but instead a former Spanish player "reinventing himself as a sports leadership guru."

12. Jere Longman, "Women's World Cup; Norway's Rivalry with U.S. Is Intense," *New York Times*, June 13, 1999, https://www.nytimes.com/1999/06/13 /sports/women-s-world-cup-norway-s-rivalry-with-us-is-intense.html.

13. "Mia Hamm and the Mental Preparation for a Historic Team USA Gold—Gold Medal Entourage," YouTube Video, 8:54, posted by the Olympic Channel, October 23, 2016, https://www.youtube.com/watch?v=3byjphnyUDM.

14. Astrid Junge, Jiri Dvorak, Dieter Rosch, Toni Graf-Baumann, Jiri Cho-miak, and Lars Peterson, "Psychological and Sport-Specific Characteristics of Football Players," *American Journal of Sports Medicine* 28, no. 5 suppl (2000): 22–28.

15. Rebecca A. Zakrajsek, Johannes Raabe, and Jedediah E. Blanton, "Psycho-logical Characteristics of Elite Athletes," in *APA Handbook of Sport and Exercise Psychology*, vol. 1, ed. Mark H. Anshel, Trent A. Petrie, and Jesse A. Steinfeldt (Washington, DC: American Psychological Association, 2019): 129–148.

16. Division 47 (Exercise and Sport Psychology) of the American Psychologi-cal Association, "Defining the Practice of Sport and Performance Psychology" (2012). https://www.apadivisions.org/division-47/about/resources/defining.pdf.

17. "CSF2–Comprehensive Soldier & Family Fitness," Joint Base Lewis-McChord Training Center, accessed June 10, 2020, https://www.lewis-mcchord

.army.mil/csf2/. Note, however, that in recent years the performance-enhancement dimension of the comprehensive soldier fitness program seems to have evolved away from this model.

18. See, for example, Robin S. Vealey, "Mental Skills Training in Sport," in *Handbook of Sport Psychology*, 3rd ed., ed. Gershon Tenenbaum and Robert C. Eklund (Hoboken, NJ: John Wiley & Sons, 2007), 285–309; Elizabeth L. Shoenfelt, *Mental Skills for Athletes: A Workbook for Competitive Success* (New York: Routledge, 2019).

19. Mark Nesti, "Performance Mind-Set," in *Soccer Science*, ed. Tony Strudwick (Champaign, IL: Human Kinetics, 2016), 419.

20. "FitStars: U.S. Women's Soccer Star Julie Foudy," Fitbottomedgirls.com (blog), July 15, 2011, https://fitbottomedgirls.com/2011/07/★fitstars-u-s-womens -soccer-star-julie-foudy/ (accessed June 11, 2020).

21. See, for example, Richard H. Cox, Matthew P. Martens, and William D. Russell, "Measuring Anxiety in Athletics: The Revised Competitive State Anxiety Inventory–2," *Journal of Sport and Exercise Psychology* 25, no. 4 (2003): 519–533.

22. "Mia Hamm and the Mental Preparation for a Historic Team USA Gold," Olympic Channel, accessed May 2, 2021, https://www.youtube.com/watch?v =3byjphnyUDM.

23. "Mia Hamm and the Mental Preparation for a Historic Team USA Gold," Olympic Channel, accessed May 2, 2021, https://www.youtube.com/watch?v =3byjphnyUDM.

24. Ben Lyttleton, *Twelve Yards: The Art and Psychology of the Perfect Penalty Kick* (New York: Penguin, 2015).

25. Lyttleton, 11.

26. Ben Lyttleton, "How Gareth Southgate Overcame England's World Cup Penalty Hoodoo," *The Guardian*, July 5, 2018, https://www.theguardian.com /football/2018/jul/05/england-gareth-southgate-penalties-overcome-hoodoo (accessed June 11, 2020).

27. Emine Saner, "How the Psychology of the England Football Team Could Change Your Life," *The Guardian*, July 10, 2018, https://www.theguardian.com /football/2018/jul/10/psychology-england-football-team-change-your-life-pippa -grange (accessed June 11, 2020).

28. Geir Jordet, "When Superstars Flop: Public Status and Choking under Pressure in International Soccer Penalty Shootouts," *Journal of Applied Sport Psychology* 21, no. 2 (2009): 125–130.

29. Peter Gröpel and Christopher Mesagno, "Choking Interventions in Sports: A Systematic Review," *International Review of Sport and Exercise Psychology* 12, no. 1 (2019): 176–201.

30. For another recent review proposing an integration of these models, see Leo J. Roberts, Mervyn S. Jackson, and Ian H. Grundy, "Choking under Pressure: Illuminating the Role of Distraction and Self-Focus," *International Review of Sport and Exercise Psychology* 12, no. 1 (2019): 49–69.

31. The original formulation of the "automatic execution model" is from R. F. Baumeister, "Choking under Pressure: Self-Consciousness and Paradoxical Effects of Incentives on Skillful Performance," *Journal of Personality and Social Psychology* 46, no. 3 (1984): 610.

32. Roy F. Baumeister, Debra G. Hutton, and Kenneth J. Cairns, "Negative Effects of Praise on Skilled Performance," *Basic and Applied Social Psychology* 11, no. 2 (1990): 131–148.

33. Sian L. Beilock, Thomas H. Carr, Clare MacMahon, and Janet L. Starkes, "When Paying Attention Becomes Counterproductive: Impact of Divided versus Skill-Focused Attention on Novice and Experienced Performance of Sensorimotor Skills," *Journal of Experimental Psychology: Applied* 8, no. 1 (2002): 6.

34. This general idea has recently coincided with the popularity of "mindfulness" as an approach to psychological well-being, with mindfulness seeming to hold some promise for applications to sports performance. For a recent review of related research, see Michael Noetel, Joseph Ciarrochi, Brooke Van Zanden, and Chris Lonsdale, "Mindfulness and Acceptance Approaches to Sporting Performance Enhancement: A Systematic Review," *International Review of Sport and Exercise Psychology* 12, no. 1 (2019): 139–175.

35. Lyttleton, *Twelve Yards*, 54.

36. Geir Jordet, Esther Hartman, and Einar Sigmundstad, "Temporal Links to Performing under Pressure in International Soccer Penalty Shootouts," *Psychology of Sport and Exercise* 10, no. 6 (2009): 621–627.

37. Jordet, Hartman, and Sigmundstad, 626.

38. "England's 27-Year History of Penalty Shoot-Out Woe: Ranked in Order of Agony," *The Telegraph*, June 28, 2017, https://www.telegraph.co.uk/football/2017/06/28/englands-27-year-history-penalty-shoot-out-woe-ranked-order/gareth-southgate-misses-penalty-euro-1996/.

39. Lyttleton, *Twelve Yards*, 44.

40. Lyttleton, 41.

41. M. Wilson, G. Wood, and G. Jordet, "The BASES Expert Statement on the Psychological Preparation for Football Penalty Shootouts," *Sport and Exercise Scientist* 38 (Winter 2013): 8–9.

42. Greg Wood, Geir Jordet, and Mark Robert Wilson, "On Winning the 'Lottery': Psychological Preparation for Football Penalty Shoot-Outs." *Journal of Sports Sciences* 33, no. 17 (2015): 1758–1765.

43. Tjerk Moll, Geir Jordet, and Gert-Jan Pepping, "Emotional Contagion in Soccer Penalty Shootouts: Celebration of Individual Success Is Associated with Ultimate Team Success," *Journal of Sports Sciences* 28, no. 9 (2010): 983–992.

44. As an academic I'm a firm believer that everyone should get a sabbatical now and then, but the idea of a professional soccer player taking an intentional break is nearly unheard of and verboten in most soccer cultures.

45. Jay Coakley, "Burnout among Adolescent Athletes: A Personal Failure or Social Problem?," *Sociology of Sport Journal* 9, no. 3 (1992): 271–285.

46. Britton W. Brewer and Albert J. Petitpas, "Athletic Identity Foreclosure," *Current Opinion in Psychology* 16 (2017): 118–122.

47. Chris Ballard, "Project: Phenom," *Sports Illustrated*, May 29, 2019, https:// www.si.com/soccer/2019/05/29/olivia-moultrie-pro-us-soccer-nwsl-portland -thorns-nike. While Moultrie may yet succeed, the record for prodigal players all over the world is not promising. Landon Donovan's predecessors in being named best boys' player in the world at the U-17 World Cup, for example, include such non-notables as the Brazilian William (in 1985), the Nigerian Philip Osundu (in 1987), the Scot James Will (in 1989), the Ghanaian Nii Lamptey (in 1991, and the one member of the list who did go on to a notable career), the Ghanaian Daniel Addo (in 1993), the Omani Mohamed Kathiri (in 1995), and the Spaniard Sergio Santamaria (in 1997).

48. Coakley, "Burnout among Adolescent Athletes," 283.

49. There are also a good number of sport psychology consultants and scholars who advocate for related "whole-person" models of sport psychology. See, for example, John Corlett, "Sophistry, Socrates, and Sport Psychology," *Sport Psychologist* 10, no. 1 (1996): 84–94.

50. Nick Firchau, "Landon Donovan's Other Legacy: Challenging the Stigma of Mental Health," MLS Soccer, October 10, 2017, https://www.mlssoccer.com /post/2015/01/04/landon-donovans-other-legacy-challenging-stigma-mental -health-word.

51. The "tears" theme in Brazilian soccer has a deeper history than 2014. There is a famous story about the goalkeeper of Brazil's 1950 World Cup team, Moacir Barbosa, whom many blame for a dramatic 2–1 loss to Uruguay in that year's World Cup final. The game was played in front of two-hundred thousand fans at Rio's famed Estádio do Maracanã and was supposed to be a coronation. Brazil was a massive favorite. When Barbosa misjudged the second goal and was beaten to the near post—always a sin for goalkeepers—he became the ultimate scape-goat, never living down public recrimination. The story told in many accounts of Barbosa's life is that he claimed the hardest moment for him was not the day of the World Cup final at the Maracanã, but instead came twenty years later when

he was shopping at a local market. There a mother pointed him out to her young child with the exclamation, "Look at him, son. He is the man that made all of Brazil cry." That moniker became the title for the ESPN 30 for 30 sports documentary, *The Man Who Made Brazil Cry*. See also Alex Caple, "Moacir Barbosa: The Goalkeeper Who Was Condemned for Life," The Versed, August 21, 2017, https://www.theversed.com/65935/moacir-barbosa-condemned-life/#.Ja1vQv1MbB.

52. Watts, "Brazil World Cup Team Calls in Psychologist."

Chapter 6: Impacts

1. Simon Kuper, *Soccer Men: Profiles of the Rogues, Geniuses, and Neurotics Who Dominate the World's Most Popular Sport* (New York: Nation Books, 2011).

2. Kuper, *Soccer Men*, xiv.

3. Kuper, xvii.

4. Kuper, xvi.

5. Sharon Kay Stoll and Jennifer M. Beller, "Moral Reasoning in Athlete Populations: A 30 Year Review," accessed June 15, 2020, https://www.webpages.uidaho.edu/center_for_ethics/research_fact_sheet.htm.

6. See, for example, David Light Shields and Brenda Light Bredemeier, "Can Sports Build Character?," in *Character Psychology and Character Education*, ed. Daniel K. Lapsley and F. Power (South Bend, IN: University of Notre Dame Press, 2005). See also David Light Shields and Brenda Light Bredemeier, *True Competition* (Champaign, IL: Human Kinetics, 2009).

7. The Scurry example is interesting enough to even have been taken up in a sport ethics text: Robert L. Simon, Cesar R. Torres, and Peter F. Hager, *Fair Play: The Ethics of Sport* (New York Routledge, 2018).

8. The Suarez example has also received academic attention in relation to postcolonialism: Tamir Bar-On, "Learning about Postcolonialism through Soccer," chap. 4 in *Beyond Soccer: International Relations and Politics as Seen through the Beautiful Game* (Lanham, MD: Rowman & Littlefield, 2017).

9. The translation of Tabarez's remark varies slightly depending on the outlet; this one is from "Tabarez Defends Suarez after 'Bite' Incident," Four Four Two, June 24, 2014, https://www.fourfourtwo.com/us/news/tabarez-defends-suarez-after-bite-incident.

10. The "essential goodness" of sport generally is discussed by sport sociologist Jay Coakley as the "Great Sport Myth." See Jay Coakley, "Assessing the Sociology of Sport: On Cultural Sensibilities and the Great Sport Myth," *International Review for the Sociology of Sport* 50, no. 4–5 (2015): 402–406.

11. Their scholarly work is summarized in Daniel Kahneman, Stewart Paul Slovic, Paul Slovic, and Amos Tversky, eds., *Judgment under Uncertainty:*

Heuristics and Biases (New York: Cambridge University Press, 1982). More accessible accounts are available in Daniel Kahneman, *Thinking, Fast and Slow* (New York: Farrar, Straus and Giroux, 2011) and Michael Lewis *The Undoing Project: A Friendship That Changed Our Minds* (New York: W.W. Norton, 2016).

12. Gerd Nufer, "An Exploration of the Halo Effect in Professional Soccer," *European Journal of Physical Education and Sport Science* 4, no. 9 (2018): 17–29.

13. Jonathan Gottschall, *The Storytelling Animal: How Stories Make Us Human* (New York: Houghton Mifflin Harcourt, 2012).

14. E. Archetti, "'And Give Joy to My Heart': Ideology and Emotions in the Argentinian Cult of Maradona," in *Entering the Field: New Perspectives on World Football*, ed. G. Armstrong and R. Giulianotti (Oxford: Berg, 1997), 31–51.

15. Archetti, 33–38.

16. Archetti, 44.

17. See Luke Norris, "How Charles Barkley's Controversial 'I Am Not a Role Model' Nike Spot Came to Be," Sportscasting, April 21, 2020, https://www .sportscasting.com/how-charles-barkleys-controversial-i-am-not-a-role-model -nike-spot-came-to-be/.

18. Andrew M. Guest and Stephanie Cox, "Using Athletes as Role Models? Conceptual and Empirical Perspectives from a Sample of Elite Women Soccer Players," *International Journal of Sports Science & Coaching* 4, no. 4 (2009): 567–581.

19. See, for example, T. W. Crosset, "Role Model: A Critical Assessment of the Application of the Term to Athletes," in *Sports in School: The Future of an Institution*, ed. J. R. Gerdy (New York: Teachers College Press, 2000), 31–41, and A. Addis, "Role Models and the Politics of Recognition," *University of Pennsylvania Law Review* 144 (1996): 1377–1468.

20. R. K. Merton, *Social Theory and Social Structure* (New York: Free Press, 1968).

21. C. Rojek, "Sports Celebrity and the Civilizing Process," *Sport in Society* 9 (2006): 674–690.

22. While we initially expected there might be some differences between players from the two teams, that did not prove true in the data—so we analyzed them together as one group of high-level women's players.

23. Eighty-two percent identified family members, compared to 36 percent who identified female soccer players and 21 percent who identified male athletes as having been role models.

24. See, for example, Kristin J. Anderson and Donna Cavallaro, "Parents or Pop Culture? Children's Heroes and Role Models," *Childhood Education* 78, no. 3 (2002): 161–168, or Johanna Vescio, Kerrie Wilde, and Janice J. Crosswhite, "Profiling Sport Role Models to Enhance Initiatives for Adolescent Girls in

Physical Education and Sport," *European Physical Education Review* 11, no. 2 (2005): 153–170.

25. Hideaki Ishigami, "Estimating the Impact of the 2011 FIFA Women's World Cup on Japanese Adolescent Girls: A Causal Analysis of Sports Role Models," *International Journal of Sport Policy and Politics* 11, no. 3 (2019): 503–519.

26. *This Is Football*: "Belief," IMDb.com, accessed June 15, 2020, https://www .imdb.com/title/tt10578796/plotsummary.

27. U. Pillay, P. Mnguni, M. Wentzel, D. Sanchez, J. Viljoen, H. Kanyane, F. Rakate, et al., "FIFA 2010 World Cup Legacy Audit: Final Report" (2011), http://www.hsrc.ac.za/en/research-data/view/5636.

28. Peliwe Mnguni, Marie Wentzel, Diana Sanchez, Johan Viljoen, Hendrick Kanyane, Faith Rakate, Vanessa Barolsky, Priscilla Wamucii, Lesego Mogami, and Elmé Vivier, "FIFA 2010 World Cup Legacy Audit" (2011), accessed June 15, 2020, http://ecommons.hsrc.ac.za/bitstream/handle/20.500.11910/3634/6986 .pdf?sequence=1&isAllowed=y.

29. Mnguni et. al., 6.

30. Pieter Koortzen and Rudolf M. Oosthuizen, "Psychological Experiences in South African Society before the 2010 FIFA World Cup from the Systems Psychodynamic and Positive Psychology Perspectives," *SA Journal of Industrial Psychology* 38, no. 2 (2012): 156–169.

31. Adapted from J. R. B. Ritchie, "Assessing the Impacts of the 1988 Olympic Winter Games: The Research Program and Initial Results," *Journal of Travel Research* 22, no. 3 (1988): 17–25, and S. Ohmann, I. Jones, and K. Wilkes, "The Perceived Social Impact of the 2006 Soccer World Cup on Munich Residents," *Journal of Sport and Tourism* 11, no. 2 (2006): 129–152, http://dx.doi.org/10.1080 /14775080601155167.

32. In a more general conceptual framework for the impact of elite sport, De Rycke and De Bosscher present ten potential categories of impact, each of which has both a positive and negative pole. See Jens De Rycke and Veerle De Bosscher, "Mapping the Potential Societal Impacts Triggered by Elite Sport: A Conceptual Framework," *International Journal of Sport Policy and Politics* 11, no. 3 (2019): 485–502.

33. David Bek, Alessandro Merendino, Kamilla Swart, and Jill Timms, "Creating an Enduring Developmental Legacy from FIFA 2010: The Football Foundation of South Africa (FFSA)," *European Sport Management Quarterly* 19, no. 4 (2019): 437–455.

34. Bek et. al., 441.

35. See, for example, Neil DeMause and Joanna Cagan, *Field of Schemes: How the Great Stadium Swindle Turns Public Money into Private Profit* (Lincoln: University of Nebraska Press, 2008); Roger G. Noll and Andrew Zimbalist, eds.,

Sports, Jobs, And Taxes: The Economic Impact of Sports Teams and Stadiums (Washington, DC: Brookings Institution Press, 2011).

36. According to a 2016 analysis by South African economists, the Mbombela stadium had the lowest "utilization rate" of any 2010 World Cup stadium post-tournament; in 2014 the stadium hosted only fifteen events with an average attendance of less than 10 percent of stadium capacity. See Luke Humphrey and Gavin Fraser, "2010 FIFA World Cup Stadium Investment: Does the Post-event Usage Justify the Expenditure?," *African Review of Economics and Finance* 8, no. 2 (2016): 3–22.

37. Marc Strydom, "Durban's Iconic Moses Mabhida Stadium Braces for Millions in Lost Revenue," Dispatch Live, April 8, 2020, https://www .dispatchlive.co.za/sport/2020-04-08-durbans-iconic-moses-mabhida-stadium -braces-for-millions-in-lost-revenue/.

38. Ashwin Desai, "Between Madiba Magic and Spectacular Capitalism: The FIFA World Cup in South Africa," in *Mega-Events and Globalization*, ed. Richard Gruneau and John Horne (New York: Routledge, 2016), 93–106.

39. Simon Kuper and Stefan Szymanski, *Soccernomics*, 2018 World Cup ed. (New York: Nation Books, 2018), 260.

40. See also Georgios Kavetsos and Stefan Szymanski, "National Well-being and International Sports Events," *Journal of Economic Psychology* 31, no. 2 (2010): 158–171.

41. Kuper and Szymanski, *Soccernomics*, 277.

42. See, for example, Jonathan Grix and Fiona Carmichael, "Why Do Governments Invest in Elite Sport? A Polemic," *International Journal of Sport Policy and Politics* 4, no. 1 (2012): 73–90.

43. The idea here is closely related to what some scholars call "sportwashing." As defined by political scientist and former U.S. Olympic soccer team member Jules Boykoff, sportwashing is "When host countries use sports mega-events to distract us from their blighted human-rights records. FIFA, in awarding the World Cup to Russia and to Qatar in 2022, has essentially franchised the practice of sportwashing, gifting its signature event to authoritarian countries as a handy-dandy PR tool to divert and deflect." See Jules Boykoff, "Sportwashing in Technicolor," *Howler*, June 21, 2018, https://www.whatahowler.com /sportwashing-in-technicolor/.

44. Though the quote is most often attributed to Churchill, it is hard to identify when he actually said it and there seems to be similar phrases circulating long before Churchill's time. See Matthew Phelan, "The History of 'History Is Written by the Victors,'" *Slate.com*, November 26, 2019, https://slate.com/culture /2019/11/history-is-written-by-the-victors-quote-origin.html.

45. See "The Tournament," Homeless World Cup Foundation, accessed June 15, 2020, https://homelessworldcup.org/tournament/.

46. See, for example, Emma Sherry, "(Re)engaging Marginalized Groups through Sport: The Homeless World Cup," *International Review for the Sociology of Sport* 45, no. 1 (2010): 59–71; and Emma Sherry and Fiona O'May, "Exploring the Impact of Sport Participation in the Homeless World Cup on Individuals with Substance Abuse or Mental Health Disorders," *Journal of Sport for Development* 1, no. 2 (2013).

47. Jonathan Magee and Ruth Jeanes, "Football's Coming Home: A Critical Evaluation of the Homeless World Cup as an Intervention to Combat Social Exclusion," *International Review for the Sociology of Sport* 48, no. 1 (2013): 3–19.

48. Magee and Jeanes, 12.

49. Magee and Jeanes, 12–13.

50. Peter Donnelly, "From War without Weapons to Sport for Development and Peace: The Janus-Face of Sport," *SAIS Review of International Affairs* 31, no. 1 (2011): 65–76.

51. Donnelly, 67.

52. Positive psychologists have posited the "broaden and build" theory of positive emotion—suggesting that simply experiencing good feelings on a regular basis has a way of building into positive mental health across life domains. See, for example, Barbara L. Fredrickson, "The Role of Positive Emotions in Positive Psychology: The Broaden-and-Build Theory of Positive Emotions," *American Psychologist* 56, no. 3 (2001): 218–226.

53. Peter Krustrup and Daniel Parnell, eds., *Football as Medicine: Prescribing Football for Global Health Promotion* (New York: Routledge, 2019).

54. See Common Goal, accessed May 2, 2021, https://www.common-goal.org/.

55. Bek et al., "Creating an Enduring Developmental Legacy," 442.

Chapter 7: Initiatives

1. This chapter is a revised version of an essay previously published as "Soccer Saves the World?" from *Playing on an Uneven Field: Essays on Exclusion and Inclusion in Sports*, ed. Yuya Kiuchi (2019), by permission of McFarland & Company, Inc., Box 611, Jefferson NC 28640, www.mcfarlandbooks.com.

2. See Peter Moszynski, "The Worst Place to be a Child," *The Independent*, 1 August 1999, https://www.independent.co.uk/news/world/the-worst-place-to-be-a-child-1110067.html.

3. Andrew Guest, "Cultures of Play during Middle Childhood: Interpretive Perspectives from Two Distinct Marginalized Communities," *Sport, Education and Society* 18, no. 2 (2013): 167–183.

4. Alexander Wolff, "Sports Save the World," *Sports Illustrated* 115, no. 12 (2011): 62–74.

5. While the organizations involved in SDP initiatives use all types of sports and play activities as tools, as the only truly global game soccer holds a privileged place in the world of SDP. One recent review of global SDP organizations found soccer was by far the most popular single sport used by SDP programs—while 384 organizations used multiple sports (often including soccer), 236 focused exclusively on soccer. Only twenty-five programs focused exclusively on the next most popular sport for SDP programs (basketball). See Per G. Svensson and Hilary Woods, "A Systematic Overview of Sport for Development and Peace Organisations," *Journal of Sport for Development* 5, no. 9 (2017): 36–48.

6. Andrew Guest, "What's the Legacy of the 2010 World Cup?," *Pacific Standard*, June 10, 2014, https://psmag.com/social-justice/soccer-football-sports -youth-centers-south-africa-whats-legacy-2010-world-cup-83031.

7. Anders Kelto, "FIFA Hits Snags in Fulfilling World Cup Vow in Africa," National Public Radio, July 27, 2010, https://www.npr.org/templates/story/story .php?storyId=128782351.

8. Available as of February 2, 2019, at https://ar.fifa.com/mm/document /afsocial/ffh-centers/02/21/92/99/fifafinalreporton20centresfor2010_neutral.pdf.

9. I had the serendipitous opportunity to visit the centers in Khayelitsha, South Africa, in June 2013 and in Iringa, Tanzania, in October 2019, and was impressed with both. Each seemed to have strong local leadership and robust programming. But neither seemed to have much footprint beyond its immediate community.

10. FIFA, *FIFA Financial Report 2010* (2011), https://resources.fifa.com/image /upload/fifa-financial-report-2010-1392045.pdf?cloudid=miuql8kpghitm7kdzha2.

11. Maikel Waardenburg, Marjolein van den Bergh, and Frank van Eekeren, "Local Meanings of a Sport Mega-event's Legacies: Stories from a South African Urban Neighbourhood," *South African Review of Sociology* 46, no. 1 (2015): 87–105.

12. David R. Black, "The Ambiguities of Development: Implications for 'Development through Sport,'" *Sport in Society* 13, no. 1 (2010): 122.

13. Black, 125.

14. Douglas Hartmann and Christina Kwauk, "Sport and Development: An Overview, Critique, and Reconstruction," *Journal of Sport and Social Issues* 35, no. 3 (2011): 284–305.

15. See Andrew M. Guest, "SDP and Sport Psychology," in *Routledge Handbook of Sport for Development and Peace*, ed. Holly Collison, Simon C. Darnell, Richard Giulianotti, and P. David Howe (New York: Routledge, 2018), 230–240; Andrew M. Guest, "Sport Psychology for Development and Peace? Critical Reflections and Constructive Suggestions," *Journal of Sport Psychology in Action* 4, no. 3 (2013): 169–180.

16. See Grassroot Soccer, "A Letter from Tommy Clark," accessed May 2, 2021, https://www.grassrootsoccer.org/a-letter-from-tommy-clark/.

17. Grassroot Soccer, April 1, 2018, www.grassrootsoccer.org.

18. Grassroot Soccer, "A Letter from Tommy Clark."

19. UNAIDS, "Report on the Global HIV/AIDS Epidemic, 2002," http://data .unaids.org/pub/report/2002/brglobal_aids_report_en_pdf_red_en.pdf. More recent estimates have revised the 33 percent figure downward, suggesting early estimates were too high.

20. Grassroot Soccer, "A Letter from Tommy Clark."

21. Grassroot Soccer, April 1, 2018, www.grassrootsoccer.org.

22. This guide was still available as of January 2019 through the Compass, a website supported by the United States Agency for International Development providing "Social and Behavior Change Resources," at https://www .thecompassforsbc.org/project-examples/generation-skillz-coachs-guide-v23.

23. Grassroot Soccer Research Report 2016, https://www.grassrootsoccer.org /wp-content/uploads/2016/04/original-grs_research_report_2016_web _version.pdf.

24. Zachary A. Kaufman, "The GOAL Trial: Sport-Based HIV Prevention in South African Schools" (diss., London School of Hygiene & Tropical Medicine, 2014), http://researchonline.lshtm.ac.uk/1941262/1/2014_EPH_PhD_Kaufman _Z%20vol1_NEW.pdf.

25. Laurence Steinberg, "Risk Taking in Adolescence: New Perspectives from Brain and Behavioral Science," *Current Directions in Psychological Science* 162 (2007): 55–59.

26. Zachary A. Kaufman, Jeff DeCelles, Kenneth Bhauti, Rebecca B. Hershow, Helen A. Weiss, Cynthia Chaibva, Netsai Moyo, Fennie Mantula et al., "A Sport-Based Intervention to Increase Uptake of Voluntary Medical Male Circumcision among Adolescent Male Students: Results from the MCUTS 2 Cluster-Randomized Trial in Bulawayo, Zimbabwe," *Journal of Acquired Immune Deficiency Syndromes* 72, suppl. 4 (2016): S297–S303.

27. Anthropologist John Fox has written an entire book about the ball as a cultural object. See John Fox, *The Ball: Discovering the Object of the Game* (New York: Harper Perennial, 2012).

28. Gwen Knapp, "Building a Better Futbol," *Sports on Earth*, June 19, 2013, http://www.sportsonearth.com/article/51102524/the-one-world-futbol-invented -by-tim-jahnigen-brings-recreation-to-impoverished-nations.

29. Ken Belson, "Joy That Lasts, on the Poorest of Playgrounds," *New York Times*, November 8, 2012, https://www.nytimes.com/2012/11/09/giving/the-one -world-futbol-promises-a-lasting-source-of-fun-in-poor-countries.html.

30. Leigh Buchanaen, "Invincible Ball Brings Joy to Kids (& Lions)," *Inc.*, November 16, 2012, https://www.inc.com/leigh-buchanan/mal-warwick-one -world-futbol-project.html.

31. The feature article offering a more positive perspective on the BOGO model was Christopher Marquis and Andrew Park, "Inside the Buy-One Give-One Model," *Stanford Social Innovation Review*, (winter 2014): 28–33. The on-line response offering a more critical perspective on BOGO was Nathan Rothstein, "The Limits of Buy-One Give-One," *Stanford Social Innovation Review*, January 28, 2014, https://ssir.org/articles/entry/the_limits_of_buy_one_give_one.

32. Rothstein.

33. Rothstein.

34. The only academic research I've been able to find on One World Futbol is an interesting analysis by communications scholar Jeffrey Kassing, who also uses publicly available information to consider the paradoxes of the initiative's model. See Jeffrey W. Kassing, "Paradox and the Gift of an Indestructible Ball: A Case Study of the One World Futbol Project," *Soccer & Society* 20, no. 4 (2019): 569–583.

35. Another particular complication of giving away soccer balls goes back to the logic of import tariffs imposed by countries such as Malawi. They have the potential to undermine local markets and fair trade efforts. One World Futbols are manufactured in Taiwan and sold by a U.S. corporation, ensuring that any primary economic value accrues outside of the developing countries the balls are designed to help. As commenter Howard Brodwin noted in the discussion around the *Stanford Social Innovation Review* article: "There are a few BOGO soccer ball companies, and the mission of providing a free soccer ball to disadvantaged communities abroad is excellent. But there are also a several fair trade soccer/sports ball manufacturers, and the BOGO competitors can have a negative impact on their ability to sell and thereby meet their mission of providing fair wage/working condition employment. No easy answers here, and since this entire space is still evolving, I'm sure we'll see a shift in how this model can be applied."

36. Mike Hower, "One World Futbol: Saving Soccer in the Developing World," *Sustainable Brands*, March 7, 2013, https://www.sustainablebrands.com/news _and_views/articles/one-world-futbol-saving-soccer-developing-world.

37. Hower.

38. *Zanzibar Soccer Queens*, directed by Florence Ayisi (Filmakers Library, 2007); *Zanzibar Soccer Dreams*, directed by Florence Ayisi and Catalin Brylla (2016); *New Generation Queens: A Zanzibar Soccer Story*, directed by Megan Shutzer (2015).

39. Abbie Wightwick, "Female Footballers Labelled 'Hooligans' and Beaten with Sticks for Playing Game They Love," *Mirror*, May 23, 2016, https://www.mirror.co.uk/news/uk-news/female-footballers-labelled-hooligans-beaten-8030051.

40. Florence Ayisi and Catalin Brylla, "The Politics of Representation and Audience Reception: Alternative Visions of Africa," *Research in African Literatures* 44, no. 2 (2013): 125–141.

41. Martha Saavedra, "Football Feminine—Development of the African Game: Senegal, Nigeria and South Africa," *Soccer & Society* 4 no. 2–3 (2003): 225–253.

42. Wightwick, "Female Footballers Labelled."

43. Wightwick.

44. *Zanzibar Soccer Queens Impact Study*, directed by Florence Ayisi and Catalin Brylla (2016).

Chapter 8: Futures

1. This iteration reminded me of debates in U.S. youth sports about whether "every child should get a trophy" or whether the essence of competition requires prizes go only to the winners.

2. Ian Plenderleith, "Soccer in Propaganda, War and Revolution," *Soccer America*, April 23, 2020, https://www.socceramerica.com/publications/article/85481/soccer-in-propaganda-war-and-revolution-author-r.html (accessed June 23, 2020).

3. Plenderleith.

4. For further discussion, see Thomas R. Bates, "Gramsci and the Theory of Hegemony," *Journal of the History of Ideas* 36, no. 2 (1975): 351–366.

5. Women's college sports in the United States offers one potential example of a hegemonic process. Prior to the 1972 Title IX legislation that mandated educational institutions provide equal resources to men's and women's sports, the NCAA was not particularly interested in women's sports. There was, however, an organization called the Association for Intercollegiate Athletics for Women that organized women's college sport using its own model—employing primarily women administrators and women coaches, and conceptualizing a different philosophy of college sports emphasizing inclusion, democratic governance, and a goal of "enriching the lives of participants." Over time, however, when the male-dominated NCAA started to realize Title IX would ensure money and status also went to women's sports, the NCAA took over and imposed its own model. The percentage of women administrators and coaches decreased, and the possibilities for a different philosophy of college sports

diminished in tandem. The NCAA, in other words, exerted its hegemony—trading the opportunity to play under its competitive and high-status model for maintaining power structures. For further discussion, see Amy Sue Wilson, "A Saga of Power, Money, and Sex in Women's Athletics: A Presidents' History of the Association for Intercollegiate Athletics for Women (AIAW)" (PhD diss., University of Iowa, 2013), https://ir.uiowa.edu/etd/2661/.

6. Daryl A. Rosenbaum, Ravi R. Sanghani, Travis Woolen, and Stephen W. Davis, "Estimation of Injury Simulation in International Women's Football," *Research in Sports Medicine* 19, no. 3 (2011): 162–169.

7. There is some data to suggest that female soccer players experience higher rates of concussions than male soccer players—potentially in part because of an emphasis on showing they can be just as tough and reckless as male athletes. See, for example, Zachary Y. Kerr, Avinash Chandran, Aliza K. Nedimyer, Alan Arakkal, Lauren A. Pierpoint, and Scott L. Zuckerman, "Concussion Incidence and Trends in 20 High School Sports," *Pediatrics* 144, no. 5 (2019).

8. The issue of access in U.S. soccer receives periodic media attention; see, for example, Les Carpenter, "'It's Only Working for the White Kids': American Soccer's Diversity Problem," *The Guardian*, June 1, 2016, https://www.theguardian.com/football/blog/2016/jun/01/us-soccer-diversity-problem-world-football.

9. See, for example, David L. Andrews, Robert Pitter, Detlev Zwick, and Darren Ambrose, "Soccer, Race, and Suburban Space," in *Sporting Dystopias: The Making and Meanings of Urban Sport Cultures*, ed. Ralph C. Wilcox, David L. Andrews, Robert Pitter, and Richard L. Irwin (Albany: State University of New York Press, 2003), 197–220.

10. Torbjörn Andersson and Hans Hognestad, "Glocal Culture, Sporting Decline? Globalization and Football in Scandinavia," *Sport in Society* 22, no. 4 (2019): 704–716.

11. Unwana Samuel Akpan, "Elite Local Leagues and Transnational Broadcast of European Football," in *Africa's Elite Football: Structure, Politics, and Everyday Challenges*, ed. Chuka Onwumechili (New York: Routledge, 2019), 34–44.

12. Millions of fans around the world do exactly that—one marketing report based on surveying hundreds of thousands of Internet users in 2015 found that 54 percent of Indonesians and Vietnamese watched the Premier League, as did 41 percent of Indians and 36 percent of South Africans. See https://insight.globalwebindex.net/hs-fs/hub/304927/file-2593818997-.

13. "Survey: Kids Quit Most Sports by Age 11," Aspen Institute Project Play, August 1, 2019, https://www.aspenprojectplay.org/national-youth-sport-survey/1.

14. U.S. Soccer Federation, "Development Academy: Frequently Asked Questions," USSoccer.com, accessed February 19, 2015, www.ussoccer.com/development-academy/faqs:

From the start of the Academy program, our goal has been to close the gap with the top footballing nations in the world. The 10-month schedule, from September through June, or July based on postseason play, is what a typical elite soccer player's schedule looks like around the rest of the world. . . . We are competing in a global marketplace. We are not just trying to prepare elite players for college and the pro ranks in the United States; we are trying to prepare players to compete against the best clubs and international teams from around the world. Therefore, our standard has to be higher.

15. "Operation Pitch Invasion," Operation Pitch Invasion, accessed June 23, 2020, http://www.pitch-invasion.org/.

16. "Timbers, Operation Pitch Invasion Unveil Futsal Courts at Tom McCall Upper Elementary School," Portland Timbers, September 28, 2018, https://www.timbers.com/post/2018/09/28/timbers-operation-pitch-invasion-unveil-futsal-courts-tom-mccall-upper-elementary.

17. David Goldblatt, *The Age of Football: Soccer and the 21st Century* (New York: W. W. Norton, 2019), 28.

INDEX

ABOUT THE AUTHOR

ANDREW M. GUEST is a professor of psychology and sociology at the University of Portland in Oregon, where he also serves as director of the Core Curriculum. He has been a Peace Corps volunteer in Malawi, a Fulbright scholar in Tanzania, a minor league professional soccer player in Ohio and Michigan, and a coach across the US at levels from pre-K to college. Drawing on a master's degree in sport studies from Miami University and a doctorate in human development from the University of Chicago, his scholarly work focuses on sports, schools, and activities as developmental spaces for youth and communities. His own thinking fandom is most often engaged by his locals: the Portland Timbers and the Portland Thorns.